Collateral D...
Lemmy Ki...
Life Beyond ...

by Alan Burridge

I.P. Verlag Jeske/Mader GbR
Haydnstr. 2
12203 Berlin
Germany

ISBN 978-3-940822-07-9
April 2016

Hello Boys and girls,
Well, Alan has written
ANOTHER BOOK !!! Do we have a possible
ACE novelist here? No, we haven't. We
have Alan Burridge, a great friend to
all the people he likes and this is
a most informative tome. Read it, why
not?
It will make you clever. (edit).

Lemmy UKA

Lemmy Kilmister (Berlin, December 11th 2015)

Dedication

When I began this book several years ago, the last thing in mind was that it would be something of an epitaph to Lemmy's musical excursions before and during his life with Motörhead. Lemmy had read my rough manuscript, as always, and commented, as helpfully as ever, and offered extra information to bring clarity.

We are also grateful and fortunate that Motörhead publicist, Ute Kromrey, asked Lemmy to write a few lines as a foreword, and I am very grateful to her, especially as he wrote it in Berlin, where Motörhead were, unknowingly at the time, playing their final show.

This is for you, Lemmy, with gratitude and love.

Alan Burridge
Poole, Dorset
January 2016

Alan Burridge would like to acknowledge with thanks the help of Lemmy Kilmister, Mick Stevenson, Tom Doherty, Steve Morris, Adrian Lee, Mick Farren, Kevin Parrott, and Martin Peel. Also, Harry Shapiro and Caesar Glebbeek for the clarification of dates in the 'Chronology' section of their book, 'Jimi Hendrix – Electric Gypsy', published by Heinemann.

A big thank you to Doro Pesch for her enlightening phone interview on 7 November 2012; thanks also to Matthias Mader and Markus Müller for arranging it. Thank you also to Sarmad Sheikh and John Tucker.

The entries listed in this book are or have been available on vinyl, tape, video, CD, DVD and download in retail format for the collector / consumer. Lemmy Kilmister has made many other appearances which have not been released in any such manner, and, should you be interested, these are listed on the Internet Movie Data Base and Wikipedia, amongst others.

Introduction

On 24 December 1945, Ian Fraser Kilmister was born into a post-war generation of young people who would go on to lay claim to their own kind of music: rock 'n' roll. Not suited to run-of-the-mill factory work nor the short-back-and-sides expected from his elders, he quickly rebelled. Filled with optimism after seeing Cliff Richard on television Ian, who by now had picked up the nickname of Lemmy, left tradition behind to strike out and forge a career in the music business.

By the mid-1960s he was making records with The Rocking Vickers, who came extremely close to pop stardom while rubbing shoulders with the likes of The Who and The Kinks, amongst many others, as a support band on the gig circuit. Later in that same decade, he made an album reflecting the music of the then very trendy and fashionable psychedelic era with Sam Gopal.

Out of that era came the hippie movement, so it was probably no big surprise that he would join, more by luck than judgement, Hawkwind, who were about the most spaced-out bunch of hippies on the planet. But after four years and a UK Top 5 hit single, 'Silver Machine', upon which he was lead vocalist, they sacked him due to his supposed instability. Never one to give in easily, Lemmy quickly formed Motörhead, and now, four decades later, practically every living soul who has an ounce of rock 'n' roll in them is familiar with the name.

But those same Motörhead fans may not be so familiar with his recorded output with bands who invited him to make a guest or cameo appearance on an album track or single by way of writing lyrics, playing bass and/or singing; or indeed, by taking a role in their film or video clip. In a once staid rock scene which previously liked to hide the fact that one particular artist might be playing on another's recording for a different record label, Lemmy had it written into his contract that he could do so at his own discretion. To Motörhead fans, it is a safe bet that if Lemmy has taken part, then the music and the artist or artists involved will not only be of a high calibre but also of extreme interest to them.

This book focuses on all of these bands and projects in Lemmy's life which he thoroughly enjoyed being part of, before and parallel to Motörhead. As he was involved in so many extra-curricular activities it has been a huge but nevertheless enjoyable task finding and cataloguing them within these pages where you will find well over 150 examples of appearances on film, TV, album tracks, singles and downloads. Hunt them all down if you wish!

Alan Burridge
Poole, Dorset
October 2015

Introduction by Doro

Lemmy Kilmister was a legend, in the true spirit of the word. Rock 'n' roll has countless larger-than-life figures, but Lemmy was bigger than them all, both in reputation and in heart.

I first met him in LA. I think it was back in 1984. I had to do a gig in front of my record label bosses and was pretty nervous. So I went into the pub next door to have a drink and relax a bit. And guess what: I just ran into Lemmy, who was sitting there with his trademark Jack Daniels and coke.

He invited me to join him for a drink or two, and of course I agreed: you don't said no, if Lemmy invites you... And obviously it did not end after a drink or two, or three, or four...

Two hours later I was staggering back to the record label to perform, but I couldn't sing at all, I forgot the lyrics and everything. Everybody was wondering what was so terribly wrong with me and when my manager asked me, I just told them the truth: "guys, I met Lemmy in that pub." All of a sudden everybody started to laugh out loud and showed great sympathy and understanding, because they all know how it ends up when you drank with Lemmy.

The next time we met was at Donington in 1986 when we were on the bill together with the Scorpions and Ozzy Osbourne. I wanted to see Ozzy's show, but the security people sent me away because I hadn't got the right pass. On the way back I bumped into Lemmy. He asked me where I was going, and I told him. So Lemmy walked up to this security guard, took the guy's pass from around his neck, gave it to me and said: "we are were going to see Ozzy right now, and you get your pass back later." What an amazing scene and what a gentleman Lemmy was.

When my beloved father passed away at the beginning of the century I had a real hard time and often felt very depressed. I recall being with my mum having dark thoughts about suicide and stuff, when suddenly my cell phone rang. I tried to ignore the call, because I wasn't in the mood to talk to anyone. But my mum persuaded me, and when I realised that it was a LA phone number I took the call – and it was Lemmy. He said that he was calling about singing a song together. This call cheered me up, and the possibility of recording with Lemmy gave me back the faith I needed so badly at that point in time.

So I went to LA to record with Lemmy and on the first night we sat in the hotel room and started talking about song ideas. He said he had this song titled 'Alone Again' which he could never put on a Motörhead album, because it just was too soft and gentle.

Next day in the studio Lemmy took the acoustic guitar and played 'Alone Again' in one take, and our jaws just dropped. He added the flamenco bit over the top of it and it just sounded great. Lemmy was an awesome player!

I really wanted to remember those days forever, so I wrote about it: the song is called 'Salvaje' and it's on my »Fight« album.

I am very proud of that, because he was a true innovator, a true individual, and a true friend. Lemmy personified the spirit of rock 'n' roll. I do miss him.
Doro

Collateral Damage

Ian Fraser Kilmister, later to become affectionately known as Lemmy of Motörhead, was born in Stoke-on-Trent on 24 December 1945. His father, a padre in the Royal Air Force, left the family when the young Ian was around three months old. His mother, Jessica, later married a former professional footballer, George Wills, who had played centre forward for Bolton Wanderers.

When he was nine years old, Ian's family moved to Almwych in North Wales, and he attended the Syr Thomas Jones High School. At this point, the Lemmy nickname came into play, which pleased him as he had never been happy with his birth name.

At 15, the young rebel was expelled from school for hitting the headmaster across the face with his own cane. The teacher had been inflicting punishment by caning the young Kilmister's hand and in doing so had split open a previously cut finger wound, with the resulting pain causing the loss of temper and the resulting retaliation.

The first music to catch Lemmy's attention was skiffle, followed by Bill Haley & His Comets' 'Rock Around The Clock', but the first record to ever give him the spinal shiver was Little Richard's 'Lucille'. Together with Jerry Lee Lewis, these two artists became the heroes of this impressionable young rocker. He also liked Buddy Holly and The Crickets, Chuck Berry, and Elvis Presley, and was most impressed after seeing Cliff Richard on the BBC television programme »Oh Boy!« where the rock 'n' roll star was surrounded by a crowd of young girls going crazy over him.

The older generation had their own music with crooners like Frank Sinatra, and big bands like The Glenn Miller Orchestra, as well as the classic symphonies by composers like Beethoven and Wagner. But skiffle came into the post-war consciousness of the younger generation by way of Lonnie Donegan, with his Number 1 hit 'Rock Island Line' in 1955. Records and radio had spread the popularity of different styles and genres of music across the continents, and 'Rock Island Line' had originally been an American blues /folk song popularised in 1937 by Lead Belly (Huddie William Ledbetter). The younger generation took this American blues and rock 'n' roll music as their own, and now that the records could be imported from the United States there were no limits, other than actually finding their whereabouts (usually the larger record shops in the major cities), and having the money to buy them. Later in his life with Motörhead, Lemmy told me he would define rock 'n' roll music as "any music which a teenager would play in their bedroom, and have their parents shouting up the stairs to turn that damned noise down!" And as every generation has an idol creating that scenario, from The Beatles to Eminem and beyond, rock 'n' roll will be with us forever.

But this, what was also known as beat music, inspired the younger generation to form a group and play the music for themselves, and as The Rolling Stones and The Beatles copied this American music in their own way and started to become popular, many other youngsters wanted to do the same. Growing their hair long in stark contrast to the short-back-and-sides style of previous generations, these young men became known as Beatniks, and were regarded as undesirables. But for young men, growing their hair long was all about rebellion: it was all about being non-conformist, demonstrating that they were young and trendy with a mind of their own.

It was the time of a huge culture change by the youth who had been born at the tail-end of World War II. Parents and grandparents were still counting the cost of family losses, and were understandably nervous – after two world wars had followed one after the other so closely – that everything was not as stable as it seemed. But the young felt the need to cheer up that dismal world by not only enjoying some of the new forms of music to which radio had introduced them, but also by copying it, and making music of their own.

From the practically sedate performances and polite applause of the older generation, rock 'n' roll became the target of outrage. Female teenage audiences became hysterical at seeing their idols live in concert, so much so they would be screaming and crying in the theatre, some even emptying their bladder as they stood or sat through the hysteria of the performance; and often the male audience members would become over-excited, leading to seats being ripped from the floor of the venues, and even, on occasion, the band's equipment, such as it was at that time, being completely destroyed.

But this, along with this unique brand of music, gave the youth a voice, and a message that they were important. They were teenagers, and they would have their say and they would play their kind of music. It was an amazing time to be young and involved, and a unique point in history.

So skiffle groups began forming everywhere. It only took an acoustic guitar, (amplified music had yet to be fully developed), a small drum kit, and a bass made from a tea chest, a broom stick, and a length of thick parcel string. Meanwhile, Fender and Gibson in America had pioneered electric guitars and amplification from 1944 onwards, mass-producing affordable instruments and small amplifiers which found their way to musical instrument shops in England. On occasion, American soldiers had brought some of these highly desirable guitars to England and hocked them in pawn shops, not surviving the conflict to return and collect them. Having seen such an attractive object in a shop window, prospective guitar players wishing to learn how to emulate the sounds of their heroes would naturally want to own one of these beautiful guitars, and as they managed to afford them so the bands became electrified and louder. With records now being manufactured in durable vinyl, and in a more manageable 7" size, the younger generation began buying more of them, and found that young people just like themselves had formed bands successfully and were now in the popular music (or 'pop') charts.

Now well into his teenage years and frequenting local cafés where juke boxes played the music which he wanted to hear, Lemmy also found that the fruit machines in such places were an attraction. There are stories that his nickname reputedly arose from asking friends to 'lend me a fiver' to spend on these machines, but in his autobiography »White Line Fever« he sets the record straight: "when my mum and stepfather married, we moved to this house in Benllech, a seaside resort on Anglesey. It was about this time that I began to be known as Lemmy – it was a Welsh thing, I believe. I was in a very bad school, being the only English kid among about seven hundred Welsh – that was made for fun and profit, right? So I've been known as Lemmy since I was around ten."

The youthful Lemmy had started playing guitar for the simple reason that he had noticed that if you were in a band, there were always plenty of girls around you. Back in the late 1950s, and aware of his non-film star looks, he saw a crowd of kids who were showing off with their guitars; even though they only knew a couple of chords, as soon as they hit the strings the girls surrounded them. From Lemmy's point of view this looked the business, and by 1959 he knew that he wanted to be out there at the front playing in the band, rather than being just another onlooker in the audience.

Other members of his family were musically gifted. His mother, Jessica, had played Hawaiian guitar in her younger days, and an uncle played banjo. The Hawaiian guitar had been hanging around the house for years, so when rock 'n' roll arrived Lemmy picked it up and began playing. A friend showed him a few chords, and from there, with a little family help, he went straight into it, playing in his bedroom, the toilet, the bathroom, in fact anywhere he could just sit and play. There was no holding him back, and as soon as he realised that he could strum a few tunes, he was away. Later, as he found that his confidence had built up enough to play a song in front of an audience, he found that friends looked upon him in a completely different light. For Lemmy, this was it. This was the way his life was meant to go.

Jessica bought a smallholding in the Conwy Valley, in Wales, and Lemmy needed a job. George worked as a machine shop fitter at the local Hotpoint electrical company factory at Llandudno Junction (long since redeveloped into a housing estate) and Lemmy found a job there, too, milling in the machine shop on the night shift. Here, the legendary tale of Lemmy and a fellow long-haired beatnik type being sent home on the end of a threat to 'wear a hair net on the factory floor, or get your hair cut!' left him in no doubt as to what to do. So while his fellow-worker returned to the factory with his hair cut in the regulation short-back-and-sides, Lemmy simply left the job.

Losing his job in preference to cutting his hair didn't go down at all well with Jessica and George. Arguments ensued, leading to Lemmy being thrown out of the family home. Another legendary tale arose from this, in that he went to live with a friend in the tunnels, caves and abandoned mine workings in The Great Orme, a prominent limestone headland in Llandudno. But he had a second-hand guitar with mother-of-pearl inlays which his grandmother had bought for him, and although life without work was hard, he spent it wisely continuing to learn how to play.

The Beatles were big news, and The Cavern rock 'n' roll club, opened in Liverpool in 1957, had its own reputation as a place to go for the up-and-coming musician. The Beatles had first performed there on 9 February 1961, and at some point Lemmy hitchhiked from Llandudno to Liverpool to see them play. If he had had his doubts before, from that moment, for him, there was definitely no other option but working in the music business.

Lemmy's first public appearance was with another guitarist and a bass player at a café in Rhyl in North Wales, where he sang Rick Nelson's 'Travelling Man'. A few gigs later, the trio were joined by a drummer who played with Gigster kit brushes, which was the in-thing for drummers of that period, giving the music a jazzy feel.

In 1962, Lemmy saw a Manchester-based band called The Rainmakers (an apt name, as the city is well-known for its high rainfall), who were originally known as The Rave-Ons. The Rainmakers were very popular, and played quite frequently along the north Wales coast with this very trendy coffee bar in Rhyl being was one of their regular gigs. One day Lemmy went to see The Rainmakers play. He was regarded as one of these beatniks, with a scruffy parka and a bed roll strapped into a small haversack of belongings. Legend has it that he and a friend asked the band if they could have a lift back to Manchester. They agreed, and he played a few songs on the journey. The Rainmakers were impressed, and offered him a job playing rhythm guitar and second lead to give the band a fuller sound. But Lemmy's image within the band didn't really fit, so after a short time he left.

The Rainmakers didn't record anything in their day, and neither did Lemmy's next band, The Motown Sect. He played guitar and was their vocalist from 1962 until 1965. This band used to get gigs on the strength of their name. With popular youth culture split into Mods and Rockers, a great deal of the Mods loved Detroit-based Tamla Motown-style soul music, so they were the band's target audience. This was rather an obscure but clever move, as The Motown Sect preferred playing rhythm 'n' blues, along with cover versions of songs by The Pretty Things, Chuck Berry and Them. But they threw in a few Motown soul classics to keep the punters happy, even though the band didn't really enjoy playing them. Typical of Lemmy's sense of humour even then, he would announce "this is a song by The Four Tops," and as the crowd cheered the band would play 'Don't Bring Me Down' by The Pretty Things, and laugh about it.

Following these stints came Lemmy's first band of any consequence, recording-wise; The Rocking Vickers. He had seen them play The Oasis Club in Manchester and thought they were fabulous, mainly because they brought out the rebel in him. In complete contrast to Mod style, The Rocking Vickers were an extremely scruffy bunch with hair down to their armpits. When Lemmy joined them in 1965, they had one single to their name, a cover version of Neil Sedaka's 'I Go Ape', released on Decca Records.

The band's correct name was Reverend Black and The Rockin' Vicars, and they would wear the dog collars of the clergy onstage to clarify the image. However, their record company tended to disagree, taking the typically Sixties' staid point of view that the name, and this additional attire, could offend both church and public alike. In an effort to appease them and keep their contract, the band had to suffer the indignity of an enforced name change to The Rocking Vickers for the sake of promotional posters and on their records.

Managed by Jack Venet, a Manchester crockery salesman, and later by Gail Colson, by this time the band consisted of Lemmy Kilmister on lead guitar, Harry Feeney on vocals, Ciggy Shaw on drums, and Steve Morris on bass. They successfully toured Lapland – and there's not many bands that can say that! – with The Move supporting them, and upon their return were whisked into a photo shoot wearing the Finnish National Costume they'd acquired during the tour. They also had the dubious distinction of being one of the first Western rock bands to play behind the Iron Curtain, in Yugoslavia, as part of a cultural exchange for The Red Army Youth Orchestra. Which country did best out of the deal is for the reader to try and figure out!

The Rocking Vickers' next single, 'Zing! Went The Strings Of My Heart', was only released in Finland and Ireland, mainly because the band were very popular in both countries (touring Finland, where their first single had reached Number 1 in the charts, their itinerary included playing to 10,000 screaming fans at the Olympic Stadium in Helsinki). It was perhaps an odd choice for a single but it was something of a standard at the time; The Move also included it in their repertoire.

Following on from this, the band moved to CBS Records, and went straight into the studio with future producer of The Who, Glynn Johns. The Vickers' sound was very The Who-orientated, and they were big friends with them, even down to Keith Moon making an occasional guest appearance with The Vickers at some of their gigs. The Glynn Johns sessions resulted in the recording of the Pete Townshend song 'It's Alright'; this early version of 'The Kids Are All Right' was officially recorded by The Who on their »My Generation« album. The Rocking Vickers' cut was released as a single on 11 March 1966.

The band's next CBS release was a cover version of The Kinks' Ray Davies' song, 'Dandy'. Released in August 1966 it came very close to scoring The Rocking Vickers a minor chart hit. But the song was being recorded by several other artists at the time, notably Herman's Hermits and The Kinks themselves. The Vickers ended up in an almost toss-of-the-coin situation to appear on »Top Of The Pops«, but solo singer Clinton Ford, who had also covered the song, won the coveted slot on the weekly show. But all was not lost. CBS released The Rocking Vickers' version of 'Dandy' in America where it reached Number 93 in the Billboard Charts. This proved beyond all doubt that the rib-tickling rumour that the Vickers were only famous around the Manchester area was a complete myth.

Investigation into the band's murky past has unearthed the fact that they broadcast two or three tracks on the pirate station Radio Caroline. A fairly good quality tape is also known to exist which highlights The Rocking Vickers as they truly were: thrashing, heavy, and feedback-laden. In essence, if The Who hadn't made it, The Rocking Vickers almost certainly would have!

The 1960s' chart supremo Shel Talmy produced the 'Dandy' single. American by birth, Talmy had found fame producing early singles by The Who and The Kinks, and also had The Creation and The Birds (two of Lemmy's favourite bands) on his books. The Birds were one of The Faces' and The Rolling Stones' guitarist Ronnie Wood's early bands, and Lemmy liked their cover of the Holland / Dozier / Holland Tamla Motown song 'Leaving Here' so much that Motörhead later recorded it, and played it in their live set for many years. The song was also covered in the early 1960s by The Who, and in latter years by Pearl Jam. The Birds started out as a loud rhythm 'n' blues based band with Tamla Motown-like vocal harmonies, much like The Motown Sect and The Rocking Vickers, under the name The Thunderbirds. As this conflicted with Chris Farlowe's backing band it was shortened to The Birds. More confusion arose when the American band The Byrds began releasing records ('Mr Tambourine Man', 'So You Want To Be A Rock 'n' Roll Star' etc) and touring the UK. The Birds split up, and Ronnie Wood and bassist Kim Gardner joined The Creation, another excellent Sixties' band who were also produced by Shel Talmy and had their ground-breaking singles 'Making Time' and 'Painter Man' (with pre-Jimmy Page violin-bowed guitar) released on his Planet record label. Ronnie Wood then moved on to The Jeff Beck Group, playing bass on the »Truth« and »Beck-Ola« albums, before joining The Faces, and later, The Rolling Stones.

By the time The Rocking Vickers split up in 1967 they had probably been banned from more venues than would actually book them. Their stage show consisted of the band shaking their heads, whilst pumping out songs like Jay & The Americans' 'Living Above Your Head', 'Gloria' by Them, PJ Proby's 'Rockin' Pneumonia And The Boogie-Woogie Flu', Sam The Sham & The Pharaohs 'Woolly Bully', Bo Diddley's 'I Can Tell', Bill Haley & His Comets' 'Skinny Minnie' and The Coasters' 'I'm A Hog For You, Baby'. The act would climax with Harry Feeney, and maybe one of the other guitarists, stripping down to his grubby underwear, and making obscene gestures to the girls in the audience: surprising though it may sound, they always seemed to pull!

Bassist Steve Morris was interviewed by fan club member Adrian Lee in the August 1984 edition of the Motörheadbangers fanzine. "The Rocking Vickers were always out-and-out rock 'n' roll, which is where Lemmy's bit comes from. The numbers we played at gigs weren't necessarily those we recorded, like 'Dandy' and 'I Don't Need Your Kind'. Actually, the bottleneck guitar on 'I Don't Need Your Kind' was Lemmy! He always gave out this heavy influence, and we changed our material to compensate when he joined the band. Our version of 'Dandy' got a lot of airplay on Radio Caroline, for fun, and DJ John Peel, who was working for the station when 'It's All Right' was released, said it had the worst guitar solo of all time."

Lee's contact with Steve Morris brought about a small-scale Rocking Vickers reunion during Motörhead's UK tour in November 1984, when Steve and Harry Feeney met up with Lemmy at The King George's Hall, Blackburn, a meeting which all concerned seemed to thoroughly enjoy. These days, Harry breeds poodles, and Steve is a taxi driver. The reunion also led to Ciggy Shaw making contact with Lemmy who, at the time, was living on a houseboat; accepting Lemmy's invite to join him the two former bandmates had a great time catching up on the old days.

The Rocking Vickers »The Complete It's Alright!«
RPM Records (RPM 196)

Compilation album released in 1999
Tracks: 'I Go Ape' (1964 A-Side) / 'Someone Like You' (1964 B-Side) / 'Zing! Went The Strings Of My Heart' (1965 A-Side) / 'Stella' (1965 B-Side) / 'It's Alright' (1966 A-Side) / 'Stay By Me' (1966 B-Side) / 'Dandy' (1966 A-Side) / 'I Don't Need Your Kind' (1966 B-Side) / 'Baby Never Say Goodbye'* / 'I Just Stand There'* / 'Say Mama'* / 'Shake Rattle & Roll'* / 'What's The Matter Jane'* / 'Little Rosy'*
* Previously unreleased
Harry Feeney: vocals, Ian 'Lemmy' Willis: guitar, Steve 'Mogsy' Morris: bass, Cyril 'Ciggy' Shaw: drums
Lemmy played on three of the above recorded tracks, 'Dandy', 'I Don't Need Your Kind', and 'It's Alright'.

With little or no effects for the guitars other than a very primitive fuzz box, the tremolo arm or 'whammy-bar', reverb, and physical changes made by palm-muting and string bending, The Rocking Vickers sound very much the Sixties' band that they were. Amplification was in its infancy, and most guitarists shared one Vox AC30 30 watt amplifier, one each being a luxury. The Beatles, of course, could afford that luxury, but even those three 30 watt amps were drowned out by a concert hall filled with screaming girls. Something louder had to be found.

The Who's Pete Townshend, Deep Purple's Ritchie Blackmore and top session man Big Jim Sullivan all worked with London music shop owner Jim Marshall to overcome the shortcomings of the amps available at that time. Marshall worked with his repair man Ken Bran and Dudley Craven, an EMI sound technician, to produce the first Marshall amps. With their characteristic 'Marshall Crunch' they offered the sound that every rock guitarist was after, and with the development of electronics leading to the Wah-Wah and other effects pedals, the rest is down to rock 'n' roll history.[1]

"The Vickers were all right," Lemmy told me once. "We were earning £200 a week each. We had a house, a speedboat, and a couple of flash cars. We didn't pay the taxman, though!" he added.

With the demise of The Rocking Vickers Lemmy moved to London permanently in September 1967. Jimi Hendrix Experience roadie Neville Chesters

---

[1] In 2008, to honour the longstanding relationship with Marshall amps and Motörhead, Jim Marshall OBE (1923-2012) worked with Lemmy to produce the Signature Marshall 1992LEM 100 watt Super Bass unit, modelled on Lemmy's own modified 'Murder One' amplifier.

had invited him down to the metropolis by offering the temporary accommodation of sleeping on the floor in Hendrix bassist Noel Redding's flat in Harrington Gardens, South Kensington, to start with. This was a good move as straight off the bat Lemmy began earning some cash as a roadie with The Nice for a couple of months. Keith Emerson (keyboards), Lee Jackson (bass and vocals), Brian Davison (drums) and Davy O'List (guitars) were playing on the UK's small, sweaty and smoky blues club circuit, along with other up-and-coming acts like Fleetwood Mac, Chicken Shack, The Savoy Brown Blues Band, and John Mayall's Bluesbreakers.

The Nice had only formed in May 1967 as a backing group for American singer P.P. Arnold, who had UK hits with her version of Cat Stevens' 'The First Cut Is The Deepest' and then with 'Angel Of The Morning'. P.P. had been one of the dancers and backing vocalists, known as The Ikettes, in The Ike & Tina Turner Revue, and she agreed that The Nice could warm-up the audience with a twenty-minute set of their own before she joined them onstage. But P.P. often didn't turn up for her gigs so The Nice had to play the whole show to appease the ticket-paying punters, and the songs they chose (among them 'Rondo', their radically updated version of Dave Brubeck's 'Blue Rondo A La Turk') quickly won them a reputation and an audience of their own.

Keith Emerson was and still is an extremely gifted and flamboyant keyboard player who often physically rode and bounced his Hammond organ around the stage, stabbing the keyboard with daggers to hold the keys down; this created wild feedback, especially during their now show-stopping variation of 'Rondo'.[2]

Their music reflected the psychedelic rock era of the time, along with classical and jazz influences from Emerson's early piano training. P.P. Arnold's visa allowing her to work in the UK ran out, but by then The Nice were regarded as something of a rock phenomenon. The author remembers seeing them play a blues club in Bournemouth named The Ritz on two or three occasions between August and October 1967 as one of the 'must-see' bands of the era, and they were indeed phenomenal. Lemmy and the band's van driver were their only road crew during these formative years.

The Nice recorded their first album and single, both titled »The Thoughts Of Emerlist Davjack«, for the Immediate Records label in time for the Jimi Hendrix / Pink Floyd / Move UK tour. In the space of a few months, they had become hot property on the underground club scene. The tour started on 14 November 1967 and ended on 5 December 1967, playing 30 shows – two shows per venue with a matinee and an evening performance in fifteen large towns or cities the length and breadth of the UK. The bands played on a revolving stage, so that as one performance ended the platform revolved through 180 degrees and next band would appear. Out of sight as the next

2 *Keith Emerson's autobiography »Pictures Of An Exhibitionist« states that the knives he used onstage during the band's act were Hitler Jugend (Youth) daggers, gifted to Emerson by one of his roadies, named Lemmie [sic]. During his Motörhead years in the future, Lemmy's fascination with Spanish forged and designed steel daggers had not abated, and led to him owning a huge collection, some of which were shown in the 2010 »Lemmy« documentary.*

band played their set, the roadies for all the different bands worked together clearing the equipment, and then setting up again for the next band, and so on throughout the show. With so many bands on the bill this changeover had to be slick, and the less well-known bands did not have much time. The performances ran to the following schedule: Outer Limits played for eight minutes, as did Eire Apparent; Pink Floyd had seventeen minutes, and The Move then played for half-an-hour, including their then current hits 'Fire Brigade', a cover of Eddie Cochran's 'Something Else', 'Flowers In The Rain', and 'Night Of Fear'.

After an interval The Nice then restarted proceedings with a twelve-minute set, playing their single and album title track 'The Thoughts Of Emerlist Davjack' and their wild, show-stopping version of 'Rondo'. Amen Corner then played for fifteen minutes, and included their hits 'Gin House' and 'Bend Me Shape Me', before The Jimi Hendrix Experience played a headline forty-minute set featuring the likes of 'Foxy Lady', 'Fire', 'Hey Joe', 'The Burning Of The Midnight Lamp', 'Spanish Castle Magic', 'The Wind Cries Mary', and 'Purple Haze'. This was Jimi Hendrix's second major tour of the UK. The author had also 'experienced' him at Bournemouth's Winter Gardens on 29 April 1967 on the diverse Walker Brothers, Cat Stevens, Jimi Hendrix and Engelbert Humperdinck package. Between the UK tours Jimi had returned to America and played his infamous and legendary guitar burning and smashing performance at The Monterey Pop Festival on 18 June 1967.

Lemmy enjoyed sitting in the wings of the theatres each night watching Jimi Hendrix play, and never did work out how he did it. Lemmy had won his place as a road crew member from working for The Nice, but all the roadies for the different bands worked together to ensure the performances went without a hitch. He remembers being paid £10 a week at the time, which for 1967 was quite generous. "In those days there wasn't a road crew as such, it was just me and Neville [Chesters] looking after all of Hendrix's shit," he recalled. "I didn't do anything technical, I just lifted and carried, and Neville plugged it in. I don't know how we did it, but it always sounded great to me. They used the house PA for the vocals, and there were no mikes on the drums. There was no sound desk or sound engineer, they didn't exist, and that was how it was done."[3]

In June of the following year, 1968, The Nice would create something of a major public outcry with the release of their wildly updated instrumental version of Leonard Bernstein's 'America' (a song was from his musical »West Side Story«). During live performances, they would often set fire to the Stars and Stripes flag as a protest against America's involvement and waste of young human life in the Vietnam War. But although The Nice were popular and their albums sold, they were still regarded as an underground success,

3 *This quote came from a press interview, but I cannot locate the source. Sorry.*

so the band members became frustrated by their lack of mainstream popularity, and broke up in 1970. Keith Emerson, along with ex-King Crimson bass player and vocalist Greg Lake, and Atomic Rooster drummer, Carl Palmer, then formed the Emerson, Lake and Palmer super-group, who achieved that aim with several multi-platinum selling albums, where again, as well as writing their own songs, they transformed a great many classical music favourites into the electric rock medium.

On the same smoky blues club circuit as The Nice and their peers were The Sam Gopal Dream, who were regarded as 'charming' for their use of tablas, (a hand percussion instrument of Indian origin) instead of drums which in the hippie / flower power era, where The Beatles and The Rolling Stones had experimented with Indian instruments like the sitar with some considerable success, was quite fashionable.

When Lemmy joined the band on rhythm guitar and vocals a transition occurred and the band dropped the 'Dream' part of the name to become known simply as Sam Gopal. Other personnel included Sam Gopal himself, on tablas and percussion, Roger D'Elia on lead and rhythm guitar and backing vocals, and Phil Duke on bass.

On December 22 1967 the Jimi Hendrix connection came into play once more when he topped the bill at The Christmas On Earth Continued Festival, at Olympia in London, with an extraordinary support bill consisting of The Who, Eric Burdon and The Animals, The Move, Pink Floyd, Keith West & Tomorrow, Soft Machine, Paper Blitz Tissue, Traffic, The Graham Bond Organisation, and, last but by no means least, Sam Gopal. Jimi Hendrix must have been suitably impressed as he went along to the Sam Gopal gig at The Speakeasy a couple of nights later to jam with them onstage.

Sam Gopal continued picking up gigs, and were signed up by the little known Stable Records label. During October and November 1968, they went into De Lane Lea and Morgan Sound studios to record an album and »Escalator« was released in March 1969. Besides the cover versions of Donovan's 'Season Of The Witch' and 'Angry Faces', written by Davidson, all of the remaining songs were written by Lemmy, although he credited some to 'Group' to give everyone a share of the royalties. Many fans have been confused by the fact that »Escalator« credits Lemmy as Ian Lemmy Willis. The reason for this is that after his birth father left Lemmy preferred to ignore his father's surname of Kilmister in favour of his mother's re-married name of Willis. But because of travelling abroad with bands and the necessary passport and visa paraphernalia that such things require, he found it less hassle to revert to his birth certificate surname of Kilmister, which he had used ever since.

»Escalator« was by no means a major hit album, but Lemmy wrote nine original songs which appeared on it. Since that time, two acetate pressings have emerged, both containing the same songs: 'Horse' (credited to Group), and 'Back Door Man', a Willie Dixon song. These were different takes, and the tracks had not appeared on the album, but have been frequently bootlegged and pirated over the years. A very rare four-track EP was also pressed in minor quantities, too. This was something of an odd item as it shares the same catalogue number as the album (SLE 8001). The EP was in fact a white label test pressing with a Stable Records label glued over the top. This was a good move by Stable as it offered a far more professional looking sampler for DJs, rather than a normal white label with hand-written titles.

If there was a problem, though, it was that Sam Gopal were a rather difficult band to bring over to an audience in the live arena. However, they played dates around the UK and, like The Nice, visited amongst many other venues The Ritz on Bournemouth's west cliff sea front in 1968.

Fellow Stable artists The Deviants (with whom sci-fi author Mick Farren was vocalist) were good friends of the band, and Farren recalled his memories of the Sam Gopal times for a Motörheadbangers Fan Club interview. "There was always a problem because they didn't have regular drums. They had tablas, which required every microphone in the house, as the PA systems were very primitive in those days. There would be howling, screaming feedback, and we'd be waiting to go on, and they'd be hauling those tablas off and putting the regular stuff back on. Raga rock was a strange concept."

Sam Gopal »Escalator«
Stable Records (SLE 8001)

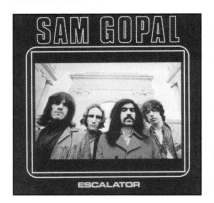

Released 1969
CD re-Issue by Breathless Records (52005) released 3 March 2000
Tracks: 'Cold Embrace' / 'The Dark Lord' / 'The Sky Is Burning' / 'You're Alone Now' / 'Grass' / 'It's Only Love' / 'Horse' / 'Escalator' / 'Angry Faces' / 'Midsummer Night's Dream' / 'Season Of The Witch' / 'Yesterlove' / 'Back Door Man'
Sam Gopal: tablas and percussion, Ian 'Lemmy' Willis: vocals, lead and rhythm guitars, Roger Delia: lead, acoustic, and rhythm guitars, Phil Duke: bass.

Recorded at De Lane Lea Studios, from 10 October to 26 November 1968 and Morgan Sound Studios on 10, 12 and 15 November 1968

Produced by Trevor Walters; engineered by Barry Ainsworth and Andy Johns. Backing vocalists Sue and Sunny. Cover art Paul Francis.

The 'Horse' and 'Back Door Man' tracks were not included on the original »Escalator« album. They were released as a single by Stable Records, catalogue # STA 5602.

As soon as Lemmy found fame in Hawkwind the original vinyl LP of the »Escalator« album moved from selling at under £1 in record shop bargain bins to highly priced collectors' pieces, changing hands for several hundred pounds. Since then, it has been pirated and re-released on a regular basis, both on vinyl and CD, with some versions boasting 'extra tablas added by Sam Gopal.' But much like The Rocking Vickers' release, had Lemmy not become a household name both bands' recordings would be regarded as little more than beat and psychedelic rock curios. Lemmy recalled in a Motörheadbangers interview: "we played The Speakeasy and got a standing ovation. I wrote all the songs on the »Escalator« album (except 'Angry Faces', 'Back Door Man', and 'Season Of The Witch' on the above release), but credited some to 'Group' to share the royalties around."

On 27th May 2010 a short black and white promo film of the Sam Gopal band miming to 'The Sky Is Burning' was uploaded to YouTube. Where this rare gem had been tucked away since 1969 we can only guess, but are grateful nevertheless. Filmed on a small boat on the River Thames near London's Tower Bridge, after a short introduction (by a French male voice), Lemmy Willis, as he was then known, dressed in a fringed suede jacket (as he was on the album cover), sunglasses, and playing a Fender Telecaster, appears with the other three members of the band. Such an early promo film as this presupposes high expectations of the Sam Gopal band as hit makers, as films like this were both uncommon and expensive to make around this time and usually only made if a sure-fire hit could recoup the outlay. The film might have been made for »Top Of The Pops« or a French TV pop station, but we may never know for certain. But it is quite something to have such an early piece of Lemmy's history emerge on film from the vaults to be enjoyed by his fans around the world.

After Sam Gopal had finally ended their days, Lemmy rehearsed with and auditioned for countless acts, including the strangely named Follow That Buffalo. It was a dismal time, and nothing fruitful happened. But whatever Lemmy did, his focus was always on the music business, and his self-imposed tunnel-vision did not waver. Not once did he run back to live with his parents, or take work outside music. He was always there, seeing bands, helping them shift gear, making sure they had whatever they needed, and being a part of the vibrant London music scene.

During 1970, for a brief four months, Lemmy joined Opal Butterfly, but didn't record anything with them. Opal Butterfly had been formed in 1967 by vocalist Allan Love, who recruited Tom Doherty (guitar / vocals), Robbie Milne (guitar), Richard Bardey (bass and vocals), and Simon King (drums) via an advertisement in the weekly Melody Maker music paper. They rehearsed for several months before playing some local dates and then auditioned for CBS Records, signing to them in February 1968 and releasing their debut single 'Beautiful Beige'.

After several tours, which included support slots to acts such as Argent, Graham Bond, The Bonzo Dog Do-Dah Band, Fat Mattress, and The Move, Opal Butterfly released a second single, titled 'Mary Ann With The Shaky Hand', a cover version of a Pete Townshend song from »The Who Sell Out« album. By this time though the band had gone through several line-up changes. Allan Love had left, and it was decided that they would remain as a four-piece. Tom Doherty and Richard Bardey now shared vocals, and Ray Major replaced Robbie Milne on lead guitar. Further tours and support slots followed with bands such as Deep Purple, Steamhammer, and Atomic Rooster, by which time Opal Butterfly had built themselves a strong college and university following, and many people commented that the band sounded like a British version of Leslie West's Mountain.

During this period Tom Doherty and Simon King had a brief flirtation with the movie world, when they were asked to act as a couple of band members in the film »Groupie Girl«, starring Esme Johns. This also resulted in Opal Butterfly writing and playing on two songs which appeared on the soundtrack album. »Groupie Girl« was similar in many ways to the British 'bawdy seaside comedy' films in the »Carry On« tradition, and it did finally get a release on DVD in 2007. Some reviews of the film regarded it as mild soft porn and an online review went as far as to refer to it as "a skin-flick with some youth culture overtones, with var-

ious obnoxious hippie bands used as an excuse to display a good amount of naked female flesh on the screen."

It was just after this stab at movie stardom that Lemmy joined Opal Butterfly's ranks. His job description encompassed sharing bass, vocals and guitar duties with Tom Doherty who had taken over playing bass after the departure of Richard Bardey. To this day, Lemmy still owes the members of the band £20 for bailing him out of Chelsea police station.[4]

By late 1971 Opal Butterfly had split, and Lemmy and Simon King had joined Hawkwind. Ray Majors would later join Mott, the post-Ian Hunter incarnation of Mott The Hoople, and Tom Doherty left England to join the Chicago-based band, Shaky Jake. Today, Simon King deals in antiques, Ray Majors is a session musician, and Tom Doherty owns a record company.

Hawkwind were based in Lemmy's home territory of Ladbroke Grove in London. Guitarist, songwriter, and former street musician Dave Brock had formed Hawkwind in November 1969. They became known for their lengthy fifteen to twenty minute 'space-rock' songs, usually with dirge-riff-hypnotic 'psychedelic' tendencies, strobe light show, and lyrics favoured by fans who were drawn by-and-large from the tail-end of the waning hippie era and underground scene. From the mixture of these laid-back musical cultures, Hawkwind frequently played free concerts, benefit gigs and festivals, often from the back of a parked lorry.

Friends with Hawkwind's electronics / keyboards player, Michael 'Dik Mik' Davies, Lemmy hung around with the band frequently. At one of their free open-air gigs at Powys Square in Ladbroke Grove, the bass player Dave Anderson didn't show up. But his bass had been loaded onto the van and the band asked Lemmy to cover the shortfall, which he did: an astute rhythm guitarist, Lemmy just played chords on the bass like a rhythm guitar, and he, Dave Brock (guitar) and Simon House (drums) formed a powerhouse three-piece rock band at the focal point of Hawkwind, whilst Dik Mik's oscillator and Nik Turner (saxophone) played cosmic sounds and almost free-form jazz respectively over the top, while amongst all that Stacia danced either naked or semi-naked.

Lemmy enjoyed the freedom of this avant-garde style where songs could last twenty minutes or so, and was happy when he was taken on as Hawkwind's bass player and backing vocalist. The first release which he appeared on was

---

[4] *Probably for possession of a small amount of marijuana, although this has never been made clear*

»Greasy Truckers Party« which captured Hawkwind, Brinsley Schwarz, Man, Magic Michael and Friends, and DJ Andy Dunkley, live at The Roundhouse, Chalk Farm, London, on 13 February 1972.[5] The album was originally released on 28 April 1972 as a limited edition (of 20,000 copies) double vinyl album, and sold for £1.50. The proceeds from the gig and the album went towards building and running a hostel at Notting Hill Gate in London.

Various Artists »Greasy Truckers Party«
EMI Records (0999 503235 2 4)

Original twelve track (ten song) double vinyl album released 28 April 1972; this box set re-released 22 October 2007

Engineered by Vic Maile; executive Producers: Douglas Smith & Dave Robinson.

The original album featured just two Hawkwind songs ('Master Of the Universe' and 'Born To Go'), taking up the fourth side of the LP. On the CD re-issue, the third CD is given over to their set: 'Announcement – Apology' / 'This Is Your Captain Speaking (Breakdown)' / 'This Is Your Captain Speaking' / 'You Shouldn't Do That' / 'The Awakening' / 'Master Of The Universe' / 'Paranoia' / 'Earth Calling' / 'Silver Machine' / 'Welcome To The Future' / 'Born To Go' / 'Brainstorm (Jam)'.

Putting the 'Announcement – Apology' title into historic perspective, wage disputes between unions and the government had led to electricity power cuts during this era, which occurred at any time. The lack of power during the show led to Hawkwind's synthesisers being temperamental, and the band having to re-start after '(Breakdown)', performing 'This Is Your Captain Speaking' in two parts.

After the double LP had become a long-deleted collector's item, this expanded CD box set release was more than welcome. Freshly re-mixed from the original multi-track master tapes and featuring the whole set (rather than the small selection of tracks on the original LP), it breathed a new lease of life not only into the recordings, but also into the generation of rock rans, now in their late fifties and early sixties, who were either there in person or who remember it as part of their rock heritage. It is also a classic for all younger rock historians to study, as gigs and events like this are something which can never be re-created, but just re-lived on record or film. All tracks feature Lemmy Kilmister on bass.

5 *Built in 1847, The Roundhouse was a circular railway engine shed containing a turntable, enabling locomotives to take a 360 degree swing around for their return journey. After ten years or so, its usage as such stopped, and it became a storage facility, and during World War II, it was left empty. Some 25 years later it was updated, and then housed a theatre company, and later also staged some rock concerts, one such being known as Greasy Truckers Party.*

History was made in that although Robert Calvert sang 'Silver Machine' on the original recording, the backing track with Lemmy's re-recorded vocals ended up as the best-selling single which brought the band's (and Lemmy's) name to public attention, fame, and fortune.

Hawkwind 'Silver Machine' / '7 By 7'
United Artists Records (UP 35381)

Released 9 June 1972
Produced by Hawkwind & Dr. Technical; recorded live at The Roundhouse on 13 February 1972 with overdubs (Lemmy's vocals) and mixing at Morgan Studios, London. Reached Number 3 in the UK Top Forty.

Recorded live at Greasy Truckers, this version was first made available, along with 'Welcome To The Future' (also from that Roundhouse gig) on the »Glastonbury Fayre« triple vinyl album in April 1972. This was limited to a pressing of 5,000 copies, and included a 32 page booklet, PVC outer album sleeve, a poster, and a foldable silver pyramid, all designed by Barney Bubbles.

It comprised tracks by some of the bands who performed at the Glastonbury Festival, at Pilton in Somerset, England, on the 22 to 26 June 1971. Although tracks by The Pink Fairies, The Edgar Broughton Band, Mighty Baby and Daevid Allen & Gong were recorded live at the event, others, like Hawkwind's, and those by The Grateful Dead, David Bowie, Marc Bolan, Skin Alley, Brinsley Schwarz and Pete Townshend, were recorded elsewhere but donated for use on this release.

The »Glastonbury Fayre 1971« DVD (released 8 June 2009) is an 87 minute film of the event by Nick Roeg. Unseen for over 30 years since its original cinema release, it has been digitally restored, and captures the optimistic spirit of the hippie generation before it faded into obscurity.

The actual festival also included Terry Reid, Traffic, Melanie, Quintessence, Henry Cow, Fairport Convention, Joan Baez, Help Yourself, Family, and Arthur Brown, some of whom, whilst they did not appear on the album, are included on the DVD which is an important and compelling document of rock and music festival history.

As a member of Hawkwind, Lemmy would appear on the next three studio releases as well as live albums resulting from them.

Hawkwind »Doremi Fasol Latido«
EMI Records (7243 5 30031 2 8)

Released 1972; this CD re-issue 2001
Tracks: 'Brainstorm' / 'Space Is Deep' /
'One Change' / 'Lord Of Light' / 'Down
Through The Night' / 'Time We Left This
World Today' / 'The Watcher'
CD bonus tracks: 'Urban Guerrilla' / 'Brainbox
Pollution' / 'Lord Of Light' (single version) /
'Ejection' (previously unreleased version)
Recorded at Rockfield Studios, Monmouth-
shire, Wales, during October and November
1972, the album reached Number 14 in the
UK chart. This was Hawkwind's third studio al-
bum (although their first with Lemmy) and
was preceded by »Hawkwind« in 1970, and »In Search Of Space« the following year.
Drummer Simon King and Lemmy's so-called heavy influence became immediately
apparent on »Doremi Fasol Latido«, despite Lemmy pointing out in the re-issue
sleeve notes that "it was not very well recorded, it's very thin and tinny."
'The Watcher' was written by Lemmy, the first song he wrote for the band, on
which he also took lead vocals. The song lyric is about a god or an alien ex-
traterrestrial watching the people of Earth destroying themselves through their
own greed, and would be one of the songs which Lemmy took with him into
Motörhead, featuring both on their early albums, and in the live arena.

Hawkwind »At The BBC – 1972«
EMI Records (50999-609929-2-5 HAWK 7)

Released 15 March 2010
Tracks – CD 1: Johnny Walker Radio 1 Session
recorded at Maida Vale Studio 5 on 2 August
1972: 'Brainstorm' / 'Silver Machine'
In Concert (mono version), recorded at the Paris
Theatre, London, on 28 September 1972:
'Countdown' (0.56) / 'Born To Go' (11.26) /
'The Black Corridor' (2.24) / 'Seven By Seven'
(7.06) / 'Brainstorm' (10.17) / 'Electronic No. 1'
(2.44) / 'Master Of The Universe' (7.30) / 'Paranoia' (5.56) / 'Earth Calling' (3.03) / 'Silver Machine' (5.10) / 'Welcome To The Future' (3.02)

Tracks – CD 2: In Concert (stereo version)*: Recorded at the Paris Theatre, London, on September 28th 1972: 'Countdown' (1.08) / 'Born To Go' (11.22) / 'The Black Corridor' (2.26) 'Seven By Seven' (7.07) / 'Brainstorm' (6.14) / 'Electronic No. 1' (2.04) / 'Master Of The Universe' (7.31) / 'Paranoia' (5.56) / 'Earth Calling' (3.03) / 'Silver Machine' (5.11) / 'Welcome To The Future' (2.53) Recordings were produced by Jeff Griffin, and engineered by Chris Lycett.

Neither the Johnny Walker session tracks nor the stereo version of the in concert tracks had officially been released until this package came along. The mono tracks had been released before on Windsong Records in 1991, and the stereo version was an 'off-air' bootleg, unimaginatively titled »Broadcast«. Of course, as an official BBC release, this set boasts an unsurpassable sound quality. With photos from the era included in the CD booklet, this timely release killed off the other sub-standard and bootleg travesties.

The show was recorded just after the band had enjoyed their chart hit with 'Silver Machine', and this was the reason it was included in what normally constituted 'The Space Ritual' set. The Space Ritual itself was later recorded by the band on the tour bearing that name, so this BBC recording is a precursor to that phenomenal album and live event, which so many fans proudly thrust out their chests to boast that 'I was there!'

Hawkwind »The Space Ritual – Alive In Liverpool And London« EMI Records (HAWKSR4)

Originally released 11 May 1973, this special collectors' edition was released 25 June 2007

CD 1 / DVD: 'Earth Calling / 'Born To Go' / 'Down Through The Night' / 'The Awakening' /' Lord Of Light' / 'Black Corridor' / 'Space Is Deep' / 'Electronic No. 1' / 'Orgone Accumulator' / 'Upside Down' / '10 Seconds Of Forever' / 'Brainstorm' #.
CD 2 / DVD: '7 By 7' / 'Sonic Attack' / 'Time We Left This World Today' / 'Master Of The Universe' / 'Welcome To The Future' / 'You Shouldn't Do That'* / 'Orgone Accumulator'+ / 'Time We Left This World Today'+ / 'You Shouldn't Do That'

Plus DVD video section 'Silver Machine' (original promo film) / 'Urban Guerrilla' (original promo film)

Recorded live at Liverpool Stadium on 22 November 1972, and at Brixton Sundown on 30 December 1972 by Vic Maile and the Pye Mobile. Mixed at Olympic

Studios by Anton Matthews and Vic Maile. Sleeve art by Barney Bubbles a.k.a Colin Fulcher (1942-1983). Digital re-mastering and new mixes by Peter Mew and Nigel Reeve at Abbey Road Studios, London, assisted by Mirek Stiles. Produced by Hawkwind.

* Previously unreleased.

Previously unreleased complete version.

+ Alternate night's performance.

The album reached Number 9 in the UK album charts, and Number 179 in the Billboard Top 200.

Recorded during the tour to promote the »Doremi Fasol Latido« album, The Space Ritual attempted to create by way of sound, vision and artwork, travelling through space and time. It featured dancers and a light show by Liquid Len. The original live double LP had long become worn out and scratched with constant playing by its owner, stoned and stumbling in the dark to turn the records over. Released on CD before, this 2007 special edition is just about the most definitive release of this classic live album as you can get. It has all the extras, including the 'Silver Machine' promo film in its entirety, which in the past seemed to have either been shown on »Top Of The Pops« before we had VCR, or as incomplete segments. If you're reading this and have never experienced The Space Ritual, may I suggest that you remedy the situation as soon as possible. If you are a fan of Lemmy's unique bass playing style, this album is a great indication of its early development and power.

Hawkwind »The 1999 Party«
EMI Records (72143 8 33333.2 5)

Released 17 November 1997
CD1: 'Intro' / 'Standing On The Edge' / 'Brainbox Pollution' / 'It's So Easy' / 'You Know You're Only Dreaming' / 'Veteran Of A Thousand Psychic Wars' / 'Brainstorm' / 'Seven By Seven'
CD2: 'The Watcher' / 'The Awakening' / 'Paradox' / 'You'd Better Believe It' / 'The Psychedelic Warlords (Disappear In Smoke)' / 'Sonic Attack' / 'Master Of The Universe' / 'Welcome To The Future'
Recorded 21 March 1974 at the Chicago Auditorium Theatre and engineered by Roy Thomas Baker with the Paragon remote. Mixed and digitally edited by Dave Brock and Paul Cobbold, February / March 1997. Executive producer: Douglas Smith.

This was Hawkwind's second American tour, running from 1 March to 15 April, with support from Welsh blues rock band Man. It featured a revamped Space Ritual set, with only three songs and three poems remaining from it. Two Michael Moorcock poems, which ended up being reworked, would later be released on the »Warrior On The Edge Of Time« album, and five tracks would later appear on »Hall Of The Mountain Grill«. The stand-out track for Hawkwind and Motörhead fans is the inclusion of a live rendition of 'The Watcher'.

Hawkwind »Hall Of The Mountain Grill«
EMI Records (7243 5 30035 2 4 LC 0542)

Originally released in September 1974
Tracks: 'The Psychedelic Warlords (Disappear In Smoke)' / 'Wind Of Change' / 'D-Rider' / 'Web Weaver' / 'You'd Better Believe It' / 'Hall Of The Mountain Grill' / 'Lost Johnny' / 'Goat Willow'
Bonus tracks: 'You'd Better Believe It' (single version) / 'The Psychedelic Warlords (Disappear In Smoke)' (single version) / 'Paradox' (remix single edit) / 'It's So Easy'
Dave Brock: lead guitar, 12 string guitar, synthesiser, organ and vocals, Lemmy: bass, vocals, (rhythm and lead guitar on 'Lost Johnny'), Simon House: keyboards, synthesiser and vocals, Nik Turner: sax, oboe, flute and vocals, Del Dettmar: keyboards, synthesiser and kalimba, Simon King: drums and percussion

Recorded at Olympic Studios, Barnes, London, from May through June 1974, with tracks 5, 9, 10, 12 and 13 recorded live at Edmonton Sundown, 26 January 1974. Produced by Hawkwind and Doug Bennett.

»Hall Of The Mountain Grill« has been heralded by critics and fans alike as one of – if not actually – Hawkwind's best, although it peaked at Number 16 in the UK chart, the lowest placed of the albums on which Lemmy appeared. Lemmy, of course, played bass and added vocals throughout this album, but he had also put music to Mick Farren's 'Lost Johnny' lyric, on which he also played rhythm and lead guitars, and took the lead vocal.

In their younger days, Lemmy and Mick Farren had bumped into one another on London's psychedelic music nightclub scene, and had also shared the same record label in Stable Records, with Sam Gopal for Lemmy, and The Deviants for Farren. A science fiction writer both then and now, Farren captured a rather fantastic stream of sci-fi consciousness within the lyrics of 'Lost Johnny'. Reminiscent of those Pete Brown wrote for Cream in that they throw cinematic images into your consciousness with every line, Lemmy took the song onwards into Motörhead, often introducing it as 'Misplaced Durex' – a 'Johnny' being English slang for a condom, of which Durex is one of the leading brands.

Robert Calvert »Captain Lockheed And The Starfighters« Eclectic Discs (ECLCD1056)

Originally released 1974; expanded re-issue 2007

Tracks: 'Franz Josef Strauss, Defence Minster, Reviews The Luftwaffe In 1958, Finding It Somewhat Lacking In Image Potential' 1:40 / 'The Aerospace Inferno' 4:36 / 'Aircraft Salesman (A Door In The Foot)' 1:41 / 'The Widow Maker' 2:42 / 'Two Test Pilots Discuss The Starfighter's Performance' 0:41 / 'The Right Stuff' 4:23 / 'Board Meeting (Seen Through A Contact Lens)' 0:58 / 'The Song Of The Gremlin (Part One)' 3:22 / 'Ground Crew (Last Minute Reassembly Before Take Off)' 3:17 / 'Hero With A Wing' 3:20 / 'Ground Control To Pilot' 0:52 / 'Ejection' 3:35 / 'Interview' 3:56 / 'I Resign' 0:27 / 'The Song Of The Gremlin (Part Two)' / 'Bier Garten' 0:39 / 'Catch A Falling Starfighter' 2:54

Bonus tracks: 'The Right Stuff' (extended version – previously unreleased) 8:07 / 'Ejection' (single version) 3:47 / 'Catch A Falling Starfighter' (single version) 3:00 (single released on United Artists (UP35543) in 1973)

Recorded at Olympic Studios on 17th August 1973

Musicians: Paul Rudolph: lead, rhythm and bass guitars, Lemmy: bass and rhythm guitars, Simon King: drums, Brian Peter George St John Le Batiste De La Salle[6]: synthesiser and electronic effects, Del Dettmar: synthesiser, Nik Turner: saxophones, Dave Brock: lead guitar ('The Widow Maker'), Twink: funeral drum ('Catch A Falling Starfighter'), Bob Calvert: voice, percussion, Arthur Brown: voice ('The Song Of The Gremlin'), Adrian Wagner: keyboards and Series III ('The Song Of The Gremlin') (keyboards and Series III by courtesy of Robert Moog), The Ladbroke Grove Hermaphroditic Voice Ensemble: back-up vocals

[6] *Or Brian Eno to his friends*

Actors: Vivian Stanshall, Jim Capaldi, Tom Mittledorf, Richard Ealing and Bob Calvert

Technicians: Phil Brown, Frank Owen, Rufus Cartwright, Anton Matthews, Phil Chapman

Produced by Roy Baker, co-ordination by Douglas Smith. Recorded at Island, Olympic, Radio Luxembourg (dialogue) Studios between March 1973 and January 1974; re-mixed at Trident Studios

All words by Bob Calvert, and all music apart from 'The Widow Maker' (Dave Brock) and 'The Song Of The Gremlin' (Adrian Wagner, Arthur Brown)

Poet, writer and musician, Robert Calvert (1944-1988) was the intermittent frontman / vocalist for Hawkwind between 1972 and 1979. He co-wrote 'Silver Machine', the lyrics for which were about his bicycle.

During his time away from Hawkwind, Calvert worked on a number of solo projects, this album being the first. Lemmy, Hawkwind, some of The Pink Fairies, and various other Ladbroke Grove musicians worked on getting this strange Robert Calvert concept album together.

Is it a stage play with music, a rock opera, or just Calvert's eccentricity?

Hawkwind »Warrior On The Edge Of Time« Rock Fever Music (RFM 011)

Originally released May 1975: gatefold re-release with bonus tracks, 2001

Tracks: 'Assault & Battery Part 1' / 'The Golden Void Part 2' / 'The Wizard Blew His Horn' / 'Opa-Loka' / 'The Demented Man' / 'Magnu' / 'Standing At The Edge' / 'Spiral Galaxy 28948' / 'Warriors' / 'Dying Seas' / 'Kings Of Speed'

Bonus tracks: 'Motörhead' / 'Kings Of Speed' (live)

Dave Brock: guitar, synth, bass track and vocals, Nik Turner: tenor and soprano sax, flute and vocals, Lemmy: bass guitar, Simon House: mellotron, moog, piano, synth and violin, Simon King: drums and percussion, Allan Powell: drums and percussion, Mike Moorcock – vocal (tracks 3 and 9)

Produced by Hawkwind. Recorded at Rockfield Studios, March 1975. Engineered by Dave Charles. Mixed at Olympic Studios, March 1975, engineered by Phil Chapman and Steve Owen.

Reached Number 13 in the UK album charts, and Number 50 in America's Billboard chart.

»Warrior On The Edge Of Time« would be Lemmy Kilmister's final album with space rockers Hawkwind. Lemmy's verdict? "The album was a fuck-up from start to finish," he noted on the re-issue sleeve notes. "That 'Opa-Loka' was a lot of fucking rubbish. I wasn't even on that. That was the drummer's thing, that track. We were kind of complacent anyway. If you have a hit album, you're complacent, and if you have two, you really are in trouble. With them, they had four, because they had »In Search Of Space« before me. There's some great stuff on all them albums. »The Golden Void« was a beautiful track, but by then I was well out of favour."[7]

Lemmy's sacking from Hawkwind during their third American tour has been well documented over the years. After being caught by customs officials with a small amount of amphetamine sulphate (otherwise known as speed) at the border entering Canada from Detroit, he was locked up for three days. Customs had believed the drug to be cocaine, which carries a more serious charge, but finding this not to be the case Lemmy was released; speed was not regarded as an illegal substance at the time.

But his fellow musicians were not amused as the tour had been placed in jeopardy: some previous grudges also came to a head which resulted in a band vote and in Lemmy being sacked.

Returning to Ladbroke Grove where he shared an apartment with Motorcycle Irene[8], he was determined to start a band of his own, and the grounds that if it was his band, then he could never be sacked again. Their first gig, on 20 July 1975 at The Roundhouse, saw them supporting Greenslade, one of the progressive rock bands of the time who would soon feel the backlash of the nascent punk movement. Motörhead identified more with the stripped-down return to rock 'n' roll basics of the punk rock scene. "We were part of it, except we had long hair," Lemmy said in one Motörheadbangers interview, and after meeting them on the gigging circuit and also sharing the same label

[7] *Please note: there have been numerous releases and re-releases from Hawkwind with Lemmy but, for the sake of brevity, only the official and original releases have been included here. For a complete Hawkwind story, Carol Clerk's »The Saga Of Hawkwind« (Omnibus Press ISBN 1-84449-832-8) is recommended reading.*

[8] *In a double-page feature in Sounds weekly music paper in the 1980s, Irene Thoeduru, whom Lemmy later nicknamed Motorcycle Irene after the song by American psychedelic rockers, Moby Grape, said that she had met Lemmy when he turned up as a candidate to share her apartment. She said that he'd thumbed through her album collection to find out what her tastes were and, deeming these acceptable, took on the arrangement. They became friends and Irene hung out with the band, becoming Motörhead's unofficial photographer: many of her casual photos appear on the inner sleeve of the Chiswick »Motörhead« album. Later, as Motörhead's popularity increased, Irene worked for Douglas Smith's Greybray management team at 15 Great Western Road, and, for some time, she and Phil Taylor were a couple. Reputedly, Irene had nicknamed him as a Philthy Animal due to his sexual tastes, and like her nickname, it stuck. The band occasionally referred to Douglas as Drugless in a similar manner.*

in Stiff Records, Motörhead were sandwiched between The Damned and The Adverts at another Roundhouse gig on 24 April 1977.[9]

Motörhead had slogged their way around the UK gig circuit, mainly playing clubs to get their name known. They had recorded an album at Rockfield Studios in South Wales for Hawkwind's record company, United Artists, but this remained unreleased until the band's fame began escalating. Original drummer, Lucas Fox, left the band during the recording to be replaced by Phil Taylor, who overdubbed the drums. Eddie Clarke had also replaced Larry Wallis, and they had recorded the 'White Line Fever' / 'Leaving Here' single for Stiff Records.

From Lemmy's passion for amphetamines, the fast-and-furious music of the punk rock scene suited Motörhead's driving music extremely well, so it would be natural that with no barriers from conflicting record companies, he would indulge his passion of joining forces with other musicians to play live onstage, or record, with The Damned. By now, Motörhead's contract with Stiff Records had ended, and by coincidence rather than design, like The Damned, they would also sign up with the Chiswick Records label. But one of Lemmy's live appearances with them would emerge on a bootleg some thirty years after the event.

The Doomed »Live at The Electric Ballroom, Camden, London, September 5, 1978« Bootleg

Limited edition pressing of 235 vinyl copies. Lemmy Kilmister: bass and vocals, Dave Vanian: vocals, Rat Scabies: drums, Captain Sensible: guitar
Side A: 'Introduction' / 'Jet Boy, Jet Girl' / 'Stretcher Case Baby' / 'Antipope' / 'Second Time Around' / 'Problem Child' / 'Silver Machine'
Side B: 'Burglar' / 'Help' / 'Kill' / 'Stab Your Back' / 'City Kids' / 'New Rose'
When the opportunity arose, Lemmy enjoyed nothing more than joining The Damned onstage for a gig. They did so under the band names of The Doomed or Les Punks.

This is a typical bootleg LP, with 'Fuck Off A' and 'Fuck Off B' scratched into the run-off as a means of identity. It has a white paper inner sleeve, and a white cardboard outer sleeve, with a colour photocopy giving details and tracks on the recording, and cut-and-paste images of the band members involved. Despite the belief by some fans that this is a hand-held recording made in the audience, the

[9] *The Damned had formed in 1976, and, mainly due to the endeavours of lead singer Dave Vanian, were the forerunners of the gothic-punk genre. Guitarist Captain Sensible wore sunglasses and a red beret onstage as protection against the punk audience habit of spitting at the bands. With Rat Scabies on drums, these three members have been fairly constant throughout the history of the band. The Adverts were also formed in 1976, by guitarist TV Smith and bassist Gaye Advert, whom many regard as the first female punk star. They made their name at The Roxy, which had earned its reputation as London's first live punk venue.*

quality is excellent bearing in mind the technology available in 1978, so this may well be a sound desk recording of the event, which has somehow made it onto the bootleg circuit during 2008. Unnumbered PC-burned CD copies were also doing the rounds, but these tend to foul up, skip and jump, despite their supposed indestructibility. Vinyl will last forever in the hands of the caring record collector. A legitimate release of this historic gig would not go amiss.

In April 1977, Motörhead had become so frustrated at enjoying appreciative live audiences but not having records to back them up that they decided to split up. With a final show pencilled in for the Marquee Club in London on 1 April, the band felt that they wanted something – anything – as a recorded testament to their existence. Lemmy asked Ted Carroll of Chiswick Records to record the gig, but as he didn't have the money to hire a mobile studio he agreed to give them two days in a studio to record a single. This Motörhead did in late April, but with their live show so well rehearsed, they were able to record enough backing tracks for an album over the 48 hour time-span. After hearing the tracks Carroll, along with his business partner Roger Armstrong, agreed to let Motörhead have some extra time to add vocals to the songs.

In June, the rift between Lemmy and Hawkwind had healed somewhat when Motörhead supported them for just over two weeks on a short UK tour. With the album for Chiswick Records on the horizon for release in the August, Motörhead hit the road again with Chiswick label-mates The Count Bishops for the Beyond The Threshold Of Pain tour. This was fated when Phil Taylor broke his hand in a fight.

Up and running again and with Tony Secunda as their manager, the Chiswick »Motörhead« album was released, reaching Number 43 in the UK album charts. Secunda booked the band some more gigs around Scotland, the North of England, and the Midlands, to keep the wolf from the door during late 1977.

In January 1978 a string of ten shows saw the band through until 18 February, when Secunda, seeing the opportunity of Chiswick Records recording The Count Bishops live at The Roundhouse, paid 33% of the costs to have the Motörhead set also recorded. For this show, the band appeared as Iron Fist & The Hordes From Hell, and the live tracks were released five years to the day later under the title of »What's Words Worth?«

Despite this, Secunda didn't get the band where they really wanted to be, and an argument between him and Carroll and Armstrong at Chiswick Records spoiled any opportunity of making another album for the label. The band split with Secunda and his Wizard Management. Phil Taylor and Eddie Clarke formed a pick-up band to earn themselves a few quid as The Muggers, whilst Lemmy looked to return to Hawkwind's Douglas Smith for management.[10] Meanwhile, the trio spent a day in the studios with old pals The Damned to record a couple of tracks for fun.

[10] *Douglas Smith was Hawkwind's manager, and Lemmy met him when he joined the band. Rather like the first United Artists Motörhead album, »On Parole«, Lemmy had contracts with both UA and Douglas at the time, so although Lemmy was fired from Hawkwind, there were still certain contractual obligations still running. Incidentally, although on album sleeves or in the press he might have been called Doug Smith, to his face, he was and is always Douglas. He is one of those people who just need his full name, in the same way as, say, David Coverdale is never known as Dave.*

The Damned 'I Just Can't Be Happy Today' / 'Ballroom Blitz' / 'The Turkey Song'
Chiswick Records (CHIS 120)

Released 26 November 1979
This is currently the best way of finding the 'Ballroom Blitz' track, featuring a superb Lemmy bass solo. The single peaked at Number 46 in the UK charts.

The Damned »Marvellous - The Best Of The Damned«
Big Beat Records (CDWIKK 198)

Released 6 December 1999
Tracks: 'Love Song' / 'Smash It Up' / 'I Just Can't Be Happy Today' / 'Ballroom Blitz' / 'White Rabbit' / 'Wait For The Blackout' / 'The History Of The World (Part 1)' / 'Disco Man' / 'Therapy' / 'Looking At You'
Line-up for this album: Dave Vanian: vocals, Rat Scabies: drums, Captain Sensible: guitar, Algy Ward: bass, (who after forming Tank was replaced by Paul Gray: bass).
Chiswick Records label-mates as Motörhead and The Damned were at the time, they spent the day of 14 May 1979 at Workhouse Studios. 'Ballroom Blitz' was one of the two resulting tracks, and was released on the above 45 single and later re-issued on this CD. The Damned were using Workhouse Studios at this time, (amongst several others), recording their »Machine Gun Etiquette« album.

Motördamn 'Over The Top' / 'Ballroom Blitz'
Devils Jukebox Records (DJB66613)

Released 2009, limited edition of 666 numbered copies on red, white or blue vinyl Also released by Devils Jukebox as a limited edition of 100 in a Marlboro cigarettes style pack of all three coloured pressings.

The session featured Dave Vanian, Lemmy, Rat Scabies, Philthy Animal Taylor, Captain Sensible, Fast Eddie Clarke and Algy Ward, and both tracks result from the 14 May 1979 Workhouse Studios session on The Old Kent Road, in South East London. The sleeve notes call this "the sum total of a day's recording with Motörhead and The Damned. Some have described it as a 'piss-up with instruments', others as 'the two greatest rock 'n' roll bands of the time in unholy union'. We go with the latter. OK, so with 'Over The Top' by the seven-headed beast safely in the can, Lemmy was the only member of Motörhead left standing by the time they came to stick 'Ballroom Blitz' down on tape, but phew, it's only rock 'n' roll... and we love it."

At Motörhead's Portsmouth Guildhall gig on the Ace Up Your Sleeve tour on 13 November 1980, in an interview for Motörhead Magazine, Lemmy told the author: "it was just that us and The Damned wanted to put a record out, all together, seven of us in the studio. What we were gonna do was 'Ballroom Blitz' and 'Over The Top'. So, we all got down to the studio at about four in the afternoon, which was too late anyway, as we were all still pissed from lunch time. Only two of them were there, and Dave Vanian arrived stone cold sober, just as we were getting even more pissed. But we had the backing tracks down, but we didn't get any vocals or lead guitar, and people were going home ill. In the end it was me, Algy, and Vanian, and Vanian went home because he was pissed off with it. So Algy and I put vocals on 'Ballroom Blitz' and 'Over The Top'. It was great fun from what I remember of it, which is very little."

'Over The Top' by Motördamn had previously only been available on The Damned album »The Long Lost Weekend«, released by Chiswick Records (WIK 80) in 1988.

By now Douglas Smith had realised that Motörhead had an audience despite their bad luck at securing a record company to release their impending output. But he had no better luck until he came across Bronze Records, a small label which had been instigated by Uriah Heep tour manager, Gerry Bron. Being fairly insignificant in the now large record industry, Bronze were just about the last port of call. But after going along to a Motörhead gig at Dingwalls in Camden at Douglas's behest, their A&R man Howard Thompson saw a promise in the band previously unnoticed by others. Thompson convinced the powers that be at Bronze to try Motörhead out with a single, and if it made the charts, to sign them for an album.

At Phil Taylor's suggestion, Motörhead recorded their version of the well tried and tested standard 'Louie Louie'. Written by Richard Berry, 'Louie...' had been covered by just about everyone both live and on record, but Motörhead's version, full of pent-up aggression and anger at being ignored for so long but now set free on vinyl, excelled.

Generally, bands go on tour to sell records, new releases being a favourite, and 'Louie Louie' was no exception. But it was underlined by a refreshed kinship with Chiswick Records after the dismay created by Tony Secunda; the company re-released the »Motörhead« album on white vinyl as extra product. 'Louie...' also brought the band their first appearance on »Top Of The Pops«, the 'must-see' TV show for every music fan, mid-tour on 24 October. Both the tour and sales were good enough for Bronze to sign the band for further recordings, and from December 1978 through to January 1979 Motörhead rehearsed and recorded what would become the »Overkill« album.

The album was released on 24 March, with the Overkill tour with Girlschool as support starting the day after. The title track was and still is a tour-de-force which made the rock world sit up and take a lot of notice. A sound like that on 'Overkill' (the song) had never been heard by humanity before. With double-bass drums thundering out a staccato machine gun beat, Philthy Animal Taylor had come up with the riff which every drummer wished they had thought up first. The whole five-minute track with its two false endings still sounds like World War III in a telephone box, and those drums, that riveting bass guitar and Lemmy's rasping vocals, along with Fast Eddie Clarke's slicing six-string, feedback-laden lead and rhythm guitar, have yet to be surpassed. The bonus was the selection of Jimmy Miller as producer, a man whose expertise at recording drums was at the time unparalleled, and as such this original recording is still a sheer delight to listen to some 35 years later.

Suddenly accepted as a serious driving force on the rock scene, Motörhead were invited to play the prestigious Radio 1 'In Concert', with seven songs being broadcast on 26 May. In late June, Bronze released 'No Class' from the album as the second single, and on 7 July Motörhead started recording for the second time that year for the »Bomber« album. Mid-sessions on 24 August, the band played the Reading Festival, allowing fans a 'sneak preview' of their new album by playing the 'Step Down' track, with Fast Eddie Clarke on vocals. Late October and the early part of November saw Motörhead playing some warm-up gigs in

France and Germany as a prelude to the Bomber tour which, with Saxon supporting, kicked off at Bracknell Sports Centre on 10 November.

Motörhead were in their element. Finally, they were playing the larger venues, and thousands of loyal fans as well as newcomers – through the success of these two new albums within twelve months – could go and see them live. The band barely had time to have a day off, as dates at a break-neck speed took them through to 14 December.

Bracknell Sports Centre was a strange venue to play a gig. Motörhead had not played it before, or since. It would be the date that my old school friend and fellow heavy rock music fan Eric Billett and I would meet the band face-to-face for the first time.

Hawkwind had never had a fan club per se; their super-fan Brian Tawn had published his Hawkfan fanzine as such, and upon Lemmy's exit from the band, and Brian's will to see his new band play (and with the punk-era fanzine craze at its height) he created a fanzine titled 'Lemmy Hear Motörhead' in an effort to keep Motörhead in the rock music public eye.

A reader and keen writer all my life, at my day job I worked an offset litho printing machine for the company for an afternoon every weekday, printing letterheads, flyers and suchlike. Information about Motörhead was scarce. Eric and I had seen them at Poole Arts Centre in 1978, and at Portsmouth Guildhall on 1979's Overkill tour. We had played what few albums and singles we had to death trying but failing to get 'bored' with Motörhead. Between us, Eric and I decided that we would try and 'overkill' the band by going to four gigs on the upcoming November 1979 Bomber UK tour. My idea was to write gig reviews of each, and cobble a fanzine together with the idea of other fans also writing gig and album reviews to gain a pool of knowledge about Motörhead.

Brian Tawn had also published a small Motörhead discography, which he advertised via a vinyl record information sharing column in Sounds music paper, called Wax Fax, edited by a guy named Barry Lazell. I sent Brian a postal order for the discography, outlining my plans for a fanzine dedicated to all things Motörhead, and what a rotter he was for publishing his discography, as it was something I had been planning to include in my first edition. Brian replied with the discography, saying that he had a wife and young family, which did not leave enough time to produce fanzines about Hawkwind and Motörhead, and, as I had a printer at my disposal, could I take over the Motörhead side of things. My answer was, of course, YES!

Brian arranged with then Motörhead manager Douglas Smith for backstage passes to be made available for Eric and I at our planned four shows – Bracknell, Bristol, Portsmouth, and Bournemouth Winter Gardens which was a real on-the-doorstep gig for us. Eric had a blue Mini at the time. We too had wives and young children, so such a cheap-to-run car was a necessity. Despite it being November, we arrived at Bracknell Sports Centre in the daylight. A crowd of fans had already started queueing, but just as we were approaching, a young couple wearing tennis whites and holding rackets, walked out of an exit door. Before it shut, I grabbed it, and we walked in. Bold-faced bravado maybe, but hey, we were Motörhead's guests with a backstage pass each awaiting us!

The main sports centre hall had, of course, been emptied ready for the Motörhead show. Somehow, Eric and I found ourselves in space adjacent to the main hall, where the sports gear – pommel horses, mats, badminton nets, trampolines and suchlike – had been stored. A door to our left was just ajar, and I looked in to see Motörhead's amps set up on the stage, the brand new and never-er-before-seen Bomber lighting rig above it, and Lemmy walking toward us. I ducked back and said to Eric, "Fucking hell! Lemmy's walking this way!"

Of course, every rock fan worth his salt knew Lemmy's fearsome no bullshit reputation. Brian had explained that he had written to Lemmy saying that we would be coming along to the show, but we could never imagine quite how we would meet him. I knew that if he walked through that door and saw us and we didn't introduce ourselves, we would look complete idiots later on. So when Lemmy emerged I stepped up to him, offered my hand, and explained my will to produce a Motörhead fanzine, whilst also uttering the hopefully magic words, 'Brian Tawn'.

Lemmy shook my hand, and also Eric's, smiled, said "Ah, yes, Brian, I remember, come on in!" Two-thirds of the way back from the stage in the centre of the floor was the sound desk riser and, standing on it, Fast Eddie Clarke, Philthy Animal Taylor, his drum roadie Paul Cummings, and Douglas Smith. Lemmy introduced us to one another, and we hit it off straight away – and have never looked back.

It was a great show, and we were thrilled to be backstage living the dream of experiencing what went on behind the scenes at a Motörhead gig. The band, Douglas, and tour manager Graham Mitchell were very friendly and helpful. At some point after the show, from Lemmy's liaison on The Young And Moody Band with The Nolan Sisters, Linda Nolan arrived to see him. Before we left for home, Lemmy offered a chug from his bottle of Southern Comfort, which I gratefully accepted, whilst assuring him that we would be seeing them again for the other three shows.

At the Bournemouth show I took along my wife Jane and Eric took his then wife Angie. Both women were treated with the greatest of respect by everyone in the band and crew; Lemmy, Eddie, Phil and the roadies may well have had a top-notch womanising reputation, but only to women who make it known that they are available. Other than that, they were true gentlemen.

Never could I have imagined that the fanzine, later to become the Motörhead-bangers Fan Club, would go on for so many years. In 2009, I took it upon myself to travel by rail to the Motörhead gig at Plymouth Pavilions on 11 November, not only for the Motörhead gig, but also to remind Lemmy that we had first met 30 *years and one day previously at the Bracknell show. He later reminded the crowd that evening that the Bomber tour had taken place 30 years earlier, and dedicated 'Dirty Love' to me for reminding him.*

1980 would not see the pace slacken for the band. Again with Saxon, Motörhead, after dates in Belfast and Dublin, tore through France, Germany, Belgium and Italy between 7 February and 25 March. Despite Motörhead being in his mind for every living and breathing moment of his life now, Lemmy was still keen to record with others, and helped out on a track by his Hawkwind / Hawklords pal, Robert Calvert.

Robert Calvert 'Lord Of The Hornets' / 'The Greenfly And The Rose' Flicknife Records (FLS204)

Released 1980
These tracks were recorded as demos in preparation for Calvert's »Hype« album, and they were issued as a single by Flicknife Records in 1980. The band used for this session was a unique combination of former Hawkwind members, except for Gary Cooper who was Calvert's literary agent at the time.

Robert Calvert »Freq« Cleopatra Records (CLEO94672)

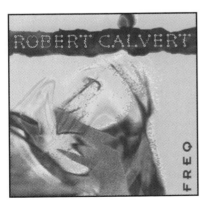

Originally released January 1985; this version released June 1994
Tracks: 'Ned Ludd' / 'Talk 1' / 'Acid Rain' / 'Talk 2' / 'All The Machines Are Quiet' / 'Talk 3' / 'Picket Line' / 'Talk 4' / 'The Cool Courage Of The Bomb Squad Officers' / 'Talk 5' / 'Work Song'
Bonus tracks: 'Lord Of The Hornets' / 'The Greenfly And The Rose'
Recorded at Computer Music, London, August 1984
Rather like his »Captain Lockheed...« album, »Freq« is also a play with music, this time based on 1984-1985 British miners' strike.
Lemmy plays bass on 'Lord Of The Hornets'.

Motörhead recorded a gig at the Apollo Theatre, Oxford, and four tracks were quickly mixed and released as »The Golden Years« live EP in late April. It hit Number 8 in the UK charts, and was also released in The Netherlands as »Lochem Pop '80«, a plug for the Lochem festival which they played in May 1980 (although, of course, it still features the Oxford songs). The band then headlined the Over-The-Top Heavy Metal Brain Damage Party at Bingley Hall in Staffordshire, where they were presented with silver discs for sales of the »Bomber« album.

Phil Taylor's sister Helen, and her boyfriend Paul Hadwen, were running the Motörheadbangers Fan Club at the time. Helen called me and explained that she, and other people she'd chosen from the membership, were organising coaches to take fans to the Bingley Hall gig, and would I like to do so for the south of England. I agreed, and phoned a few local coach companies to get prices. Sea View Coaches in nearby Parkstone offered the best deal, so I booked a 52 seater coach, whilst Helen gave my name in the fan club newsletters as a contact.

On the day, we had 27 fans from around the south, collected at various pick-up points, the last one being Southampton. My wife Jane was travelling pregnant with our second child, who the following October would be born as Steven Alan Burridge. He had already attended Motörhead's West Runton Pavilion gig in the March of 1980, in his early days of looking out of the belly button window.

We were informed by the elderly coach driver to place any empty lager cans in the black bin liners provided, to prevent one rolling beneath the clutch, brake or accelerator pedal and creating a problem. We only had half a coach full, yet after one refreshment/toilet stop, two of the fans were arguing over who was sitting in whose seat. Feeling rather like a school teacher on a day-trip with infants, I went to sort them out.

"He was sitting in my seat," one protested.

"For fuck's sake," I replied, perhaps unsympathetically; "we have half the coach empty; sit somewhere else!"

The whiff of dope overpowered the cigarette smoke in those wonderful times when we could smoke anywhere with no repercussions. The driver did not seem to notice or complain, and not wishing to be the headmaster again, I just let it ride. Finally, we were now in Staffordshire, and by way of a small dirigible hanging in the air with 'Motörhead' and 'Girlschool' logos emblazoned upon it, we aimed for Bingley Hall.

Everyone bailed out to do their own thing once we reached the car park. As luck would have it Douglas Smith was walking towards us: perfect timing. "Around the back, Alan," he said, after a smile and a handshake. "I'll get your backstage passes."

Thank you, Douglas.

We had taken a box of Motörhead Magazines, which I was publishing at the time, hand-in-hand with Helen and Paul with their Motörheadbangers' fanzine. The idea was that we and Helen would have stalls inside to sell magazines, and in Helen's instance, to sign up more fans to the club. Inside, with passes securely clipped on, we had a table alongside Mozz Morris, who was running the Saxon fan club.

Bingley Hall was a large brick-built barn used for cattle auctions. Hosed out, of course, and smelling sweetly, all we suffered from was the July heat. Phil and Helen's parents introduced themselves, and seeing Jane's tummy, invited her backstage, where it was a vastly different air-conditioned paradise. She enjoyed five-star treatment to ensure that she did not fall and injure herself or the unborn child, and we have always been grateful for that special care and attention offered that day.

Photography student Ric Saunders, whom I knew through letters (as he had approached Douglas asking to photograph the band as a University project) approached the stall. "The band asked me to take you backstage, Al. I'll show you the way."

I explained my predicament of not wishing to abandon the stall, and asked him to bring Jane back down, after which I'd be more than pleased to accompany him to this refrigerated heaven upstairs. Half an hour or so passed, and they returned, Jane suitably refreshed and Ric keen to go. As ever, it was great to see Fast Eddie and Philthy again, and we exchanged handshakes and pleasantries. Lemmy was not immediately to be seen, but there was a lounge area which the members of Girlschool were enjoying, so I joined them for a sit down.

They had small A5 sized booklets with Motörhead on the cover. I asked what it was and where had they come from. Kim pointed and smiled to a crashed-out moustachioed guy in an armchair, whom I quickly realised was John Muir. John had approached me some months before with a view to publishing a book about Motörhead. He had his own publishing company, Babylon Books, in Manchester, had sent for my first few magazines, and had been visiting a fellow publisher, who had a paste-up for a proposed book titled »Practical Motörhead«. The title had been 'borrowed' from a British monthly magazine titled »Practical Motoring«, and John had looked at the artwork, told his friend it was crap, and that he knew "the only bloke who ought to be writing a Motörhead book!"

That was me.

We had only spoken on the phone, but I had gathered that John was a bit of a lad. Seeing him lolled there drunk and stoned, I walked over and gave him a nudge. John had come across some black and white photos of Lemmy and Philthy, taken at an early rehearsal session, and he asked me to provide the words to accompany them in a publication. He had approached Douglas to do this with some degree of being approved by the band, and the books Girlschool were looking at were the first print run.

When John came round and I'd introduced myself, he explained that Douglas was happy with the book, but to be fair, there were not enough photos of Fast Eddie. The Fast one had been elsewhere, or turned up after the photographer had left, or some such story, on the day. So, on that proviso that Douglas had agreed to provide more Fast Eddie photos, John had agreed to a second print run.

We chatted for a while, and Lemmy finally appeared looking a bit knackered, and history would dictate (after he had a funny turn during the show) that he had

enjoyed three blow-jobs from the two chicks who were hanging around him that day. Nice one, Lemmy; that's rock 'n' roll, baby!

Bingley was like a rock festival, but indoors, with a good list of bands, like Angel Witch, Vardis, White Spirit, Saxon, and Girlschool, with Motörhead topping the bill. As a special event, Motörhead were presented onstage, by Her Majesty the Queen look-alike Jeanette Charles, with silver discs for sales of »Bomber«.

Afterwards, somehow, we got out of there and found our coach, and with all passengers present and correct, the ride home would drop everyone off in the reverse order to the outward journey. Darkness swallowed the trip back home well, and it seemed as though the return trek was quicker. We were all knackered, drunk, and some a little bit stoned. We dropped the Southampton fans, and others at places I don't remember. By Ferndown in Dorset we were almost home, and most people had been dropped off. A few miles closer, and we arrived at a set of traffic lights near a place named Longham. I'm not sure now what time in the early hours of the morning it was, but the lights changed from red, to amber, to green, and the coach did not move an inch. The old chap driving had nodded off.

"Hey, driver, the lights have changed!" I barked.

At the sound of my voice he kind of shook himself awake, apologised, and set off. We were on the final leg of our way home, after one of the most amazing gigs in Motörhead's early history.

In August Motörhead entered Jackson's Studios in Rickmansworth with producer Vic Maile to record another album, and mid-month, they recorded their set for the »Rock Stage« TV show at the Theatre Royal in Nottingham. Two months later, in early October, they appeared on »Top Of The Pops« with their 'Ace Of Spades' single, and the album, now regarded as a classic, was released on 20 October.

The massive Ace Up Your Sleeve tour began two days later, and culminated in no less than four nights at the prestigious Hammersmith Odeon. At their 2 December appearance in Belfast, Phil Taylor suffered three cracked vertebrae following drunken horseplay with fans after the show.

The following January, the three members of Motörhead, kicking their heels at their drummer's incapacity (none more than Philthy himself), dropped in on Girlschool who were making an album, again with producer Vic Maile at Jackson's. Vic suggested that the two bands record something together, and Lemmy's idea of a cover of Johnny Kidd & the Pirates 'Please Don't Touch' was met with approval from all concerned. This was released quite aptly, on 14 February, as »The St Valentine's Day Massacre EP«, and was a resounding success, peaking in the UK charts at Number 3.

Douglas Smith invited Jane and me up to London to see, and review for Motörhead Magazine, a gig at the Marquee club by ex-Damned bassist Algy Ward's new band Tank, whom he also managed.

We arrived at the Greybray offices in Great Western Road mid-afternoon. Motorcycle Irene took us under her wing, and, later in the day, she went with us by taxi to the famous London rock venue. Irene was accompanied by Lightning Raider's guitarist John Hodge, who, much like everyone within Motörhead's inner circle, was a great guy.

We met up with Algy and the Brabbs brothers, Mark and Pete (Tank's guitarist and drummer respectively) and after conversation and a few drinks I took a few photos of the band to accompany the fanzine review. Who the support band was, I cannot remember now, but Tank's set, (bearing in mind that Algy had learned to play bass from listening to Motörhead records), was quite blistering, heavy, and loud.

After the show, Irene and John took us back to the place Irene shared with, among others, Lemmy. Her bedroom had pillar box red walls and a black ceiling; it was carpeted, with a splendid-looking bed, a huge branch from a tree, and a kind of bookcase of glass with another branch inside it, around which was curled a massive snake, maybe a boa constrictor. Irene smiled and showed us her pet, adding that she would not be letting it roam free and use the other tree branch while we were there.

Irene was sweet and gave us her bed for the night. She and John went off elsewhere and Jane and I looked at one another in amazement. We thought we might get a sofa to sleep on (and indeed, that was about all we expected), so this was a real treat and a wonderful gesture by Irene.

We'd had not eaten much though, other than crisps and salted peanuts bought from the Marquee bar. As Irene had given us a key we decided to try our luck – it was now past 3 am – on the cold, mid-January 1981 Ladbroke Grove streets to try to find something more substantial to eat. Like most capital cities, London never closes, and we quickly found a Kentucky Fried Chicken and bought a large helping each. Sitting on Irene's bed, we felt much better after eating, but still eyed this huge, but seemingly dormant boa constrictor in the glass bookcase with much trepidation. It looked safe enough, so we tried to put it out of our heads...

KFC is fine, but there are always bones remaining. After a while we were awoken by some strange noises in the room. We had not shut the door properly (or maybe it didn't shut) and after switching on the light we found a mixture of six or seven cats and kittens at the foot of the bed, finishing off those KFC bones and what little meat there was remaining. Cat lovers as we are, we enjoyed their company, and before long they disappeared, leaving only the empty cartons.

Having got back to sleep, we were woken by some boots thundering up and down the uncarpeted stairs outside, interrupted in the middle by the sound of the toilet flushing, and then we heard a record being played – 'Please Don't Touch' which we knew Motörhead had recently recorded with Girlschool (also managed by Douglas back then) for release in a few weeks' time. As ever with his nocturnal lifestyle, Lemmy had obviously returned from his usual nightly outings around the clubs (probably The Embassy Club, which was his favourite around that time) with a friend or friends.

Hearing the song was a joy rather than a nuisance: we were getting a sneak preview of the track, which Lemmy had most likely had recorded onto a studio acetate at the time. In fact, we enjoyed it three or four times more, and I cannot think of many better golden rock 'n' roll moments in my life than lying in Motorcycle Irene's bed with my wife, a massive boa constrictor just a few feet away, and Lemmy downstairs playing 'Please Don't Touch' in the early hours of the morning.

We did not meet Lemmy face-to-face on that occasion, but we had a great and memorable time with Irene, John, Tank and the cats, and Lemmy playing his records downstairs. Douglas was always very kind and found a little job for us to do, and that morning back at the Great Western Road offices we spent a few hours working on hundreds of Black Sabbath tour programmes. There had been an error in the printing, so Jane and I had been given wads of sticky-back, glossy printed sheets, which we had to peel and stick over the page containing the error. There were thousands of them, and there was no way that we could finish the job, but Douglas's idea was that if we worked for three hours or so, it would be enough for him to pay us, and the amount would cover our train fares to London and back. He was very thoughtful like that on more than one occasion, and never a rich man and with young children at home, I always felt grateful for his kindness.

As well as the collaboration with Girlschool, during Motörhead's enforced time off due to Philthy's neck injury at this time Lemmy was invited to participate in a track with something of a superstar line-up, which was released later that year.

The Young & Moody Band 'Don't Do That'
Bronze Records (BRO 130)

Released September 1981

The Young & Moody Band were Bob Young (a roadie for Status Quo): vocals, Micky Moody (ex-Whitesnake): guitar, Lemmy: bass, Cozy Powell: drums, and Colleen and Linda Nolan (from The Nolan Sisters): vocals

This was a seemingly unlikely combination of talent with heavy rock superstars rubbing shoulders with two of the five pop darlings known as The Nolans or The Nolan Sisters. Bob Young had worked as a roadie from the mid-Sixties onwards for bands like Amen Corner, The Nice, and The Herd (Peter Frampton's early chart band) so there were connections here from Lemmy's Sixties roots. From this groundwork, he was offered a job as a roadie by Status Quo's management after their 1968 'Pictures Of Matchstick Men' hit single. A musician and writer, anyway, Bob began writing lyrics for Quo, notably 'Paper Plane', 'Caroline', and 'Down, Down'. Meanwhile, after a stint with 'Who Do You Love' chart band Juicy Lucy, guitarist Micky Moody had a band, Snafu, who toured as support for Status Quo. This led to Young and Moody founding a band together, firstly known as Young & Moody and then in 1976 becoming The Young & Moody Band. Cozy Powell had played with The Jeff Beck Group, Bedlam and Rainbow, and was currently a member of the Michael Schenker Group. Whitesnake and Black Sabbath would follow. He enjoyed chart success with drumming-based songs produced by hit guru Mickey Most, namely 'Dance With The Devil', 'The Man In Black' and 'Na Na Na'. The Nolans, or The Nolan Sisters, were an Irish group famous for their 1979 hit single 'I'm In The Mood For Dancing'. So along with Lemmy and Motörhead's image and reputation, this was about the most unlikely line-up of all time, and bound to cause a few heads to turn; it achieved modest success, peaking at Number 63 in the UK chart. Lemmy said of this one-off collaboration: "They offered me money to do it, and with the Nolan Sisters being around, it sounded like fun". A video was made but has rarely been shown, perhaps once or twice on UK TV around the time that the single was released. It can now be found on YouTube.

Motörhead and Girlschool took on an extensive tour of France during March, and returned home (bearing in mind Philthy's recent injuries) for The Short, Sharp, Pain In The Neck tour, with two dates in Newcastle and one in Leeds (27 – 30

March) being recorded for the live »No Sleep 'Til Hammersmith« album. From mid-April they were guests on Ozzy Osbourne's Blizzard of Ozz US tour until the end of June. But with »No Sleep 'Til Hammersmith« going straight into the UK charts at Number 1, it proved beyond all doubt – not that any proof was needed – that Motörhead fans wanted, needed, and now had an album of the band where they were at their best – live in concert. With Black Sabbath pulling out of the headline slot of the Heavy Metal Holocaust festival, at Port Vale Football Stadium, in Stoke-on-Trent, on 1 August, special guests Motörhead were promoted to headliners and as a kind of return favour had Blizzard Of Ozz added in their place as the bill's special guest.

On 1 October Motörhead were invited to the BBC's Maida Vale Studio 4 to record a session for the David 'Kid'

Jensen Radio 1 show. The songs were broadcast five days later and, until the archive »BBC Live & In Concert« double CD was released in February 2008, these sessions had been hidden well under the fans' radar; unlike other Motörhead BBC recordings, the Kid Jensen session had not been one of the cassettes doing the rounds on the bootleg circuit. Jensen's show was broadcast daily during what is now termed as 'drive-time', when people are driving home from work, and it appeared as though most if not all fans had missed these gems. But thankfully, the album researchers did a great job in uncovering them for us.

The No Sleep 'Til Christmas European tour began on 20 November, with Algy Ward's Tank as special guests. Travelling through Scandinavia, Germany and Spain, two dates in Ireland, and one at Belfast's Wickla Hall, brought the tour to a close on 23 December.

January 1982 saw Fast Eddie Clarke producing Tank's »Filth Hounds Of Hades« album at The Who's Ramport Studios in South London. This was where the rot began setting in regarding the relationship between Eddie, Phil and Lemmy. In truth, the time should have been spent rehearsing new Motörhead material for their follow up to »No Sleep 'Til Hammersmith«. Instead, once the Tank album was completed Motörhead used an odd couple of days remaining from those sessions at Ramport, before moving on to record the bulk of what would become the »Iron Fist« album at Morgan Studios during February.

With little time to draw breath, as Motörhead were now the hottest property on the rock scene, the Iron Fist tour began, again with Tank as support, in mid-March. At the same time, the band's relationship with Bronze began getting strained, as the album was released late – two weeks into the tour, in fact – at the start of April. The idea is to play your new album in concert and, the following day, fans, suitably impressed, go out and buy it. But the initial thrust of this fortnight of playing the shows without the album being in the shops was a major concern for the band. However, between the tour's end on 12 April and the next set of band commitments, Lemmy spent some time with some friends recording.

Speed Queen »Speed Queen«
CBS Records (CBS 25101)

Only released in France, in 1982
Side 1: 'Haute Tension' / 'Revanche' / 'Travesti' / 'Contre-Courant' /' Cool It Down'
Side 2: 'Aeroplane Man' / 'Les Maudits' / 'Viens Faire Un Tour' / 'Pas Tout Seul' / 'Rien Qu'une Histoire'
Stevie: vocals, Joel Montemagni: guitars, Terry Smadja: bass guitar, Gerard Jelch: drums
The album was recorded at Island Records Studios in Basing Street, London, in April 1982 and mixed at Scorpio Sound, London, the following month. A rock band from France, Speed Queen supported Motörhead at their Hammersmith Odeon show on 27 November 1979, where they became acquainted with Lemmy. Meeting up again when recording the album in London, Speed Queen invited Lemmy to sing back up vocals on the chorus for the 'Revanche' [revanche is French for revenge] track.

Another American tour had been lined up to begin in the second week of May; but before that, another amalgamation of talent, rather like the 'Please Don't Touch' single with Girlschool, had been organised for the band in Toronto, with punk priestess Wendy O Williams and her band The Plasmatics.

Fast Eddie had muttered words of discontent about the proposed session in a Radio 1 interview with all three members before they flew out, so it seemed as if the die had been cast even then and the sessions, at Eastern Sound Studios in

Toronto, were fraught from the offset, leading to disagreements. The CNE Coliseum show on 12 May was, thankfully, recorded and later released, as it would be Fast Eddie's penultimate gig with Motörhead, after which he resigned from the band. What came to be regarded as Motörhead's 'classic line-up' was no more. Lips from Canadian band Anvil was approached firstly as a temporary replacement to complete the tour. He declined, and ex-Thin Lizzy / Wild Horses guitarist Brian Robertson was next on the list. His first gig was at the Aragon Ballroom in Chicago, on 22 May. A handful of Japanese dates followed in June, followed by Motörhead headlining two outdoor shows, firstly at Wrexham Football Club stadium in Wales, and the day after at Hackney Speedway Stadium in London. New York's Twisted Sister had come to Lemmy's attention and appeared at both these events, and then went on to play at the Reading Festival, a show which was caught for posterity on film.

Twisted Sister »Under The Blade«
Armoury Records (ARMCD532 GAS 0000532AMY)
Special Edition CD + DVD

Released 30 May 2011
»Under The Blade« special edition: 'What You Don't Know (Sure Can Hurt You)' / 'Bad Boys (Of Rock 'N' Roll)' / 'Run For Your Life' / 'Sin After Sin' / 'Shoot 'Em Down' / 'Destroyer' / 'Under The Blade' / 'Tear It Loose' / 'Day Of The Rocker'
Bonus tracks – the »Ruff Cuts«' EP: 'What You Don't Know (Sure Can Hurt You)' / 'Under The Blade' / 'Leader Of The Pack' / 'Shoot 'Em Down'
DVD from the 1982 Reading Festival: 'What You Don't Know (Sure Can Hurt You)' / 'Sin After Sin' / 'Bad Boys (Rock 'N' Roll)' / 'Destroyer' / 'Shoot 'Em Down' / 'Tear It Loose' / 'Under The Blade' / 'It's Only Rock 'N' Roll' / Bonus interviews
The original version of »Under The Blade« album was released in 1982; Twisted Sister's Reading Festival performance took place on 29 August 1982
Dee Snider: lead and backing vocals, Jay Jay French: guitar, Eddie Ojeda: guitar and backing vocals, Mark 'The Animal' Mendoza: bass guitar and backing vocals, A.J. Pero: drums and backing vocals

Famously described by vocalist Dee Snider as like "Slade meets the Sex Pistols" (and Alice Cooper, of course) Twisted Sister were an American band who wore women's make-up but played driving hard rock. Lemmy supported them from the word go, as he could see behind the façade and enjoyed the music for what it was: powerful rock 'n' roll. The Reading gig was never supposed to have been filmed or recorded in its entirety, and the bands were told that the cameras were there only for broadcasting the performance to the VIP tent, so there are sound and vision limitations. But fans were pleased that such an historic performance had survived for almost thirty years. During a jam on The Rolling Stones' 'It's Only Rock 'N' Roll' Lemmy, Fast Eddie Clarke, and ex-UFO bassist, Pete Way, joined Twisted Sister onstage. Less than three months after Fast Eddie had left Motörhead during their American tour, Dee Snider helped heal any wounds by getting Lemmy and Eddie back onstage together. Pete Way was producing the »Under The Blade« album sessions for Twisted Sister at this time, on which Eddie played the guitar solo on 'Tear It Loose', and together Way and Clarke were also in the early stages of forming the first (and very short-lived) Fastway line-up.

In September, 'Stand By Your Man', the ill-fated collaboration between Motörhead' and Wendy O Williams, was released in the UK, but it did not achieve anything like the success of Motörhead's earlier association with Girlschool. With Brian Robertson now regarded as Motörhead's permanent guitarist, the band undertook a European tour from mid-October through to mid-November.

Twisted Sister »The Video Years«
Rhino DVD (R2 127868)

Released 16 July 2007 (total running time 131 minutes)

The first song on this collection is from »The Tube«, UK Channel 4's TV rock show, from December 1982. Twisted Sister were playing The Rolling Stones' 'It's Only Rock 'N' Roll (But I Like It)' and, seemingly worried about how the TV audience would take to them on this very popular Friday evening peak-viewing-time show, vocalist Dee Snider removed his make-up on-camera to show that they were just a basic good-time rock 'n' roll band underneath the face paint. To cement their credibility, Snider invited "Lemmy Kilmister and Brian 'Robbo' Robertson from Motörhead" to join the band onstage for the song. Lemmy and Robbo walked quickly through the audience (with a cameraman right behind them) to pick up their guitars and speed the song back up, ending in Lemmy announcing: "Twisted Sister, all right!" to seal the band's standing forever. Also included is a 2007 interview with Lemmy talking about the event, and he talks later in the DVD about Dee Snider as a frontman.

Lemmy later told me that Brian Robertson had only signed with Motörhead to do one album. This was recorded in February and March 1983 at Olympic and Eel Pie Studios in London, with producer Tony Platt. Released as »Another Perfect Day« on 27 May, it heralded the Another Perfect tour, which started on the same date, and ran through until 5 July with three dates at the Marquee Club in London to help celebrate its Silver Jubilee.

With the 'I Got Mine' single about to be released as the precursor to the full album, Douglas Smith invited me up to London for a preview. Some months before, I had been fortunate enough to enjoy another invite to rehearsals for the album. Algy Ward from Tank was also there, and Robbo, sporting a black eye from some recent pub brawl, along with Lemmy and Philthy, had played a rough rendition of 'I Got Mine' before it had its name and lyrics. It was easy to enjoy that wonderfully memorable riff, and be familiar with it when the single was released.

But this time the band were at Nomis, a huge Georgian house turned into a great many soundproof rehearsal rooms in London, owned by Simon Napier Bell who had made his fortune with John's Children, Boney M, The Yardbirds, Wham, and the many other bands he'd managed and, from the glimpse taken passing the reception desk, The Kinks, Rory Gallagher, and Spandau Ballet were also rehearsing in their own private soundproof rooms.

Motörhead were not set up to play live. This was just a press release kind of day, and Lemmy, Philthy and Robbo welcomed me into the room with the then customary can of Carlsberg Special Brew. After a catch-up chat, and bubbling enthusiasm about the »Another Perfect Day« sessions and recordings, Lemmy and Philthy invited me over to a space they had prepared. Two wooden chairs were facing each other, one vacant, the other with Philthy's ghetto blaster sitting on it. With another can of Special Brew thrust into my hands, I was invited to sit down to enjoy a preview of the album. It was on cassette, and Lemmy pressed the 'play' button, after which he and Philthy retired to a safe distance, leaving me to it.

What an album that was and still is! Other than 'Die You Bastard' each and every track was a prospective single. Lemmy walked across from time to time, shouting out different things to listen for, one being the piano on the 'Rock It' track – "piano on a Motörhead album!" he enthused, with a beaming smile. So different from the albums made with Fast Eddie Clarke yet, for my money, still a powerful and expressive exhibition of Motörhead's talent.

One of the road crew brought in a Chinese take-away menu, we all chose what we wanted, put the money on the table, and off he went off to get the order in. It was a welcome break, and very tasty: chicken balls and chips for me were appetising albeit not that adventurous, but most enjoyable nevertheless. But as ever in the company of Motörhead, time is never a good friend, as it passes far too quickly. Lemmy ordered me a cab for Waterloo railway station, then the three of them dedicated and signed a copy of the 'I Got Mine' 12" single, taken from a heap they had for promo purposes. Reception phoned to say that my cab was waiting, so it was quick goodbyes and handshakes, and 'see you on the tour.' Indeed I did, and at the Portsmouth Guildhall gig, for the second or third time, I was fortunate enough to meet and enjoy some time and conversation with Lemmy's mother Jessica and his step-father George Willis. Living in nearby Salisbury as they did, south coast gigs, which is my neck of the woods anyway, were favourites for them to pay a visit to see their son / stepson. They were a lovely couple, and I had met them at Bournemouth Winter Gardens, Southampton Guildhall and, come to think of it, Boscombe Academy shows. One time, Lemmy reminded them of how they once argued about his long hair, yet now it was part of what earned him a living. A wonderful couple, now both sadly deceased, but a privilege to have met and known them.

At the Poole Arts Centre gig my wife Jane learned a very important lesson in life. We were backstage, had shaken hands with the band and some of the road crew, and been welcomed. Lemmy offered us a drink. From a cool-box brimming with cans and ice cubes, I accepted a can of Fosters. Jane foolishly said that she would have whatever Lemmy was having!

At the time, his drink of choice was Smirnoff blue label vodka, 50/50 in a pint beer glass with fresh orange juice. He duly obliged her request, and prepared the drink. It took her a while to get through it, but by the end of the gig, she had done so. Bear in mind that Lemmy had probably drunk a couple before we arrived, had two or maybe three more, then went onstage, and played the gig; Jane however was all over the place, pissed as a fart as they say. The band did an autograph session a while after. They were sitting at a desk and a fairly large number of fans were in a queue, and we were standing behind the band. Well, I was. A local fan / friend, Eddie Evans, smiled and waved. "Where's Jane?" he asked. "Down here," I replied, pointing at the tortured soul of my wife lying in a dishevelled heap on the floor and not knowing nor caring where she was, or what day of the week it might be.

The moral of the story is that you should never ask for whatever Lemmy was drinking at the time.

An American tour with The Rods and Virgin Steele took place from mid-July until mid-August. But the mid-October European tour with Vulcain would see cracks appearing in this all-too-fragile line-up, and Brian Robertson played his last date with Motörhead in November.

Hawkwind 'Night Of The Hawks' from »The Earth Ritual EP« Flicknife Records (FLEP 104)

Released 1983
This track also featured on the compilation album:

»Born To Lose - Live To Win - The Best of Lemmy« Connoisseur Collection (VSOP CD 296)

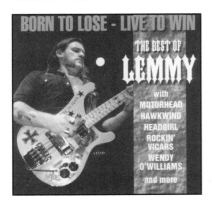

Released 1994
Tracks: 'It's Alright' - The Rocking Vickers / 'The Watcher' - Hawkwind / 'Lost Johnny' - Hawkwind / 'Iron Horse' / 'Born To Lose' - Motörhead / 'Leaving Here' - Motörhead / 'Motörhead' - Motörhead / 'Louie Louie' - Motörhead / 'Dead Men Tell No Tales' - Motörhead / 'Stay Clean' - Motörhead / 'Ace Of Spades' - Motörhead / 'Please Don't Touch' - Head Girl (Motörhead and Girlschool) / Motörhead (live) – 'Motörhead' / 'Stand By Your Man' - Wendy O Williams and Lemmy Kilmister / 'Night Of The Hawks' - Hawkwind / 'Countdown' - Lemmy Kilmister and The Albert Jarvinen Band / 'Blue Suede Shoes' - Lemmy and The Upsetters featuring Mick Green / 'Paradise' - Lemmy and The Upsetters featuring Mick Green.

'Night Of The Hawks' features Lemmy on bass guitar and vocals. Lemmy has performed this live with Hawkwind on several occasions, and it is a fast, driving track which suits the Lemmy / Motörhead blueprint exceptionally well. An anecdote about Lemmy going to Dave Brock's studio in Bideford, Devon, and recording his contribution was in the air at the time, so we can only presume it to be true.

A replacement for Brian Robertson was required. His departure was widely reported in the UK music press, and tapes from guitarists all around the world began flooding into the band's offices at 15 Great Western Road, London.

Whittling the demos down to just two prospective guitarists, Mick 'Würzel' Burston and Phil Campbell joined Motörhead for its twin-guitar line-up in early February. On St Valentine's Day, the new four-piece recorded their legendary appearance for the BBC TV comedy show »The Young Ones«, although before it was televised in early May, Philthy had also left Motörhead. Phil Campbell had heard that ex-Saxon drummer Pete Gill was available. Pete joined the band in March, and after rehearsals and six warm-up gigs in Finland, the new Motörhead line-up made their UK debut at Hammersmith Odeon on 7 May.

A week later, the band went into Pink Floyd's Britannia Row Studios in London, to record six new tracks. Bronze Records, seeing Fast Eddie leaving, a dip in the Motörhead graph during Brian Robertson's tenure, and a 'new' Motörhead built around its founder, had decided that a greatest hits compilation album was in order. This angered Lemmy. This was not the death of Motörhead, but a brand new start, with three young and eager musicians straining at the leash. So Lemmy would agree to this compilation album, but only if the new line-up was also represented, and so the band found themselves in Britannia Row to record four new songs (one for the end of each side of the double LP) plus two for a single.

The band then set out on an extensive tour of New Zealand and Australia from mid-July through to late August. The double album, titled »No Remorse«, was released mid-September to reach Number 14 in the UK, with the 'Killed By Death' single peaking at Number 51. Four dates in Hungary and Yugoslavia preceded the No Remorse Death On The Road UK tour in late October, which ended on 7 November at Hammersmith Odeon. The year was then seen out with an American tour with Mercyful Fate, and five dates in Germany for the Christmas Metal Meeting.

Manager Douglas Smith often asked me up to London to see the band and what they were up to. To facilitate this, I would ask Jane to phone in to my employer, saying that I was ill with a bug, and would be back tomorrow. By the time she was doing that, I would already have caught the Weymouth to Waterloo train at Poole railway station, and be speeding my way there.

From Waterloo, I'd get the underground to Westbourne Park tube station, emerge on to the street and be in Great Western Road, where Douglas's office was situated at No. 15, on the opposite side of the road. The building was and maybe still is a bit uncared for, but to save staff running up and down stairs to let people in, it had an electronic door-opener fixed to the wall. Pressing the appropriate button would buzz the office and a voice would ask who was at the door. Upon answering, if they wanted you to enter, they pressed a button which released the door catch. You had to be a bit quick here, and push on the door so that it opened when the electronics had released it, or it would automatically relock. So, once in the know, and having pushed gently on the door, you were in. The office reception to the right housed the office staff like Motorcycle Irene and Sue Manly. More often than not by this time, around 11:45, they would be giggling and well on their way through a bottle of vodka, but nevertheless, always welcoming.

There followed tea or coffee and an exchange of pleasantries and any news either way. Often, other male staff like Dave Gilligan and Adrian Davidson would be there in the rear portion of the office, and like the women were always busy, but never too busy to have some time for you. If Douglas was busy, they might suggest going down to the pub rather than just sitting there smoking cigarettes as, after all, they had work to do. The pub was a short walk back down the road towards the tube station, but I'm unable to remember its name. It has a canal running at the side of it, and an alfresco area with tables and chairs for sitting, drinking and eating – they served nice food there, too, and lunch was always a 'must.'

But on this occasion I stayed in the bar area, and a while after the food, a couple of beers and cigarettes, Lemmy arrived. Handshakes and a fresh drink each, and as ever he was on the one-arm-bandit, the gambling machine. During the conversation, Würzel arrived. After exchanging pleasantries, Lemmy mentioned that he had written some lyrics for a Finnish rock band, and sung them on a backing track which they had sent him. Of course, this was interesting stuff. He didn't know if and when it would be released, and after speaking to Würzel, who was due to go back to the rented house the band then shared, the guitarist agreed to bring the cassette back with him when he returned. We didn't have a machine to play the cassette on, so Lemmy suggested I take it home, have a listen, and then post it back to him.

When I arrived home and played it, I realised that Würzel had picked up the cassette with backing track on, rather then the copy with Lemmy's lyrics and vocals. Through Irene or Sue at the office, I got the address for the Finnish record company, who had released the track, called 'Countdown', by The Albert Jarvinen Band. They were prepared to sell 12" pressings of the single, so I sent out a newsletter asking fans if they'd like a copy to send me the appropriate costs for the record and postage. It is one hell of a heavy track, and the lyrics quite unusual for Lemmy, but nevertheless excellent, as are his vocals. I can't remember how many copies I ordered now but it was quite a lot, maybe well over 150 perhaps, and the fans who bought it were thrilled with their purchase. The 12" pressing is now quite rare and fetches a good price, but it has been licensed for Lemmy compilation albums from time to time and can be heard there to save paying out a small fortune.

Albert Jarvinen Band 'Countdown'
City Boy Records (MS 1002)

Released 1984
This track also featured on the compilation album:

»Born To Lose - Live To Win - The Best of Lemmy«
Connoisseur Collection (VSOP CD 296)

Released 1994
Tracks as before: 'Countdown' – Lemmy wrote the lyrics for, sang on, and produced the song.

As mentioned above, Finnish blues rockers The Albert Jarvinen Band sent Lemmy a cassette of a blues/rock backing track via Douglas Smith's Greybray management office in London. Albert asked Lemmy if he would like to write a lyric for the backing track and, suitably impressed with the song and the musicianship, when Motörhead were on tour in Finland around that time, Lemmy got together with them in the studio, adding his vocals and production skills to the track.

The Motörheadbangers fan club contacted Polarvox Records, who released the original 12" single at the time under the City Boy record label, and imported copies which were then sold on to interested fan club members. It is a superb addition to the above much-underrated compilation CD.

Ramones »Bonzo Goes To Bitburg« 12" EP
Beggars Banquet Records (BEG 140T)

Released 1984
Tracks: 'Bonzo Goes To Bitburg' / 'Go Home Ann' / 'Daytime Dilemma (Dangers of Love)'
'Go Home Anne' mixed by Lemmy Kilmister and Guy Bidmead
Echoing the cover artwork illustration, the 'Bonzo Goes To Bitburg' song is about US President Ronald [Bonzo] Reagan's controversial visit to the German city of Bitburg, and subsequent meeting there with West German Chancellor Helmut Kohl as part of a plan to observe the 40th Anniversary of VE Day by attending the G7 Economic Summit in Bonn. In November 1984, Helmut Kohl had visited the White House in an effort to symbolise reconciliation between the two countries after their steadfast opposition regarding the Soviet Pershing Missile crisis, which had threatened America and Europe.

Lemmy had been friends with The Ramones since they first played dates in the UK, supporting The Flamin' Groovies at Roundhouse 4 July 1976. Guy Bidmead had been producer Vic Maile's apprentice and engineer, but moved up into the producer's seat for Motörhead's »No Sleep At All« album (amongst others), co-producing it with the band. Despite not being too comfortable on the production side of recording sessions, Lemmy was happy co-producing the 'Go Home Ann'

track with Guy Bidmead during these rare Ramones London recording sessions. This EP was released in the UK, and only available in the United States on import. Later re-titled 'My Brain Is Hanging Upside Down (Bonzo Goes To Bitburg)', the song appeared on The Ramones 1986 »Animal Boy« album, produced by Jean Beauvoir. So this EP is something of a rarity for Lemmy and Motörhead collectors.

In January 1985, 'Mean Machine' and 'Nothing Up My Sleeve' were scheduled to be released as Motörhead's next single. But by then, the ill-feeling between the band and Bronze had escalated to a point where Motörhead wanted to leave the label. But their contract was still valid, so Bronze placed a court order on the band stopping them recording for anyone else.

Bronze could not, however, deprive the band from earning a living by playing live, and in April they made the most of that fact by making an appearance on a new UK rock show, titled »ECT« (supposedly short for 'Extra Celestial Transmission'). The presentation of the show gave the impression that the programme was being transmitted from another planet, by way of static displayed on the TV screen giving way to tuning into the programme. Motörhead were the first band to appear on »ECT«, and gave Bronze the finger by playing those two new songs, along with 'Bomber', for fans to record by way of their VCRs.

Motörhead were booked to be the first band on this radical new rock show. Via manager Douglas Smith, the fan club had been alerted, a newsletter mailed out, and for those who were able to attend, tickets provided. And on 12 April 1985, with my friend

Eric's then wife Frances, we set out by rail for the »ECT« Studio at Wembley, Middlesex. It was close to Hanger Lane tube station on the North Circular Road, and entry was between 4.45 and 5.15, with the show being broadcast live at 6.00 pm, I believe. It was packed, as you can imagine, with plenty of fans and fan club members. The ticket told us to 'wear something outrageous, or we may not be allowed in.' For me and most other fans, our leather biker jackets were outrageous enough, and we had no problems.

It was still the time of the Lemmy, Pete Gill, Würzel and Phil Campbell line-up, and at a few minutes to six, the band walked onstage to play 'Jailbait' as their warm-up and soundcheck. They too were dressed outrageously. Lemmy in white jacket, black shirt and white tie, with a scar across his face, provided by the make-up girls, as if he had been whupped by pool cue. The other three band members were sporting tuxedos.

As men do, I had noticed before we left that Frances was bra-less, and aware of her as the rebel she was, knew that if Lemmy had asked, as he often did when introducing 'Jailbait', for a female to "show us your tits!" then she would have done so without hesitation. It's a girl thing, isn't it, even at the festivals. The chicks get on their boyfriends' shoulders, and it's a safe bet that a cameraman will pick up on them, and if they do show us their tits, then that's a bonus. Sadly, on this occasion, that event was not to be, despite Frances insistence of trying to sit on my shoulders. She was not a heavy lady by any means, but a lifetime of back injuries would not allow me the luxury of having her perched there.

Suddenly, we were live on air, and Motörhead rattled through 'Nothing Up My Sleeve', 'Bomber', and 'Mean Machine'. Thunderous applause followed, and as far as people who were watching this from home, it was the commercial break, or the adverts. But in the studio, which had four stages, the cameramen and the crowd moved slightly for the next band on, The Lords Of The New Church. Just in time, the 'on-air' lights lit up again, and the band launched into their mini-set of songs. Always a danger with live shows, vocalist Stiv Bators almost had the whole thing taken off-air by mentioning heroin during his introduction. No time to bleep him, but luckily, the show went on. Other bands on the agenda were Magnum, during their »On A Storyteller's Night« era, and an American band called Madam X.

The drummer and lead guitarist for Madam X were sisters, Roxy and Maxine Petrucci, who were plugging their »We Reserve The Right« debut album (still, incidentally, a favourite of mine). Maxine, the guitarist, wore leather boots, pantyhose/tights, and pink panties, and a top, of course, and one Motörheadbanger, who shall remain nameless, went backstage to see her after the show and ask if he could have those pink panties as a souvenir. But much as he tried, Maxine would not part with "part of my stage outfit". On this, their first trip to England, Madam X had arranged with the TV company to play an extra couple of songs off-air for their own or promo use, so all bands did two or three songs on-air, and in addition we enjoyed an extra two from Madam X, when the show had officially ended.

After the show, we went backstage to see the band, only to find Philthy Animal Taylor, had come along, too. We were all fired up with adrenaline from the show, and enjoyed a few drinks and conversations with many in attendance.

The tube and train rides home were uneventful, and Frances and I were tired from the long day. When we arrived back at the apartment Frances shared with Eric, as a surprise, my wife Jane was there, too, and she and Eric were bursting to show us the VHS tape they had recorded of the show. From memory, as I haven't watched the tape for some years, Frances and I were swallowed up by the crowd, and not visible on any of the camera shots. But it had been quite an experience, and one that Frances and I enjoyed. She and Eric divorced a few years later, and along with many other great times spent in her company, »ECT« was another golden moment.

Whilst Radio 1's »The Friday Rock Show« DJ Tommy Vance was on holiday, Lemmy was given the two-hour spot to play many of his favourite tracks by other artists.

Still kicking their heels, and again as a poke in the eye to Bronze, Lemmy and Würzel became part of The Crowd, by singing on the charity track 'You'll Never Walk Alone'. Providing their services for free, this move did nothing to provoke a reaction from Bronze, and the single went to Number 1 in mid-June, with a video of the session featuring everyone who participated. Lemmy and Würzel, along with everyone else involved, were presented with a gold disc for sales of the record.

Much to the surprise of many, but not to the band or their fans, Motörhead were ten years old, and played two nights at Hammersmith Odeon to celebrate the occasion. The It Never Gets Dark Scandinavian tour followed, with dates going through the whole of July and early August. In mid-November, an American tour over Wendy O Williams and Megadeth burned up a sheaf of dates until 21 December.

The Crowd 'You'll Never Walk Alone'
Spartan Records (12BRAD1)

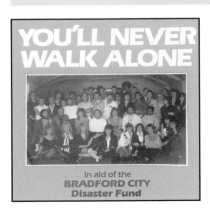

Released 1985

A charity record in aid of the Bradford City Disaster Fund, which Lemmy and Würzel took part in when they were 'banned from recording' due to their Bronze Records legal battle. But there was no harm adding their vocals for free, so they joined The Crowd when this song was chosen in solidarity with Bradford City Football Club following the Valley Parade fire at their ground in 1985 when 56 spectators died, and many more were injured.

Gerry Marsden, of the Sixties' band, Gerry & the Pacemakers fame, was behind the idea for this charity single, but artists including Lemmy, Würzel, Paul Mc-Cartney, artist and entertainer Rolf Harris, Heavy Metal Kids vocalist and actor Gary Holton, members Girlschool, disc jockey Dave Lee Travis, entertainer Bruce Forsythe, The Nolans, The Who's John Entwhistle, singer Kiki Dee, keyboard player Rick Wakeman and many more also joined in on the day of recording. The single went straight to Number 1 in the UK charts, and all the stars who gave their services received a gold disc for sales. A video was made of the recording, which was shown on »Top Of The Pops«, and is now on YouTube, showing Lemmy singing his heart out. However, neither he nor Würzel were present when the front cover photograph was taken.

The European Team 'Sport Alive'
Mausoleum Records 7" (KICK 8420) / 12" (SPORT 83100)

Released 1985
Recorded in memory of the Heysel Stadium disaster in Brussels, Belgium, where thirty-nine fans were killed when hooligans from opposing teams – Liverpool and Juventus – clashed and started fighting.

Again, Lemmy and Würzel joined in and gave their vocals to the song during the ongoing Bronze court battle. The record was not very successful and sales were low, as the song didn't have the required 'anthemic qualities' to grab the European record buyers. The record also included vocal contributions from Doro Pesch, Girlschool, Rock Goddess, Uriah Heap, Slade, Robin George, Debbie Bonham, Venom, Rogue Male, Waysted and Lionheart, amongst others.

Boys Don't Cry 'I Wanna Be A Cowboy' /
'Turn Over (I Like It Better That Way)'
Legacy Records (LGY28)

Released 1985
Motörhead's then manager, Douglas Smith, had signed Boys Don't Cry to his GWR Records label offshoot, Legacy Records. The band's name originated from the 10cc hit 'I'm Not In Love' lyric "big boys don't cry" and the novelty single was described as the perfect musical realisation of a spaghetti western movie, including kitsch references and dead-pan humour in the lyrics.

The band asked if Lemmy could do them a favour by appearing in their video for the song. As ever, Lemmy did so just for the fun of it; in this case it was just a cameo role, because he took no part in the actual recording. The clip is usually available on YouTube. 'I Wanna Be A Cowboy' achieved Number 12 in the Hot 100 in 1986, and charted around the world, going into the Top 10 in Australia and South Africa. So the video would have been aired hundreds of times, in turn giving Lemmy and Motörhead a plug.

Wendy O Williams »Bump 'n' Grind«
Cherry Red Films (CRDVD120)

Released 22 March 2006
Tracks: 'Goin' Wild' / 'Pedal To The Metal' / 'You'll Succeed' / 'No Class' / 'Party' / 'Jamming' / 'Live To Rock' / 'Jailbait' / 'Ain't None Of Your Business' / 'Bump 'N' Grind' / 'Fuck That Booty' / 'Fuck 'N' Roll.
Wendy Orleans Williams (1949-1998) was the leader and lead vocalist for the American punk band, The Plasmatics, who were known for stage theatrics such as blowing up cars, and chain-sawing guitars. An ex-porn movie star, Wendy frequently appeared onstage scantily dressed, often appearing in little more than tiny panties and electrical tape covering her nipples. Wearing her hair in the punk mohawk style, whilst band member Richie Stotts wore a ballet dancer's tutu and fishnet pantyhose / tights, it was quite some surprise when Wendy was named as the Queen of Shock Rock. With their Hammersmith Odeon show cancelled on safety grounds in 1981, and the press calling them 'anarchists', they quite naturally came to Lemmy's attention. It was the recording of Tammy Wynette's 'Stand By Your Man' with Wendy O Williams which led to Motörhead's guitarist Fast Eddie Clarke leaving the band.
In 1985, a series of these live shows were recorded at the Camden Palace, and Motörhead record label-mates Girlschool also had their appearance at the same

venue released on video and DVD. Great friends as Lemmy was with Wendy and the band from recording 'Stand By Your Man', it was no surprise that, with Motörhead not being on tour at the time, Lemmy would go along and see their show. 'No Class' was already in Wendy's set and, with Lemmy and Würzel being a two-headed monster on the London scene at the time and going everywhere together, it was only natural that they would both turn up, and put in a special guest appearance on 'Jailbait'.

A great show, recorded on 1 October 1985, and a valuable timepiece in Wendy's career of her visit to London.

Warfare »Metal Anarchy«
Neat Records (NEAT 1029)

Released January 1986
Side Metal: 'Intro' / 'Electric Mayhem' / 'Warfare' / 'Death Vigilance' / 'Wrecked Society'.
Side Anarchy: 'Living For The Past Days' / 'Disgrace' / 'Military Shadow' / 'Metal Anarchy' / 'Psycho Express'.
Evo: drums and lead vocals, Falken: bass, Gunner: guitars.
Recorded at Ezee Studios, London; produced by Lemmy Kilmister and Guy Bidmead.
Würzel: guest guitar on 'Metal Anarchy.'
Re-released on CD as an Expanded Edition in August 2007 with seven bonus tracks, (which were from different sessions, and not produced by Lemmy) on Sanctuary Records (CMRCD1536).

Drummer Evo split from The Angelic Upstarts to form Warfare. A mate of Tank / The Damned bassist Algy Ward, Evo approached Lemmy at a Tank gig at Dingwalls, asking if he would like to produce the album. A huge Motörhead fan, Evo and his band recorded »Metal Anarchy« over a three day stretch at Ezee Studios, with Lemmy and Guy Bidmead producing. At the band's request, Würzel came in and recorded a blistering guitar solo on the song 'Metal Anarchy' on the second day of the sessions.

Inspiration for Warfare and the album very much came from Motörhead, and although at first glance Lemmy might not have seemed the obvious choice to twiddle the proverbial knobs Evo thought that it was a logical step. "To me, without Motörhead there wouldn't be any metal scene as we know it today. I'm not even sure that Lemmy himself knew what he created; it was, and is, a monster. They were really flying the flag for our sort of music. He was also well-educated and extremely good company, and was far from being the crazy guy who drinks huge amounts of alcohol, as the media often described him.

"Lemmy's a cracking producer," Evo said in a Motörheadbangers interview. "He knows what is required and how to get it. And he really pushed me hard, more than I was used to. We had three days to do it to fit in with Motörhead's touring schedule, and we did it, effectively, live, which suits us, coming from a punk background."

Early 1986 saw Motörhead in Master Rock Studios, in Kilburn, London. The litigation with Bronze Records went in the band's favour, and ownership of the master tapes for the albums recorded with the label was also granted to them and manager Douglas Smith. The band celebrated by playing the seven-date Easter Metal Blast with dates in Germany, Switzerland, and Denmark in late April, adding to their set songs from the Kilburn sessions such as 'Nothing Up My Sleeve', 'Mean Machine', 'Deaf Forever', and what would be the album's stunning title track, 'Orgasmatron'.

'Deaf Forever' was selected as the single from the album, and was released in early June, with the album itself released in August, a week before the band's appearance at the Monsters Of Rock festival at Castle Donington. »Orgasmatron« peaked at Number 21, which was quite a result considering the lengthy battle with Bronze; but the band had kept themselves busy on the road, and so the fans' interest and enthusiasm had never waned.

Not content with playing just one UK festival, Lemmy made a guest appearance with Hawkwind later in the month at Reading, and this was later released via Raw Fruit Records.

Hawkwind »Friday Rock Show
Live At Reading Festival August 24th 1986«
Raw Fruit Records (FRSCD005)

Released 1 March 1992

Tracks: 'Magnu - Angels Of Death' / 'Pulsing Cavern' / 'Assault And Battery' / 'Needle Gun' / 'Master Of The Universe' / 'Utopia' / 'Dream Worker' / 'Assassins Of Allah (Hassan I Sahba)' / 'Silver Machine' (featuring special guest).

Dave Brock, Alan Davey, Harvey Bainbridge, Huw Lloyd-Langton, Danny Thomas junior

Featuring Lemmy Kilmister as special guest on bass/vocals on 'Silver Machine'; Dumpy Dunnell, of Dumpy's Rusty Nuts, was also a guest on the song.

Itinerary permitting, Lemmy enjoyed making a guest appearance with Hawkwind, particularly at festivals. The crowd loved it, having the original bass player and vocalist up there singing and playing on 'Silver Machine', the song which he made his own back in the day. For Hawkwind, well, much as they too must have enjoyed such events, it must be somewhat embarrassing having the man they unceremoniously sacked back in the fold, albeit briefly. But had Lemmy not been sacked, the world would have missed out on Motörhead; and what a tragedy that would have been!

A US tour with Megadeth and the Cro-Mags saw the band on the road from early October until late November, and on 1 December they started a string of eleven dates in Germany. However, in February 1987, drummer Pete Gill was sacked by Lemmy. A European tour followed from mid-February to the end of March, which saw the return of old fan favourite Philthy Animal Taylor to the Motörhead drum stool.

Little Bob Story »Ringolevio«
Universal Music France (984 393-7)

Released 1987, re-issued with bonus tracks 2006
Tracks: 'Ringolevio' / 'Shadow Lane' / 'Life Goes On' / 'Crosses On The Hill' / 'Hush' / 'Sad Song' / 'Motorcycle Boy' / 'Tell Everybody The Truth' / 'Green Back Dollar' / 'Roads Of Freedom' - Bonus tracks: 'Cover Girl' / 'Shooga Shooga' / 'Dancing' / 'No More Words'
Roberto Piazza: lead and vocals[11], Yves Chouard: lead guitars, keyboards, backing vocals, Gilles Mallet: rhythm guitars, backing vocals, Gilles Tynaire: bass guitars, keyboards, Nico Garotin: drums, backing vocals
Recorded and Mixed in May and June 1987 at The Greenhouse, London; produced by Pat Collier. Bonus tracks recorded and mixed in 1986 at Studio Marcadet (La Plaine St-Denis, Paris). Enginered by Stephane Sahakian
The »Ringolevio« novel was written by Emmett Grogan and published by Granada
Special thanks to Ian 'Lemmy' Kilmister for great shouting [on 'Ringolevio'] (courtesy Gill Massey and GWR Records)
Such a tenuous connection: an album starting with Lemmy shouting "listen up, sons of bitches, Little Bob's gonna tell you a story!" But Motörhead had played live with the French band on the same bill in the past, and they obviously thought enough of Lemmy to invite him to kick the album off. It's a great album anyway,

11 *That's what it says in the CD booklet!*

and as a rule of thumb, anything that Lemmy was involved with is always well worth hearing. Little Bob Story play a superb blend of blues, rock, and R'n'B in the tradition of The Nashville Teens, early Rolling Stones, The Pirates and Chuck Berry, so it is little wonder that they turned Lemmy's head enough to attract him into making this cameo appearance to introduce their album. Gill Massey worked for Douglas Smith at his Greybray management/GWR Records' London offices at Westbourne Park, and she organised this venture.

Another American tour began in early April, and rehearsals started soon afterwards for Motörhead's second album for Douglas Smith's newly-formed GWR Records label, »Rock 'N' Roll«. Lemmy had been invited to take part in the Comic Strip spoof movie »Eat The Rich« so time was taken up there until the Rock 'N' Roll UK tour began in mid-September with Sword in support. Mid-November saw them in Scandinavia on their European tour with King Diamond which took them through to their 23 December Stuff The Turkey – Eat the Rich one-off show at London's Brixton Academy.

»Eat The Rich«
New Line Home Video/ DVD (ID1370LIDVD)

You Are What You Eat!

Released October 1987

With its Motörhead soundtrack and all-star cast this British black comedy tells the story of a "ticked-off waiter who, with the aid of revolutionary cohorts, turns an upper-crust restaurant into a jet-set banquet – literally", ran the promotional blurb at the time.

The film featured, amongst others, Jennifer Saunders (»Absolutely Fabulous«), Dawn French (»The Vicar of Dibley«), Rik Mayall (»The Young Ones«), Miranda Richardson (»The Hours)«, Lemmy, Paul McCartney, Bill Wyman and Robbie Coltrane (»Cracker« and »Goldeneye«).

The movie and of course the accompanying soundtrack album, and Lemmy's part in the film as gun-runner, Spider, came about from Motörhead's appearance in »The Young Ones« BBC TV sit-com, and playing on the bill at Castle Donington, where the band formed by some of »The Young Ones« stars, known as Bad News also performed that day. »Eat The Rich« was a typically British comedy in every way, and Lemmy enjoyed his role in the film. The soundtrack album is the only way – unless you are prepared to buy the now very collectable 7" or 12" single – to enjoy a copy of Würzel's instrumental 'Bess'.

The 1988 Alice Cooper / Motörhead American tour actually began on 31 December 1987. However, the band had to temporarily pull out as they were blighted with visa problems which were not resolved until 22 January, when they re-joined the tour, which they followed with a European stretch with Girlschool in early March which started in Greece, and went on through Germany, France, Portugal and Spain. After playing a couple of summer festivals, Motörhead made a personal appearance at London's Tower Records for the release of their »No Sleep At All« live album on 17 October 1988. Another two-month American tour with Overkill and Slayer took them through to three pre-Christmas UK shows at Nottingham and Hammersmith. Four dates in Germany between Christmas and a chorus of 'Auld Lang Syne' rounded the year off.

Girlschool »Take A Bite«
Sanctuary Records (CMRCD1382)

Released 1988; this version re-released 2006 as 2-on-1 CD with »Nightmare At Maple Cross« Tracks: »Nightmare At Maple Cross« - 'All Day All Nite' / 'Play With Fire' / 'Danger Sign' / 'Never Too Late' / 'Tiger Feet' / 'Back For More' / 'Let's Go Crazy' / 'You Got Me (Under Your Spell)' / 'Let's Break Up' / 'Turn It Up' Tracks: »Take A Bite« - 'Action' / 'Fox On The Run' / 'Girls On Top' / 'Tear It Up' / 'Love At First Bite' / 'Head Over Heels' / 'Up All Night' / 'This Time' / 'Don't Walk Away' / 'Too Hot To Handle'
»Take A Bite« produced by Andre Jacquemin.

Lyrics for 'Head Over Heels' written by Lemmy Kilmister.
By now becoming renowned for his ability to come up with excellent lyrics quickly, Lemmy wrote the words for the superb 'Head Over Heels' for friends and label-mates Girlschool. Girlschool had started out as Painted Lady, and are now regarded as the longest running active all-female rock band. Kim McAuliffe (vocals and guitar) and Denise Dufort (drums) have been the main core of the band since its inception. Original bassist/vocalist Enid Williams left to embark upon an ill-fated solo career, but later returned to the fold. Unfortunately original lead guitarist Kelly Johnson passed away in 2007.

Lita Ford »Lita«
RCA / Dreamland Records (6397-2-R)

Released 1988
Tracks: 'Back To The Cave' / 'Can't Catch Me' / 'Blueberry' / 'Kiss Me Deadly' / 'Falling In And Out Of Love' / 'Fatal Passion' / 'Under The Gun' / 'Broken Dreams' / 'Close My Eyes Forever'
Lita Ford: guitar and vocals, Donnie Nossov: bass, Myron Grombacher: drums, David Ezrin: keyboards
Lyrics for 'Can't Catch Me' by Lemmy Kilmister.

Connections with ex-The Runaways lead guitarist, now solo star, Lita Ford were made when Motörhead played on the same bill as Lita on 10 June 1984 at the Heavy Sound Festival at Poperinge in Belgium. Again, Lemmy's ease of writing a top-notch lyric after being provided with a studio backing track shone yet again here on 'Can't Catch Me'. Lita and Lemmy remained great friends, appearing at several awards functions in Los Angeles together. 'Can't Catch Me' also appears on Lita Ford's 2013 album »The Bitch Is Back… Live«. Before launching into it, she tells the crowd a little about how it came about. "I went to the Rainbow and I hooked up with Lemmy, and we went back to his apartment and got really messed up. I was there for three days, I swear, and we wrote this song…"

»The Decline of Western Civilisation II: The Metal Years« New Line Cinema (PVC 3020 M) VHS Tape

Released 1988

A Penelope Spheeris film which featured amongst others Alice Cooper, Ozzy Osbourne and members of Aerosmith, Kiss, Motörhead and Poison. The filming took place in and around Hollywood and featured an interview with Lemmy and the Motörhead song 'Cradle To The Grave'. A soundtrack CD released in 1988 also included the track.

So many young hopefuls appear in the film saying 'remember my name, you'll be seeing it in lights.' Where are they now? Only those notable giants of the day are still remembered, and only those same notable giants are still here to tell it like it was and still is. Megadeath, Alice Cooper, Ozzy Osbourne, Aerosmith and Motörhead are, to many people, all that mattered in 1988, and all that matter even now. But rock documentaries were rare in 1988, so five stars for at least trying to get something on the genre out there!

A few more UK dates followed in late February/early March 1989, with five shows in Brazil following close after. Early April saw Motörhead back on the road for the Bastards Over Europe tour of Scandinavia, The Netherlands, Belgium, France and Italy. A trip to Yugoslavia was marred when Lemmy had the back of his left hand sliced open by a member of the audience throwing a razor blade super-glued to two coins at him. The couple of remaining dates were cancelled to allow the injury to heal; the worst case scenario at the time was that the injury might turn poisonous leading to fears that Lemmy might have two fingers amputated. Thankfully, antibiotics avoided this drastic measure which would have put an end to his guitar playing career.

The No Sleep At All UK tour, as mentioned above, was taking place and, with the idea of meeting Phil Campbell's parents Jack and Louise (whom I'd spoken to on the phone many times), Eric Billett and I attended the St David's Hall, Cardiff, gig on 3 March 1989.

We knew the band always had backstage passes for us, but as a precaution, and the fact that we're not spongers, we always bought a ticket anyway. There's little point travelling to a gig and there being a hiccup with the passes and so missing out on the show, so tickets were, and still are, a must-have in my opinion. On this occasion, it would pay off.

A guy named Higgy was the tour manager, and always a bit of a hard nut to crack trying to get a pass. We met him in the foyer, but he told us that there were so many friends and relations of Phil's at the gig that he'd run out of passes. Fair enough. We always regarded getting backstage as a privilege anyway, and, well, we still had that all-important ticket, and could enjoy the gig. Knowing that Jack and Louise were expecting to see us, though, I wrote to Louise the following day, outlining the story. I didn't complain or grouch: I just said that it didn't happen, and the reason why, and that we would catch up somewhere else.

Motörhead finished that short tour, had a few days off, and then flew out for the dates in Brazil. Although I didn't know it at the time, Louise had shown Phil my letter, and he'd taken it with him. On the flight to Brazil, Phil showed it to Lemmy. The story goes that Lemmy insisted on Higgy standing in the gangway of the plane and reading my letter out aloud.

At some point after Motörhead returned home I received a phone call; it was Higgy. He apologised about the lack of passes at the Cardiff gig, and said that it would never happen again.

A day or two later, Lemmy called. "Did Higgy phone you, Al?"

"Yes, he did, Lemmy; it was good of him."

"No, it wasn't good of him. It was something he HAD to do. You DO NOT come and see us after all these years and NOT get a pass."

"Oh, right, thank you."

"I told him that if Alan Burridge is at a show and there are no passes, you felt tip 'Backstage Pass' across his forehead, or even his cock, and you MAKE SURE he gets backstage!"

"Oh, right, thank you," I said again.

"No, Al, thank you. You have done a lot for us over the years, and what happened with Higgy will never happen again to you. You don't deserve it."

I expressed my grateful thanks to him. What better endorsement could there be?

The band had some time off, a rarity, but it led to them attending the Motörheadbangers Fan Club Tenth Anniversary Party at the Hippodrome in London, which Fast Eddie Clarke also attended, on 7 June. This was an excellent event, organised by Würzel's partner, Jem Reeves. Jane and I made our way to Waterloo by rail during the afternoon, and then travelled to Würzel and Jem's home in Islington by taxi.

The couple were excellent hosts, and in the early evening Würzel's brother-in-law John drove us down to London's Chinatown area where the Hippodrome was located. A few tables had been set up for a meet-and-greet where band members could sit and autograph anything the fans had brought along, and enjoy a casual conversation.

One male fan, whose name escapes me, had enjoyed more than a few drinks and, stripped to the waist, asked Lemmy, Philthy, Phil, Würzel and Fast Eddie to sign his torso with felt tip. This they did, with the fan swearing that he would have the signatures tattooed the next day. He walked over to speak to me, telling me that when the fan club fanzine arrived in the post he would read 'every word, six or seven times.' I smiled and nodded my approval, but being a bit drunk, he asked if I was taking the piss. I assured him that was not the case, and explained that it was just a joy to hear someone saying that, as I did not realise just how valued the fanzine was to the fans. He nodded and understood, and went on his way; but for one brief moment, I thought he was going to punch me on the nose.

A Finnish band called Peer Günt were booked to play and were pretty good, but with five members of Motörhead in attendance most fans were happier milling around them, enjoying the personal contact with their heroes, than listening to the music. The event had been sponsored by Black Death vodka, and I was presented with two bottles to take home. Later, Jem organised a photographer named Les to take some photos of the band and myself at the tables, with an 'MHB's 10' birthday cake.

This was an amazing gesture. There was also a five-piece female band in attendance, whose name I don't remember. They were young and attractive and wore very short skirts, but whether they ever actually made any records is anyone's guess. But Les took Lemmy's photo with them, and the photo, along with a report of the fan club's birthday party, appeared in the Daily Sport newspaper the following day.

Würzel and Jem had made plans for Jane and I to spend the night at their Islington home, for which we were and still are very grateful. By the time the event ended most trains had stopped running, so it was nice to enjoy a good night's sleep, breakfast with Würzel and Jem, and Toots, Würzel's dog, and a leisurely return home that afternoon. A splendid event, attended by two or three hundred fan club members and fans alike, which will never be forgotten.

Dates in Germany and Switzerland followed in late June/early July. The band's relationship with manager Douglas Smith and his GWR record label was, however, becoming increasingly fragile. The band wanted bigger and better things for Motörhead, especially in America where Lemmy was planning on going to live. While the rights and wrongs were being debated in court, yet again, Motörhead spent the month of October making demos at the Music Farm in Sussex, with a view to securing a new record label. The ten-date Silent Night UK tour burned up mid-December.

Nina Hagen »Nina Hagen«
Mercury Records (838 505-2)

Released 1989
Tracks: 'Move Over' / 'Super Freak Family' / 'Love Heart Attack' / 'Hold Me' / 'Las Vegas' / 'Live On Mars' / 'Dope Sucks' / 'Only Seventeen' / 'Where's The Party' / 'Michail, Michail (Gorbachev Rap)' / 'Ave Maria'
Regarded by many as the mother of punk, Nina Hagen joined the East German band Automobil and found fame as one of the country's best known young stars for their 1974 song 'Where's The Colour Film' which mocked the sterile, grey Communist state.

Back in Germany by 1977, she formed The Nina Hagen Band, and their self-titled debut album included a cover of The Tubes' 'White Punks On Dope', which had different German lyrics. Nina's vocals and the band's hard rock sound gained worldwide attention.

On 'Where's The Party' - backing vocals: The Soultanas, special thanks to Lene Lovich, Lemmy (by courtesy of Motörhead) featured on the occasional distorted bass.[12]

Lemmy is also mentioned in 'Nina's Special Love & Thanx.'

It was only natural in the world of rock 'n' roll that two such charismatic characters as Lemmy Kilmister and Nina Hagen should be attracted like magnets to record a track together.

[12] Again, this is what it says in the booklet, even though it's not exactly clear...

»Black Leather Jacket«
1988 UK Channel 4 TV documentary

Released (as a 70 minute VHS cassette by Polygram Music Video (CFV 08872) in 1989 Narrated by »Easy Rider« movie star Dennis Hopper, »Black Leather Jacket« was televised as six ten-minute weekly episodes as part of a risqué late evening cult European soft porn TV programme titled »Club X«.

Based on Mick Farren's (RIP) book of the same name, it traces the history of the black leather jacket from aviation beginnings for warmth to being a sexual fetish garment and every variation in-between; Lemmy gets a couple of short interview clips (with Würzel looking on), sitting outside a London café, talking about the benefits of wearing such a radical garment.

Segments of the »Black Leather Jacket« theme tune, which was written by Lemmy and performed as Lemmy & The Upsetters, are featured on the soundtrack. Not featured on the film, but televised on »Club X«, was the 'Black Leather Jacket' theme by Lemmy & The Upsetters, which was played in the studio by Lemmy Kilmister: vocals and piano, Phil Campbell: guitar, Philthy Animal Taylor: drums, Fast Eddie Clarke: bass, and three saxophonists hired for the session. The song was released as a part of the 2008 Motörhead »Stone Deaf Forever!« box set.

»Hard 'n' Heavy« Video Magazine Volume 1 VHS Tape
Picture Music International (MVP 9911833)

Released 1989; running time 70 minutes
"Get ready, you're about to experience the rudest, crudest, lewdest video ever! It's the world's first and only Hard Rock/Heavy Metal video-magazine," ran the promotional material for this short-lived video magazine. Alongside excerpts of videos and interviews with (in this first volume) the likes of Bruce Dickinson, Anthrax, Voi Vod and W.A.S.P. came the 'Trick Or Treat' feature in which a guest would be handed a sack and asked to comment upon the items they pulled out of it. Lemmy was the first such guest, and one of the items in the bag is a copy of the »Motörhead Babylon« book. "It's very good," says Lemmy. "They should get a petition together to get it re-printed." The video also features a short clip from the 'Eat the Rich' video.

»Hard 'n' Heavy« Video Magazine Volume 2 VHS Tape
Picture Music International (MVP 99113833)

Released 1989; running time 75 minutes
More of the same, this time featuring, amongst others, Scorpions, Steve Vai,
Femme Fatale and Vixen. The feature 'Issues Of The Issue' interviewed Lemmy
on freedom of speech.

*11 December 1989; the Silent Night UK tour had played its first show the night
before at the Mayfair in Southampton, and this, the second show, at The Academy in Bournemouth was a nice 'doorstep' show for me; just eight miles from
home.*

*At the time, I had been off sick from work for five months with a mystery illness
which, 23 years later, would resurface as Multiple Sclerosis. In 1989, it had left
me unable to drive, so this was one of the few gigs I travelled to by taxi.*

*The Academy had been known in my younger years as The Royal Ballrooms, in
Boscombe, a suburb of Bournemouth within spitting distance of the town itself.
Over the years we had seen The Faces, Thin Lizzy, Van der Graaf Generator, Led
Zeppelin, Status Quo, and many other top bands there. Under its new identity of
The Academy, I was about to see another.*

*I arrived early, and the band were backstage, although backstage was a gross
overstatement: it was more like a cloakroom, a passageway with coat hooks and
barely enough space to swing the proverbial pussy.*

It was, of course, the Lemmy, Phil, Würzel and Philthy line-up at that time, and it soon became apparent that the band were not happy with their 'dressing room', if indeed it could be called that. More to the point, Lemmy's parents, Jessica and George (who lived in nearby Salisbury) were there, and Lemmy felt pretty pissed off at this fairly inhospitable situation. I had been fortunate enough, due to geographical location, to have met Lemmy's parents before, so we chatted to each other amidst the rows of coat pegs. They were a lovely couple, smart, intelligent and hospitable, and then in their late-seventies. I had met them at Portsmouth Guildhall in 1983 when the band were touring »Another Perfect Day« and as they had given me their address from that point on I sent them a copy of the fanzine each time it was published. Jessica thanked me for doing so; as she said, "it's the only way that we can find out what Ian's [as they called him] been doing."

At this point Lemmy discovered a door which led to someone's rooms, with a TV, sofa, armchairs, table and so on, and he suggested we invade the space for some comfort. Half an hour or so later a member of staff arrived, saying that this was someone's home, and that we had to leave.

Lemmy replied, "well now it's our dressing room."

"Oh, no it isn't!" came the reply, in true time-of-the-year pantomime fashion.

"Well," said Lem, "if that's the case, there's no show!"

The man had the wind taken out of his sails. "But you might damage something..."

"If we do, we will pay for it," Lemmy snapped back.

The guy shrugged his shoulders, knowing that he was beaten, and left.

Jessica and George always smoked a couple of Lemmy's Marlboros, and quaffed a large measure of his JD and coke, but rarely stayed to watch the show – the up to three days of deafness required to get over the event was something they were not so keen on. And anyway, they had travelled here to see their son and step-son, so as far as they were concerned it was job done.

The gig went well, but afterwards, backstage, we heard news that one of the Academy 'security' guys had had a ruck with Skippy, one of the lighting crew. Apparently, the security guy had whacked him in the ribs with an aluminium pole, part of the lighting rig, and broken some ribs. Phil Campbell had taken Skippy to the local hospital by taxi to get him looked at.

Now, I've been going to gigs since I was 14 years old, and unlike football, I had never witnessed any trouble. Indeed, had I not been enjoying the honour and privilege of a backstage pass, I would not have witnessed this.

The venue was a strange one, in that everything had to be transported through the front door; there was no rear access at all. When Lemmy heard about the ruck, he found out that the crew had almost finished loading, and were ready to ship-out.

"We've got to run the gauntlet, Al," he told me. "We'll take you back to our hotel, and get you a cab from there."

'Running the gauntlet' were not words I particularly wanted to hear, but I thanked Lem and, along with Würzel, the three of us walked across the side of the stage and down some steps to the ballroom floor. The main doors, before us, centrally, were flanked by probably ten of the security guys either side. They were dressed in penguin suits, with dickie-bows, white shirts, black shoes, greased back hair, and had faces which reminded me of a bulldog licking piss from a stinging nettle.

Wearing Lemmy's always powerful confidence like an overcoat, the three of us walked towards the doors with twenty pairs of eyes looking daggers at us. Outside, a white Transit van (with seats and windows) was waiting for us. We got in, filling the last three seats, the doors slammed, and off we went.

The band were staying at Bournemouth's Royal Bath Hotel, one of, if not the best hotel in town. We baled out of the van and walked into the foyer. A woman grabbed Lemmy's arm as we stood at the reception desk where he asked the receptionist to get me a cab. Shaking my hand, Lemmy said, "see you soon, Al" – as did Würzel – before going upstairs for the night. Another unforgettable gig with Motörhead.

Another five UK dates followed in March 1990, followed by European gigs in Yugoslavia, (to make up for the shows cancelled due to Lemmy's hand injury), Bosnia, Greece, Italy and Austria. In early June, both Lemmy and Philthy relocated to Los Angeles. Motörhead had won their battle with GWR and were now free to seek another record label. Signed for management with AC/DC / Led Zeppelin manager, Phil Carson, the Music Farm demos secured a contract with Sony, and the recording of the »1916« album.

»The Last Temptation Of Elvis – Songs From His Movies«
New Musical Express Charity Double LP (NMELP 038/039)
In Aid Of The Nordoff Robins Music Therapy Centre, London

Released 1990
Side 1: Bruce Springsteen – 'Viva Las Vegas' / Sydney Youngblood – '(Let Me Be Your) Teddy Bear' / Tanita Tikaram – 'Loving You' / Robert Plant – 'Let's Have A Party' / The Pogues – 'Got A Lot Of Loving To Do' / Holly Johnson – 'Love Me Tender'
Side 2: Paul McCartney – 'It's Now Or Never' / Dion Dimucci – 'Mean Woman Blues' / The Jesus And The Mary Chain – 'Guitar Man' / Cath Carroll and Steve Albini – 'King Creole' / Aaron Neville – 'Young And Beauti-

ful' / Vivian Standshall & The Big Boys – '(There's) No Room To Rumba In A Sports Car' / The Primitives – '(You're So Square) Baby I Don't Care'
Side 3: Hall & Oates – 'Can't Help Falling In Love' / The Reggae Philharmonic Orchestra – 'Crawfish' / Ian McCulloch – 'Return To Sender' / Fuzzbox – 'Trouble' / The Hollow Men – 'Thanks To The Rolling Sea' / The Blow Monkeys – 'Follow That Dream' / Lemmy & The Upsetters with Mick Green – 'Blue Suede Shoes'
Side 4: Nancy Griffith & The Blue Moon Orchestra – 'Wooden Heart' / The Jeff Healey Band – 'Down In The Alley' / The Cramps – 'Jailhouse Rock' / Les Negresses Vertes – 'Marguerita' / Pop Will Eat Itself – 'Rock-A-Hula Baby' / Elvis Presley – 'King Of The Whole Wide World'
Executive Producer: Roy Carr.
Always keen on recording a track not only to surprise people, but also as a fun thing to do, and for charity, Lemmy jumped at the opportunity to record his version of an Elvis Presley song. Pleased with the result, the song was also released as a single.

Lemmy and the Upsetters with Mick Green
'Blue Suede Shoes' / 'Paradise'
Sunnyside Records (STYLE 777)

Released August 1990
Both songs recorded at Sunnyside Studios, Ilford, Essex; 'Blue Suede Shoes' was originally recorded for the New Musical Express / Nordoff-Robins Music Therapy Charity double LP/CD titled »The Last Temptation Of Elvis« and then released as a 7" 45rpm single b/w 'Paradise'.
Lemmy got together with long-time friend, and the man who in a different world would have been Motörhead's first guitarist, Mick Green, who played most famously with Johnny Kidd And The Pirates in the early 1960s. After Johnny Kidd's death in a road traffic accident in Lancashire in 1966, The Pirates re-formed in 1976, with Mick Green (guitar), Johnny Spence (bass) and Frank Farley (drums), and achieved fame of their own from appearances on the R&B Circuit, and an album recorded live (with songs by other bands) at The Hope & Anchor pub in Islington, London. Mick's playing on these two tracks only goes to show how well he would have suited Motörhead, what with the full-on blast of 'Blue Suede Shoes' and the more laid-back 'Paradise' showing his diversity of playing at different ends of the rock 'n' roll spectrum.

»Hardware«
4-Front Video (083 956 3) VHS

Released 1990; running time approx. 90 minutes

The publicity for the film announced: "in a radioactive wasteland, a mysterious zone-tripper discovers the remains of cyborg MARK13, a highly advanced killing machine. He sells it to Mo (Dylan McDermott), a scrap merchant, who, in turn, presents the find to his seductive girlfriend, Jill (Stacey Travis). Trapped in her apartment, Jill becomes terrified when MARK13 suddenly reconstructs itself using household appliances, and goes on a bloody rampage."

Though never a huge hit, »Hardware« was a great movie in its day and hailed as »The Terminator« of the Nineties. Dark, moody, and mysterious in every aspect, Lemmy has a cameo role as a riverboat taxi driver who ferries Mo and his pal down river; while chatting, he jams a cassette into the onboard hi-fi and plays the first few bars of 'Ace Of Spades'. As you do...

Simon Boswell »Hardware Original Motion Picture Soundtrack« CD
Varese Sarabande Records (VSD-5283)

Released 1990

Tracks: 'No Flesh Shall Be Spared' (4.11) / 'Good Morning America' (.41) with Iggy Pop as Angry Bob / 'The Order Of Death' (4.44) by Public Image Ltd. / 'Reno's Reindeer Steaks' (.09) / 'Alligator Heart' (1.25) / 'Everything Is Under Control' (2.88) / 'MARK 13' (2.37) / 'Jill Burning' (2.05) / 'Silent Night' (.50) / 'A Message From Our Sponsors' (2.41) / 'A Piece Of Pipe' (.48) by Kaduta Massi with Lemmy / 'Stigmata' (5.44) by Ministry / 'It's Horrible...I Love It... What Is It?' (2.51) / 'Cockroach Tea' (2.45) / 'Crucifixion' (2.41) / 'Hardware' (2.12)

Arranged, recorded and produced by Simon Boswell

It's quite difficult to find a copy of this CD, as film soundtracks are notoriously deleted quickly. However, this one was released with two different CD cover inserts, just to make it all the more collectable.

For the 48-second-long track 'A Piece Of Pipe' Kaduta Massi lifted Lemmy's spoken lines from the film soundtrack along with the Simon Boswell backing music. One of Lemmy's lines mentions "a piece of pipe," hence the title.

Lemmy, Phil and Würzel made a personal appearance at the HMV record store on Oxford Street in London on 21 January 1991 to launch the »1916« album, which was released in the UK on that date.

The following month Motörhead were supported by The Almighty and Cycle Sluts From Hell on the fourteen-date It Serves You Right UK tour. Three dates were cancelled due to Lemmy having the flu, but were played at a later date. Together with Cycle Sluts From Hell, Motörhead then went out on their Lights Out Over Europe European tour at the end of February; this ran into early April, after which they played the cancelled dates from the UK tour, and added several more venues to the itinerary.

»Hard 'n' Heavy« Video Magazine Volume 12 VHS Tape Picture Music International (VVD 871)

Released 1991; running time approx. 90 minutes

In this issue of the video 'zine there was an 'Ask Lemmy' feature in which he tackled viewers' personal heartaches and other assorted phobias.

The video also featured, amongst others, Dave Lee Roth, David Coverdale, Billy Idol, Rob Halford, Great White and LA Guns.

Motörhead played five shows in Japan in June; two nights in Tokyo were followed by a show apiece in Kawasaki and Nagoya, with the final gig taking place in Osaka on 17 June.

Ozzy Osbourne »No More Tears«
Epic Records (CZK 46795744987T)

Released 15 June 1991
Tracks: 'Mr. Tinker Train' / 'I Don't Want To Change The World' / 'Mama, I'm Coming Home' / 'Desire' / 'No More Tears' / 'S.I.N.' / 'Hellraiser' / 'Time After Time' / 'Zombie Stomp' / 'A.V.H.' / 'Road To Nowhere'
Ozzy Osbourne: vocals, Zakk Wylde: guitar, Randy Castillo: drums, Bob Daisley: bass, John Sinclair: keyboards, Michael Inez: bass
Recorded at A & M Studios and Devonshire Studios; produced & Engineered by Duane Baron & John Purdell

The lyrics for 'I Don't Want To Change The World', 'Mama, I'm Coming Home', 'Desire' and 'Hellraiser' written by Lemmy Kilmister. Ozzy Osbourne has admitted to not being a keen lyric or natural writer, and with music but no words to go with them he invited Lemmy to help out with four songs on this album. »No More Tears« and the single 'Mama I'm Coming Home' were massive hits, and Lemmy candidly stated on more than one occasion that he 'earned more from writing lyrics for Ozzy's album and single than I did with Motörhead for the last fifteen years.'

The Japanese shows were quickly followed with five dates on The Legendary Muthas Of Metal Australian Invasion tour, and early July would see them on The Operation Rock 'N' Roll American tour with Alice Cooper, Judas Priest, Dangerous Toys and Metal Church. But in mid-August Motörhead dropped out of the tour after Lemmy fell and broke two ribs. Back on the road in mid-December, Motörhead played six dates in Germany on The Christmas Metal Meeting tour, supported by Kreator, Sepultura, Morbid Angel, Headhunter and Wolfsbane.

In early March 1992, Phil Campbell and Würzel flew to Los Angeles to begin working on a new album. At the end of the month they took a short break to play at a Randy Rhoads Tribute concert on 28 March at Irvine Meadows in California. This would be Phil Taylor's last gig with Motörhead.

Ozzy Osbourne
»Don't Blame Me: The Tales of Ozzy Osbourne«
Epic Records DVD (EVD201815 9)

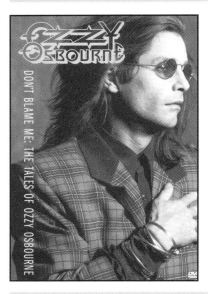

Released 16 March 1992
Songs featured: 'Twinkle, Twinkle, Little Star' (piano solo) / 'Revelation (Mother Earth)' / 'Behind The Wall Of Sleep' / 'Blue Suede Shoes' / 'Black Sabbath' / 'Fairies Wear Boots' / 'N.I.B.' / 'Iron Man' / 'War Pigs' / 'Paranoid' / 'I Don't Want To Change The World' / 'Flying High Again' / 'Demon Alcohol' / 'Hellraiser' / 'Mr. Crowley' / 'Breaking All The Rules' / 'I Don't Know' / 'Shot In The Dark' / 'Suicide Solution' / 'Crazy Train' / 'Dee' / 'Goodbye To Romance' / 'Mama, I'm Coming Home' / 'Desire' / 'No More Tears'
This is a great Ozzy documentary, featuring several short interview segments with Lemmy together with Ozzy's performances of the four songs on the »No More Tears« album for which Lemmy wrote the lyrics.

Bootsauce »Bull«
Island Records (314-512-361--2)

Released 19 May 1992
Tracks: 'Love Monkey #9' / 'Touching Cloth' / 'Whatcha Need' / 'Big, Bad & Groovy' / 'Dog Pound' / 'Outhouse Quake' / 'The 13th Psalm' / 'Misunderstood' / 'Rollercoaster's Child' / 'I Saw You There' / 'The Whole Of You' / 'Bad Dinner' / 'Hold Tight' Bootsauce were an off-the-wall Canadian rock band formed in Montreal in 1989. They were often compared to the Red Hot Chilli Peppers, playing a combination of rock, soul, funk and metal, and considered by many to be ahead of their time. On 'Hold Tight' the 'grunge vocal' is provided by Lemmy, and the 'grunge solo' by Phil 'Wizzo' Campbell.

Motörhead's new album, with Phil Taylor and Mikkey Dee playing drums on one track each, and Tommy Aldridge doing the balance, was released as »March Or Die« in August 1992. Mikkey's contribution to the album came on 'I Ain't No Nice Guy', the song which also featured a duet with Ozzy Osbourne and a solo from Slash. The following month they were on the road in America with Ozzy Osbourne and Ugly Kid Joe. Dates with Guns N' Roses and Metallica followed in October, and they also did a couple of South American shows with Alice In Chains.

Mikkey Dee was taken on as Motörhead's new drummer. Mikkey had come up through various local bands on the Copenhagen music scene, the most renowned of which was Geisha. Later, he joined King Diamond and appeared on several of his albums, coming to the notice of Lemmy and Phil Campbell when King Diamond supported them. Asked to join Motörhead on a couple of earlier occasions, Mikkey had declined as he had commitments and obligations to King Diamond, and again, felt much the same when he played with Don Dokken. But at those stages in his career he did not feel he had what he believed it took to be Motörhead's drummer; after working with them on »March Or Die« he believed that he was now ready to take on the role.

Pure Hell »The Black Box« EP
Autumn 1992 Recording Sessions

Unreleased
Formed in Philadelphia, Pure Hell (Spider, Stinker, Chip and Lenny) were the first all-black American punk rock band. They released one 45rpm picture sleeve 7" single in 1978 through Curtis Knight's Golden Sphinx Records label, a cover of Nancy Sinatra's 'These Boots Were Made For Walking' which was more heavy rock than punk, but a storming track nonetheless.

In Autumn 1992 they went into 4th Street Recording Studios in Santa Monica, California, with Lemmy as their producer and co-engineer, and recorded six tracks: 'Wild One' (on which Lemmy plays bass) / 'One Left In The Chamber' / 'American' / 'Hell Is For Heroes' / 'The Call' (with Lemmy on backing vocals) / 'Dead Girl'. These six songs make up »The Black Box« EP, and although it remains unreleased most of them are available to listen to on the band's MySpace site; they've had thousands of plays online and, given that, it would be great for a record company to license these rare tracks and release them officially.

Despite having what I would call a close relationship with Lemmy, I knew absolutely nothing about the above sessions. I've found that you have to have stumbled across something and then actually ask Lemmy directly, otherwise he wouldn't think to mention it: it would merely be filed away in his brain someplace as 'history'. However, in 1979, on Motörhead's UK »Bomber« tour the author interviewed Fast Eddie Clarke about his pre-Motörhead bands, one of which was Curtis Knight's Zeus.

Eddie had been the lead guitarist, and in America Jimi Hendrix had also been Curtis's guitarist in his Curtis Knight and the Squires band. The resulting interview appeared in the 1981 »Motörhead« book published by Babylon books. In more recent years, some of the text ended up on the internet and Kathy Knight-McConnell came across it on a search. Kathy had been the wife of the now deceased Curtis Knight, and made contact with me to ask if she could include the interview in her forthcoming book. She also asked about speaking to Eddie herself. After putting the two in contact, whereby the guitarist was aasked to add further recollections to the story, Kathy mentioned in an email that she knew Lemmy. I asked how that had come about, and she told me about the Pure Hell sessions.

Her book, titled »Curtis Knight – Living In The Shadow Of Jimi Hendrix« was published in 2010, and is recommended reading. I mentioned the recordings to Lemmy at the Plymouth, UK, date on Motörhead's 2009 UK tour and he pointed out that Pure Hell are "a great band and they're great songs; someone should release them."

Motörhead's 1980 hit single 'Ace Of Spades' had something of a rebirth in February 1993 when it was used for a TV commercial for Pot Noodle. It charted on the back of this and Motörhead enjoyed another stint on »Top Of The Pops«.

The following month Phil and Würzel flew to Los Angeles to start working on their next album with Lemmy and Mikkey. They broke off recording in April to play a couple of dates in Argentina, and crossed the world once more to spend June and the first part of July on a European tour with Terrorvision. Their contract with Sony/WTG now history, by October they had completed the recordings and signed a contract to release the »Bastards« album. Favoured by many fans as one of their best in recent years, it suffered through being released on the relatively small ZYX label; the label had poor distribution in Europe and the UK, so fans found it difficult to find and buy it.

The sleeve art, by Joe Petagno, was created in response to what he regarded as the dire artwork on the »March Or Die« album. Joe hated this and so created »Bastards« in revenge. Initially, the illustration had been sent for use as the cover to one of the Motörheadbangers fanzines, with Joe offering it also as a signed and numbered A3 poster. When the band saw the cover of the fanzine, they loved it so much that they contacted Joe, asked for a few minor adjustments and used it on the new album.

Fast Eddie Clarke »It Ain't Over Till It's Over« Chequered Flag Records (CHFCD 100)

Released 5 November 1993
Tracks: 'Snakebite' / 'Lying Ain't Right' / 'Back On The Road' / 'Naturally' / 'All Over Bar The Shouting' / 'Make My Day' / 'Laugh At The Devil' / 'No Satisfaction' / 'Lessons' / 'Hot, Straight and Normal' / 'In The City' / 'It Ain't Over 'Till It's Over'
Fast Eddie Clarke: guitars and vocals, Pete Riley: drums, Mel Gabbitas: bass, John Sloman: backing vocals
Recorded at The Point and Aosis Studios, London; produced by Will Reid Dick.

Lemmy wrote the lyrics for and recorded vocals on 'Laugh At The Devil' on this solo album by Motörhead's former guitarist. "The problem was," Lemmy recalled in a conversation with me about it, "Eddie forgot the fact that Motörhead tune down half a step to help my voice range, so I had to stand there grabbing hold of my bollocks to get the high notes!"

Always shy and not a confident vocalist, Fast Eddie Clarke did sing as little as possible in his early career, the noteable exceptions being with Motörhead on their cover version of John Mayall's Bluesbreakers with Eric Clapton 'I'm Your Witchdoctor' (released on the »Beer Drinkers & Hell Raisers« EP by Chiswick Records) and 'Step Down' on their »Bomber« album. Eddie sang 'Step Down' live for the first time at the band's appearance at the 1979 Reading Festival, and it was subsequently featured in the set list from time to time afterwards on the Bomber tour. But after a short time, Eddie's lack of confidence in his vocals led it to being dropped completely. However, his »It Ain't Over Till It's Over« solo album proved that his insecurities were unfounded. He has a great voice here although, like many fine guitarists, Eddie prefers concentrating on his playing rather than his singing.

The majority of December was taken up on the Christmas Metal Meeting European tour, with Kreator, Sodom and Skew Siskin supporting headliners Motörhead. With no respite from touring, early February through to early May saw Motörhead second on the bill to Black Sabbath on a massive Cross Purposes US tour. Mid-May saw them co-headlining a 45,000 seat stadium in Argentina with The Ramones, and a five-date Japanese tour came at the end of that month.

Shonen Knife 'Tomato Head'
Virgin Records America (v25h-38433)

Released 17 May 1994
'Tomato Head' produced by Page Porrazzo and Shonen Knife: (1) 'Z-Mix' (3:53) remixed by David Z; (2) 'Jazzy Tomato Head Mix' (4:05) remixed and additional production by The Dust Brothers (John King and Michael Simpson), additional keyboards and bass by Mark Nishita; (3) 'Lemmy In There Mix' (5:51) remixed by Howard Benson; (4) 'Love Is Like A Heat Wave' (2:50) – bonus track (not available on any album

Naoko Yamano: vocals, guitar, harmonica, Michie Nakatani: vocals, bass, keyboards, Atsuko Yamano: vocals, drums, percussion

Shonen Knife have also performed as a Ramones tribute band, named The Osaka Ramones. With Kurt Cobain a fan, Shonen Knife were special guests on Nirvana's Nevermind June/July 1992 UK tour. The band were formed in Osaka in 1981, and being influenced by Sixties' girl groups, surf sounds and punk rock, the music obviously attracted Lemmy enough to wish to become involved. There's not a great deal of Lemmy here though, just a few shouts, lecherous laughs and back-up vocals on the 'Lemmy In There Mix' of the 'Tomato Head' track, but he no doubt enjoyed himself with the three young female Japanese musicians who are Shonen Knife, nevertheless.

»Airheads«
20th Century Fox DVD (F1-SGB08602DVD)

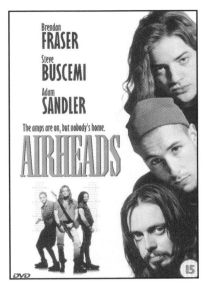

Released 3 August 1994

A spoof of the music industry: when the not-so-bright members of a band (Brendan Fraser, Steve Buscemi and Adam Sandler) decide to take drastic action after their music continually falls upon deaf ears they break into a radio station to get their demo played on the air. The DJ and the station manager refuse to play their song, and the inept trio take the entire station hostage.

Motörhead's 'Born To Raise Hell' was the title track for the movie, and Lemmy has a cameo appearance as Lemmy von Motörhead, a school newspaper reporter / rocker. Ugly Kid Joe's Whitfield Crane and Ice T were guest vocalists on the 'Born To Raise Hell' song.

On 28 January 1995 Lemmy was 'The Icon Of Heavy Metal' on UK Channel 4 TV's »Don't Forget Your Toothbrush« where he played 'Ace Of Spades' and Little Richard's 'Good Golly Miss Molly' live in the studio with Jools Holland and his band providing the backing music to Lemmy's bass and vocals. He also took part in a Motörhead quiz against MHB, Robert Kiewik.

There is a strange and memorable story behind this. »Don't Forget Your Toothbrush« was a gameshow, where the audience took their passports, enough personal belongings to last seven days, and a week's holiday leave from their job. If selected, a couple were subjected to quiz questions and, if they won, would be driven to the airport for a free week's holiday. Ideally, the audience consisted of members of the public who were under forty years of age. Each week a famous guest was featured, and a 'superfan' would do battle against the star, with quiz questions based on the star's life and career.

I had a phone call from one of the producers, Suzi Aplin, who had a voice sexy enough to melt your socks, and a strong, confident personality who did not take no for an answer. Suzi informed me that they were lining up Lemmy for the show, and wanted me to be the 'mystery fan' to do battle with him on the personal quiz. The rules were, she added, that I had never met Lemmy, and that I was under 40 years of age.

Unfortunately I did not qualify on either of those criteria: I was 44 by that time, and had met Lemmy numerous times. "Well," Suzi said, "don't worry about it, I'm sure no-one will be any the wiser." That my name had appeared on several Motörhead album sleeves wouldn't give the game away?

Well, I did worry about it. I knew Kerrang! journalist Morat (in fact, he's Motörheadbanger # 666) and he was bound to watch the show and perhaps, in all innocence, blow the whistle. So this did not sit very well with me at all. And it was not the fear of going on TV: that would have been the highpoint of my life, especially with Lemmy, for goodness sake!

My brain was going like a train, until I remembered how a Motörheadbangers fan club member from Holland, Robert Kiewik, had mentioned in recent correspondence that he had been to see Motörhead many times, but had never found the opportunity to meet them. And he was also under 40 years of age, so on both counts he could go on the show; and my conscience would be 100% clear.

I phoned Robert. Now, if someone called you and asked if you wanted to go on a nationwide TV show with Lemmy, what would your answer be? I think I know the answer...

I explained the story to Robert, and how he fitted the criteria like a jigsaw puzzle piece, rather than me going on and having to tell lies – something which I was brought up never to do. When I phoned Suzi, less than 24 hours since we had spoken, she almost had a fit. But when she had calmed down, and realised that it was the right thing to do, I gave her Robert's phone number. After speaking to Robert, Suzi called me back and agreed that he would be the right man for the job.

And so the show was broadcast live. Lemmy was in his element, singing and playing 'Ace Of Spades' and 'Good Golly Miss Molly'. He and Robert had enormous fun with the quiz, and Robert scored most points and won. Then, which was a nice touch, Lemmy and Robert each presented one another with a personal gift.

See? Honesty is the best policy. I did not watch the show with any degree of envy; more with a great deal of pride in that we had done the right thing. Motörhead and Motörhead fans are like that: we are more than friends, we are more like a family, and families help one another out, and I will never regret my decision in stepping down on that occasion.

Summer festival appearances across Europe followed, with Phil Campbell flying out to LA in early September to start working on another studio album with Lemmy and Mikkey. The band were back on the road again mid-December for The Christmas Metal Meeting with six dates in Germany which rounded off another busy year.

In March 1995 the results of their studio labours were released as the »Sacrifice« album. The following month though guitarist Mick Würzel Burston left the band. Motörhead chose not to replace him, and instead continued as a three-piece with Phil Campbell handling the guitar duties. Late April through to early June saw the band playing Motorious 95 European tour, followed by the short, three-date Sacrifice tour of the UK, culminating in the Brixton Academy gig attended by both Fast Eddie Clarke and Würzel.

July and the early days of August saw another American tour with Black Sabbath, and most of October Motörhead were playing dates across Europe with Skew Siskin, followed by four shows in the UK with Cathedral in support, ending at The Forum in Kentish Town, North London. A three-date South American jaunt took place in mid-November, with one show in Chile and two in Argentina.

Lemmy's fiftieth birthday celebrations took place early at The Whisky in Los Angeles, where Metallica played as The Lemmys, with all four members dressed in wigs, moustaches and tattoos; The Lemmys played seven Motörhead songs, and were followed by a 45 minute set by Motörhead themselves.

1996 kicked off with an American tour in early January with Motörhead, Speedball and Belladonna.

Bill Laswell »Myth: Dreams Of The World«
Dove Audio (0-7871-0734-4)

Released 23 April1996
Tracks: 'Introduction' / 'Zeus, King of the Universe' / 'Hera, Queen of the Universe' / 'Hermes, The Messenger God' / 'Apollo, The Sun God' / 'Athena, The Goddess of Wisdom' / 'Pan, The Playful God of the Country' / 'Hades, The God of the Underworld' / 'Aphrodite, The Goddess of Love' / 'Eros, Aphrodite's Son' / 'Vulcan, The God of Inventions and Metal' / 'Poseidon, The God of the Ocean and Amphitrite' / 'Mars, The God of War' / 'Artemis, The Goddess of the Hunt' / 'Cassandra, The Unheeded Prophet' / 'Dionysius, The God of Spirits' / 'Prometheus, Brought Fire to Man'

Produced by Janet Rienstra; music produced by Bill Laswell

To paraphrase the promotional text for this curio, "the Greek and Roman myths were early tales created to explain the world, and these have become inexorably woven throughout music, art, film, theatre, literature, politics and daily life... »Myth: Dreams of the World« keeps these stories vibrant..." Featuring a lengthy list of artists including Iggy Pop, George Clinton, Lori Carson, Suzanne Vega, Lemmy, Jaron Lanier and members of The Last Poets, the album also features musical contributions from Material, Anton Fier, Liu Sola, Jeff Bova and Alex Hass, Painkiller (Mick Harris, Bill Laswell, John Zorn), Divination, Automaton, Buckethead, Nicky Skopelitis, and members of Parliament Funkadelic.

Bill Laswell is an American bass player, record producer and record label owner, who has played on hundreds of albums with musicians from around the world. In the 1980s, he produced The Ramones, Public Image Ltd, and Mick Jagger amongst many others, and also Motörhead's »Orgasmatron« album and 'Eat The Rich' song.

'Mars, The God Of War' features Lemmy reciting the 'Orgasmatron' lyrics over a guitar / synthesiser backing played by Nick Skopelitis. With Lemmy's elocution sharp and crisp, the track is quickly spoken and played as the running time is just 1.52 seconds.[13]

»John Wayne Bobbitt Uncut« VHS video

Released 27 May 1996, running time approx. 77 minutes

Starring Ron Jeremy, John Wayne Bobbitt and Nikki Randall

John Wayne Bobbitt and his wife Lorena were an American couple whose difficult relationship gained worldwide notoriety when in 1993 Lorena severed John's penis with a knife. It was subsequently surgically reattached, despite being thrown from a moving car by Lorena. In this movie, Lemmy plays the part of a fictitious drunken bum who happens to catch it, and says "Oh look, a dick!" In reality, it was found in a field after a search.

Motörhead played various summer festival dates across Europe. In early August, Lemmy and Phil appeared at The Ramones' last ever show in Hollywood. The DVD of the show would be released a year later as »We're Outa Here – The Ramones Last Show«. Motörhead then undertook a short American tour during October (when the »Overnight Sensation« album was released) and November.

[13] *Thanks to Ronald Ott, who helped find a copy of this rarer than rare CD*

By mid-November they were out on another US tour, this time with Dio topping the bill, and in early December they switched places for a mass of dates through Germany with Speedball as extra support.

Ugly Kid Joe »Motel California«
Evilution Records (RAWCD 113)

Released 21 October 1996
Tracks: 'It's A Lie' / 'Dialogue' / 'Sandwich' / 'Rage Against The Answering Machine' / 'Would You Like To Be There' / 'Little Red Man' / 'Bicycle Wheels' / 'Father' / 'Undertow' / 'Shine' / 'Strange' / '12 Cents'
The band: Whit Crane, Cordell Crockett, Klaus Eichstadt, Dave Fortman, Shannon Larkin
Recorded at Sound City, Van Nuys & Disgraceland, Santa Barbara, California; produced by Ugly Kid Joe.
After an American tour with Ozzy Osbourne and Ugly Kid Joe in 1992, the band invited Lemmy to provide background vocals on 'Little Red Man'.

Skew Siskin »Electric Chair Music«
CD Maximum (CDM 0606-2538)

Released 18 November 1996
Tracks: 'Introverted' / 'My Worst Enemy' / 'No Solution' / 'Trick Or Treat' / 'Metamorphosis' / 'Revolution Of Illusion' / 'It's Alright' / 'Liquid' / 'Visible Retreat' / 'Communication Breakdown' / 'Lowside Ghetto' / 'Bloody Hierarchy' / 'Dreams Of Black' / 'Young Man'
Nina C. Alice: lead and backing vocals, Jim Voxx: guitars, Jogu Rautenberg: bass, Crash Click: drums
Berlin-based Skew Siskin are a hard-rocking band recording around the nucleus of Nina C. Alice and Jim Voxx. Lemmy described them, in a Motörheadbangers interview, as being "one of the best bands in the world right now. You've got a girl who sings like a cross between Bon Scott and Janis Joplin, who sound like AC/DC mixed with thrash."

Lemmy became aware of them in 1992, when they were touting for a record label, and the demos for their self-titled debut album landed on his manager's desk. The band's attitude is not unlike Lemmy's, and he liked the sarcasm and dark sense of humour in their lyrics as much as their superb musicianship and razor-sharp delivery and sound. Seeking them out, Lemmy found that they had a lot of common ground, and began working on the music together. Keen to promote their music to the masses, Motörhead invited Skew Siskin to join them on tour from time to time as their special guests.

'Introverted', 'No Solution', 'Trick Or Treat' and 'Metamorphosis' all feature lyrics co-written by Lemmy.

In January 1997, Motörhead played a one-off show at The Astoria Theatre in London. This was followed a few days later by the Motörhead / Mass Murderers European tour going through to early March. With hardly two days to draw their breath, they set off to start the Overnight Sensation Scandinavian tour with Skunk Anansie. Four dates in Japan followed in late May, then it was back to the US to tour with WASP.

»Dragon Attack – A Tribute To Queen«
Revolver Records (REV XD 209)

Released 21 July 1997
Featuring Lemmy, Glenn Hughes, Yngwie Malmsteen, Ted Nugent, Bob Kulick, Marty Friedman, Carmine Appice, Rudy Sarzo, Scott Ian and many others
Tracks: 'I Want It All' / 'Sheer Heart Attack' / 'Another One Bites The Dust' / 'Save Me' / 'We Will Rock You' / 'We Are The Champions' / 'Tie Your Mother Down' / 'Get Down Make Love' / 'Keep Yourself Alive' / 'One Vision' / 'It's Late'
Produced, recorded and mixed by Billy Sherwood

'Tie Your Mother Down' features Lemmy: vocals and rhythm guitar, Ted Nugent: lead guitar, Bob Kulick: rhythm guitar, Rudy Sarzo: bass, Tommy Aldridge: drums

Lemmy enjoyed projects such as this where he could stretch himself outside of Motörhead for the space of a few days recording a song for a tribute album, staving off boredom when not on tour or indeed recording his own music. Lemmy's management and record company contract allowed his indulgence in tracks such as this because he "enjoyed doing them" – as he told the author – as and when the occasion arose.

Skew Siskin »Voices From The War«
CD Maximum (CDM 0606 2539)

Released 1997
Tracks: 'I Can't Take It' / 'Fuck You' /
'Dead One' / 'B4' / 'Shadows Of War' /
'Genocide' / 'Who Cares' / 'Pussy Game' /
'I Don't Care'
Nina C. Alice: lead and all backing vocals,
Jim Voxx: guitars, Jogy Rautenburg: bass,
Crash Click: drums
Often spending time in between gigs during
the summer rock festival season in Skew
Siskin's Monongo Studios in Berlin, Lemmy
would join Nina C. Alice co-writing lyrics, and
add some bass and vocals when schedules
permitted. 'Dead One', 'B4' and 'I Don't Care' feature lyrics co-written by Lemmy,
who also played bass and additional vocals on 'B4'.

Motörhead played several summer festival dates in Europe, and in October the
Motörhead Overnight Sensation tour blasted through the UK with dBh and Novo-
caine as support. Four dates in Russia saw the year out.

»The World's Greatest Tribute To AC/DC«
Zebra Records (CDM ZEB 30)

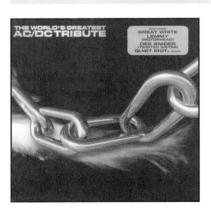

Released 17 November 1997
Tracks: Quiet Riot - 'Highway To Hell' / The
Vibrators - 'Rocker' / Lemmy Kilmister Of
Motörhead with Jake E. Lee - 'It's A Long
Way To The Top' - Mission UK Remix /
Sister Machine Gun - 'TNT' / The Dwarves
- 'Big Balls' / Joe Lyn Turner Of Rainbow
and Phil Collen Of Def Leppard - 'Back In
Black' Die Krupps Remix / Aggression -
'Touch Too Much' / Joined At The Head -
'Whole Lotta Rosie' Controlled Bleeding
Mix / Great White - 'Sin City' / Dee Snider
Of Twisted Sister and Scott Ian Of Anthrax
- 'Walk All Over You' Synical Remix / Razed In Black - 'Hell's Bells' / Genitor-
turers - 'Squealer' / Godflesh - 'For Those About To Rock'

Another tribute album track on this release dedicated to AC/DC's fabulous music; this time, with ex-Ozzy Osbourne guitarist, Jake E. Lee, Lemmy made a superb job of the classic track 'It's A Long Way To The Top'. A great many other top stars also appear.

»We're Outa Here – The Ramones Last Show«
Eagle Records (EAGCD010)

Released 27 November 1997
Tracks: 'Durango 95' / 'Teenage Lobotomy' / 'Do You Remember Rock And Roll Radio' / 'I Believe In Miracles' / 'Gimme Gimme Shock Treatment' / 'Rock 'n Roll High School' / 'I Wanna Be Sedated' / 'Spider-Man' / 'The K.K.K. Took My Baby Away' / 'I Just Want To Have Something To Do' / 'Commando' / 'Sheena Is A Punk Rocker' / 'Rockaway Beach' / 'Pet Sematary' / 'The Crusher' / 'Love Kills' / 'Do You Wanna Dance' / 'Someone Put Something In My Drink' / 'I Don't Want You' / 'Wart Hog' / 'Cretin Hop' / 'R.A.M.O.N.E.S.' / 'Today Your Love, Tomorrow The World' / 'Pinhead' / '53rd & 3rd' / 'Listen To Your Heart' / 'We're A Happy Family' / 'Chinese Rock' / 'Beat On The Brat' / 'Any Way You Want It'
Recorded 6 August 1996 at The Palace, Los Angeles

A self-confessed Ramones fan from his love of their fast, frantic music and from meeting them at their early London shows, Lemmy played bass and sung on 'R.A.M.O.N.E.S.', the song he wrote and recorded on the »1916« album as a tribute. There's also a copy of a handwritten note which Lemmy sent to the band in the CD booklet, along with a photo of the above event live onstage.

»Tromeo And Juliet«
Troma Video (DVD 9400)

Released 17 December 1997
Described in the promotional blurb as "all the body-piercing, kinky sex and car crashes that Shakespeare wanted but never had! Join Tromeo (Will Keenan), Juliet (Jane Jensen), and Lemmy Kilmister of Motörhead as they travel through Manhattan's underground in search of climatic love, violence, and the American Way."

The film features the music of Motörhead, Superchunk, Ass Ponys and Sublime amongst others, and a soundtrack album was made available on Oglio Records.

Lemmy narrates throughout the movie and is featured in an interview chapter.

Ron Jeremy 'Freak Of The Week'

Released 1998
According to the entry in Wikipedia, Lemmy made a cameo appearance in the video for this rap song by porn star Ron Jeremy – and indeed he does, for about two seconds, along with many other stars like Ice T and Grandpa (Al Lewis) from »The Munsters«. The video is featured on YouTube for the over-eighteens, but there seems to be no trace of an actual recording being released.

The »Snake Bite Love« album was released in February 1998. To support it, Motörhead played a European tour with Skew Siskin through May, recording their live album »Everything Louder Than Everyone Else« at Hamburg Docks on

21 May. July saw them in America on the Ozzfest package, then it was back to Europe for a handful of summer festivals. The UK leg of the »Snake Bite Love« tour began in early October, and was followed later in the month with European dates, ending late November with shows in Turkey and Greece.

At the 5 October gig at Plymouth Pavilions, fellow Motörheadbangers, Mick Stevenson, Robert Kiewik and Nigel Moore enjoyed a rare treat. We were in Lemmy's dressing room when he asked us to read through some recent lyrics he'd written (three in total, I believe). Although the other two were up to Lemmy's usual high standard, the third, titled 'We Are Motörhead', particularly grabbed my attention.

The four of us were sitting around a table whilst we enjoyed these lyrical delights from the boss, but 'We Are Motörhead' truly fascinated me. After reading the lyrics through three or four times, I realised that the room had fallen silent, and everyone was looking at me. I turned and smiled at Lemmy. "Those are fucking excellent," I said. "Please don't lose them; they will make a great song as an album track, or maybe even as an album title as well!"

Lemmy said "thanks, Al."

Lemmy was always thrilled when fans enjoyed his lyrics, and little did we or I know, that in the not too distant future, 'We Are Motörhead' would not only become an album track, but also its title.

The Royal Philharmonic Orchestra »Philharmania«

Released 9 November 1998
Joey Tempest – 'Born To Run' / John Farnham – 'A Whiter Shade Of Pale' / Paul Carrack – 'No Face, No Name, No Number' / Bonnie Tyler – 'I Put A Spell On You' / Marc Almond – 'Paint It Black' / Mike Batt – 'Bright Eyes' / Roger Daltrey – 'The Boys Of Summer' / Lemmy Kilmister – 'Eve Of Destruction' / Justin Hayward – 'Nights In White Satin' / Huey Lewis – 'The Power Of Love' / Colin Blunstone – 'Owner Of A Lonely Heart' / Kim Wilde – 'Because The Night' / Status Quo – 'Not Fade Away' / Midge Ure – 'Vienna'
Produced, arranged, and conducted by Mike Batt. Batt is probably best known for creating the novelty pop group The Wombles (who wore costumes based on Elisabeth Beresford's original characters which were featured in a children's TV show of the same name), although he is a songwriter of great repute and his chart-topping hit 'Bright Eyes' (a UK Number 1 by Art Garfunkel) is also featured on this album.
'Eve Of Destruction' is a superb track which Lemmy was invited to record. It's a cover of the 1965 UK Number 3 / Billboard Number 1 hit by Barry McGuire, written by Phil F. Sloan. A better song could not have been picked for Lemmy.

His voice is very similar to McGuire's earthy original, the lyric spat out with all the venom which should accompany such a prophetic verse. With the Vietnam War in full swing, and the Cold War looking at the possibility of a nuclear holocaust at any moment, Sloan's poignant observations of the fate of planet Earth at that point in time were echoed in everyone's daily thoughts.

The other artists on this album, like Lemmy, are world-famous and at the top of their game, making this an album well worth finding.

"I met him [Mike Batt] when I first moved down to London [September 1967]" recalled Lemmy. "He had a friend, Roger, who said that he could make me a chart-topping pop star. Obviously that part of it didn't work," he smiled wryly at the thought of it. "He just got in contact and asked if I'd like to sing on the ['Eve Of Destruction'] track," he told me. "It's all right, I can take it or leave it myself." Lemmy was always very modest about his work.

The »Everything Louder Than Everyone Else« live double album was released in March 1999. Through May until early June, the band were on the road in America with the Dropkick Murphys.

Ozzy Osbourne »Ozzmosis«
Epic Records (EPC508362-2)

Released 5 April 1999

Tracks: 'Perry Mason' / 'I Just Want You' / 'Ghost Behind My Eyes' / 'Thunder Underground' / 'See You On The Other Side' / 'Tomorrow' / 'Denial' / 'My Little Man' / 'My Jekyll Doesn't Hide' / 'Old L.A. Tonight' / 'Whole World's Fallin' Down' [re-issue bonus track] / 'Aimee' [re-issue bonus track]

Band: Ozzy Osbourne: vocals, Geezer Butler: bass, Zakk Wylde: guitar, Deen Castronovo: drums

Taking shape during several writing sessions, and with writing partners including Lemmy, Steve Vai, Zakk Wilde and Geezer Butler, »Ozzmosis« highlighted Ozzy Osbourne's resilience, both as a person and as an artist.

'See You On The Other Side' – lyrics written by Lemmy, who was once again helping out his great friend Ozzy, but this time just with the one song. Lemmy talked about this once, telling me, "sometimes I write better lyrics for others than I do for my own band!"

A.N.I.M.A.L. »Usa Toda Tu Fuerza«
(398429035-2)

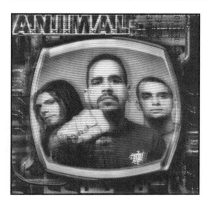

Released 1999
Tracks: 'Revolucion' / 'Cuida Tu Fe' / 'Usa Toda Tu Fuerza' / 'Barrio Batron' / 'Ganar O Berder' / 'Dios' / 'Choli Rancho' / 'Vamos Por Mas' / 'Solo' / 'Atropello' / 'Aura' / 'Highway To Hell'
Andres Gimenez: guitar and vocals, Marcelo Corvalan: bass and vocals, Andres Vilanova: drums
Recorded at Indigo Ranch Studio, Malibu, California, May 1999; produced by Richard Kaplan.
A.N.I.M.A.L. were from Argentina; the title »Usa Toda tu Fuerza« translates as 'Use All Your Strength'. 'Highway To Hell' features Lemmy on vocals. Most of the band's nu-metal lyrics dealt with the plight of the ethnic minorities and the indigenous people of Latin America, so inviting Lemmy to join them on a straightforward cover of the AC/DC classic made perfectly good sense as it was a fun cover, rather than the usual focussed material the band produced.

Summer festivals across Europe took up the middle of 1999, with spare time filled by recording a new studio album in Germany.

Skew Siskin »What The Hell«
CD-Maximum (CDM 0606-2540)

Released 13 September 1999
Tracks: 'Spend The Night With Me' / 'Life's A Bitch' / 'Sex, Love, Dance, Music' / 'Ace Against The Jack' / 'Shoot Out Your Lights' / 'Head Up Your Ass' / 'Out Of Sight, Out Of Mind' / 'Jesse James' / 'The Phantom' / 'Philosophy 101' / 'Let's Get Drunk & Screw' / 'Life Sucks' / 'How Can I Miss You' / 'Bend Over' / 'Voodoo Doll'
Nina C Alice: vocals and insults, Jim Voxx: rhythm, lead and solo guitar, Jogy Rautenberg: bass, Crash Klick: drums
Lemmy co-wrote the lyrics for 'Life's A Bitch' and 'Shoot Out Your Lights' with Nina C Alice.

Motörhead and Nashville Pussy played American dates throughout October into early November, when the band joined Manowar and Dio for the Monsters Of The Millennium Scandinavian tour. A one-off show at The Astoria in London ended another busy year for the band.

The Swing Cats »A Special Tribute To Elvis« Legacy Entertainment Inc (RWP273)

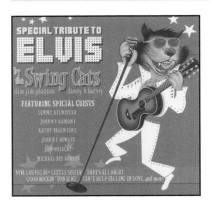

Released 14 February 2000
Tracks: 'That's All Right' / 'Little Sister' / 'Viva Las Vegas' / 'Crawfish' / 'T-R-O-U-B-L-E' / 'Good Rockin' Tonight' / 'Trying To Get To You' / 'Burning Love' / 'Tigerman' / 'I Need Someone To Lean On' / 'Steamroller Blues' / 'Stuck On You' / 'Can't Help Falling In Love'
The Swing Cats (Slim Jim Phantom and Danny B. Harvey of The Stray Cats) were supported by the likes of Lemmy, Johnny Ramone, Kathy Valentine, Johnny Rowley, Tim Polecat and Michael Des Barres. The sessions were a meeting of minds where Lemmy, Danny, and Slim Jim began recording together, which would then result in the album below. It was Lemmy's first return to Elvis Presley's music since the 'Blue Suede Shoes' track he recorded with Mick Green for the NME charity album.

Lemmy Kilmister, Slim Jim Phantom and Danny B. Harvey »Lemmy, Slim Jim, and Danny B« Cleopatra Records (CLP 0826-2)

Released 27 March 2000
Tracks: 'Big River' / 'Lawdy, Miss Clawdy' / 'You Got Me Dizzy' / 'Cut Across Shorty' / 'Tell Me How' / 'Well... All Right' /' Take Your Time' / 'Stuck On You' / 'Love's Made A Fool Of You' / 'Trying To Get To You' / 'Not Fade Away' / 'Fool's Paradise' / 'Peggy Sue Got Married' / 'Crying, Waiting, Hoping' / 'Learning The Game' / 'Matchbox' / 'True Love Ways' / 'Heartbreak Hotel'
Lemmy: vocals, acoustic guitar and harmonica, Danny B Harvey: lead guitar, bass,

keyboards, backing vocals, Slim Jim Phantom: drums, percussion, and backing vocals
Recorded at Tiki Hit Studios, Hollywood, California and Yucca Hills Studio, Agua Dulce, California, September 1999; produced by Lemmy, Slim Jim Phantom and Danny B Harvey.
Slim Jim Phantom and Danny B. Harvey of The Stray Cats were the musicians behind the »A Special Tribute To Elvis« album. Legend has it that when the sessions were complete, Lemmy picked up an acoustic guitar and started playing some of his favourite rock 'n' roll songs by people like Eddie Cochran and Buddy Holly. Slim Jim and Danny B knew the songs and joined in. Afterwards, Lemmy told them that he would like to record a selection of these songs, and the idea blossomed with this album. In typical Lemmy style, he later decided to take the band on the road during his time off from Motörhead, and used an amalgamation of The Stray Cats and Motörhead names to come up with The Head Cat. The album was re-released under The Head Cat name in 2006, titled »Fool's Paradise«.

Back at the day job, Lemmy and Motörhead played dates in Brazil, Mexico and Argentina in early-to-mid-May. While they were out and about »We Are Motörhead« was released on 16 May, 2000. These dates were quickly followed by another massive US tour with Nashville Pussy through to late June.

Boetz »Call To Arms«
Balls Out Records (41360AM-01)

Released 9 June 2000
Tracks: 'Call To Arms' / 'Green Back Crack' / 'Weak In The Knees' / 'Rock 'N' Roll Is Good' / 'Shinin'' / 'Getting Over You' / 'Oh Boy' / 'Don't Mean A Thing' / 'Wish' / 'Almost To Scotland'
Ernest Robert Boetz: vocals, guitars, bass, Tim Golden: drums
Lemmy – vocals on 'Call To Arms'
Recorded on 24 track analogue tape at Exocet Studios in Atlanta, Georgia: produced by Ernest Robert Boetz, engineered and mixed by Bruce Bennett, mastered by Rodney Mills.
Lemmy's track engineered by Bob Kulick and Bruce Bennett
With a CD sticker flagging "includes the single 'Call To Arms' featuring Lemmy Kilmister" as a come-hither sales point, you might think that Lemmy's track

was the album's saving grace. But it is actually a thoroughly decent rock album (and Lemmy wouldn't have had anything to do with any of his offshoot tracks such as this were they not), and Boetz's guitar playing is pretty razor-sharp throughout. It's rather AC/DC influenced, but in my book that only adds to its appeal.

Summer festivals across Europe and four shows in Japan kept Motörhead busy. The weekend of 21/22 October provided fans with a guest appearance at the Hawkestra Hawkwind Reunion at Brixton Academy on the Saturday, followed by Motörhead's 25th Anniversary show at the same venue on the Sunday.

Doro »Calling The Wild«
Koch Records (KOC CD-8151)

Released 2 October 2000
Tracks: 'Terrorvision' / 'I Give My Blood' / 'White Wedding' / 'I Wanna Live' / 'Kiss Me Like A Cobra' / 'Love Me Forever' / 'Pain' / 'Scarred' / 'Now Or Never' / 'Alone Again' / 'Constant Danger' / 'Burn It Up'
Doro: vocals, Bob Kulick: electric guitars, Lemmy Kilmister: acoustic and bass guitar (and acoustic guitar solo on 'Alone Again'), Joe Taylor: guitar, Eric Singer: drums
Produced and mixed by Lemmy Kilmister, Doro Pesch, Bob Kulick and Bruce Bouillet

Born in Düsseldorf in 1964, Doro – Dorothee Pesch – first came to prominence as lead vocalist for the German heavy metal band Warlock in 1984, with their debut album »Burning The Witches«. In 1986, she was the first woman to front a metal band at the Monsters Of Rock festival at Castle Donington, where Warlock shared the billing with Bad News, Motörhead, Def Leppard, Scorpions and Ozzy Osbourne. The mix of power ballads and heavy metal music, plus Doro's stage presence and vocals, led to success in the male dominated Eighties' rock/metal scene. After three more successful albums with Warlock, »Calling The Wild« was her seventh solo album.

Doro has always been keen to duet on songs with well known metal acts, and has done so with Udo Dirkschneider, Twisted Sister, Saxon, Girlschool, Sister Sin and many, many more, but this album featured her first vocal with Lemmy.

»Citizen Toxic: The Toxic Avenger IV«
Troma Team Video DVD (9235)

Released 2000
Running time 90 minutes
Troma strike again! It's a bit hard to argue with the promotional outline for this one: "when the notorious Diaper Mafia take hostage the Tromaville School for The Very Special, only The Toxic Avenger and his morbidly obese sidekick Lardass can save Tromaville. However, a horrific explosion creates a dimensional portal between Tromaville and its dimensional mirror image, Amortville. While The Toxic Avenger (Toxie) is trapped in Amorville, Tromaville comes under the control of Toxie's evil doppelganger, The Noxious Offender (Noxie)."
Lemmy appears and plays the role of Good Lemmy / Bad Lemmy.

A headlining European tour with Speeddealer in October and November took in shows mainly in Germany, but also Scandinavia.
Early December saw four dates in Russia, and without sparing any horses Motörhead carried on into Europe. But unfortunately the tour was cut short due to Lemmy being unwell.

The Pretenders »Greatest Hits«
Warner Music Vision (8573-858005-2)

Released 22 January 2001
In the early- to mid-1970s when they were just two young women intent on making it big in rock 'n' roll, Chrissie Hynde and Sonja Kristina (who would join Curved Air) were part of the then Ladbroke Grove scene in London. Like any starving musicians, the girls teamed up as backing singers when the occasion – and a few quid for doing so – came their way. One such session was for Mick Farren's »Vampire's Stole My Lunch Money« album, and rumours that they did likewise on the »Motörhead« Chiswick album (despite a tight budget and very little spare recording time) seem to be true, although the takes remain in the archives.

This documentary is well worth watching, and Chrissie's tale of however much she tried she just couldn't get a band going at the time, and Lemmy's attitude towards her pleading and whining (and classically, his answer) is just what you would have expected from him.

As well as videos for twenty of The Pretenders' greatest hits, (including 'Brass In Pocket', 'Don't Get Me Wrong', 'Kid', 'Talk Of The Town' and so on) this DVD includes a 45 minute documentary 'No Turn Left Unstoned' featuring interview excerpts with Lemmy, Nick Lowe, Bono, Rosanna Arquette, Kate Pearson, and Don Letts.

»Terror Firmer«
Troma Video DVD (9020) two DVD set

Released 23 January 2001
Another from the Troma stable, and inspired by director Lloyd Kaufman's book »All I Need To Know About Film Making I Learned From The Toxic Avenger«, »Terror Firmer« is the story of a low-budget film crew.
Lemmy plays a TV interviewer, and Motörhead feature on the soundtrack.

»Frezno Smooth« Original Motion Picture Soundtrack
Spitfire Records (6-70211-5160-2)

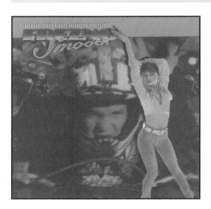

Released 6 February 2001
Tracks: 'Intro' - J-Bone & Fro / 'Hardcore' - Lemmy / 'We Got The Beat' - 4 Gazm / 'Gimme' - Alice Cooper / 'Freak' - 96 Decibel Freaks / 'Shout At The Devil' - Mötley Crue / 'Counterfeit God' - Black Label Society / 'Fear Death By Water' - Sixty Watt Shaman / 'We're Not Gonna Take It' (live version) - Dee Snider / 'Riding The Snake' - Testament / 'Chevy' - Convoy / 'Disco Ball' - Whitekaps / 'Chalis' - Dio / 'Motörhead' (live version) - Motörhead.

Executive producer Skinny G; co-executive producer Phil Carson
'Hardcore (Lemmy's Song)' was written by Twisted Sister's Dee Snider, and his version of the song (a tribute to Lemmy), appeared on his »Don't Let The Bastards Grind Ya Down« solo album; for the »Frezno Smooth« movie soundtrack, Lemmy took lead vocals on it. A live version of 'Motörhead' is also included (from the »No Sleep 'Til Hammersmith« album), although in the movie, Lemmy mimes the song with two unknown musicians.
The film »Frezno Smooth« is not currently available on DVD.

Never a band to cheat on their fans, in May 2001, Motörhead played an eight-date UK tour covering the cancelled shows from the previous December and added a couple more on top.

Impotent Sea Snakes »Everything In Excess«
Masquerade Inc.

Released 2 July 2001
Tracks: 'It's Only Life' / 'Siam Ya' / 'Without You' / 'Money' / 'Pink Lipstick' / 'Let Go O' My Thang' / 'Bleeding' / 'Talking To The Moon' / 'For The Love Of Chains' / 'The Resurrection Of Rock & Roll' / 'Cemetery'
13: vocals, Buck Futt: guitar, Tess Tease: guitar, Connie Lingus: bass, Mona Lott: drums and percussion
Songs produced and mixed by Ron Christopher.
From Atlanta, Georgia, The Impotent Sea Snakes played the Sherwood Forest gig in the UK with Motörhead in 2004, toured America on the Motörhead / WASP tour, and also played the Wacken Festival in Germany on the same bill. The Impotent Sea Snakes were, in 2007, in a state of hiatus after Buster / Todd, the fire breather, and Miduse / Brad, one of the guitarists, both committed unconnected suicides.
»Everything In Excess« featured guest appearances by Lemmy, Isaac Hayes, Jenna Jameson, Taime Downe, Moon Zappa and Rob Banks. On the 'Pink Lipstick' track, which is like a mini-rock opera, Lemmy sung the role of being the father to a cross-dressing son.

June, July and August saw Motörhead playing a dozen or so summer festival dates in Europe and Scandinava.

Jetboy »Lost And Found«
Cleopatra Records (CLP 0718-2)

Released 9 July 2001
Tracks: 'Little Teaser' / 'Me Down' / 'Feel So Good' / 'In The Alley' / 'Live And Die In A Day' / 'Dealin'' / 'Stolen People' / 'The Reading' by Lemmy Kilmister / 'Fighter's Fear' / 'Bloody Hands And Poisoned Minds' / 'No Limit'
Mickey Finn: lead vocals and harmonica, Bernie Ford: lead, rhythm and acoustic guitars and backing vocals, Billy Rowe: rhythm, slide and acoustic guitars, and backing vocals, Ron Tostenson: drums, Todd Crew: bass
Jetboy formed in San Francisco in 1983, and then moved to Los Angeles in 1986 after winning a contract with Elektra Records. Despite their hairstyles and image, with their influences ranging 'from punk rock to rock 'n' roll with a good deal of blues thrown in' one can gauge that appearances can be deceptive. Lemmy (it says on the album) "recites 'The Reading', he is also featured on backing vocals on the track, 'No Limit'."

H.O.T.D. – Hair Of The Dog »Ignite«
Spitfire Records (SPITCD145)

Released 18 September 2001
Tracks: 'Alive' / 'Over You, Under Me' / 'The Law' / 'Devil May Care' / 'Between Darkness & Light' / 'One More For Saturday Night' / 'Ignite' / 'Grit' / 'Shine' / 'Hellride'
Recorded at Track Record and Paramount Studios in Hollywood; produced, engineered and mixed by Matt Gruber. H.O.T.D. are Ryan Cook, Mike Dupke and Brian 'Boot' Saputo
A great album, very AOR, and a grand addition to any rock fan's collection as every song is a joy to listen to. Lemmy added back-up vocals on 'The Law', although he is quite far back in the mix, and if you were not aware of his presence you would probably miss his contribution. But yes, a knockout album in its own right. The CD case has a sticker flagging "Includes 'The Law' featuring Lemmy" as an eye-catcher.

»Metallic Assault – A Tribute To Metallica«
Eagle Records (EAGCD129)

Released 22 October 2001
Featuring: Lemmy Kilmister, Mikkey Dee, Gregg Bissonette, Bob Balch, John Oliva, Eric Bloom, Jimmy Bain, Jason Bonham, Whitfield Crane, Eric Singer and other artists
Tracks: 'Battery' / 'Sad But True' / 'Sanitarium' / 'The Unforgiving' / 'The Thing That Should Not Be' / 'Enter Sandman' / 'Whiplash' / 'Nothing Else Matters' / 'Seek And Destroy' / 'For Whom The Bell Tolls'
Recorded and mixed at The Office, Van Nuys, California, produced by Bob Kulick and Bruce Bouillet. 'Nothing Else Matters' features Lemmy: bass, John Oliva: vocals, Bob Black: guitar, Gregg Bissonette: drums

»Lapdance 01 The DVD«
Trinidad Entertainment (TE0001DVD)

Double DVD Released 2001. Running Time 190 minutes.
Described as "the premier renegade festival in Park City, Utah" with "a reputation as the biggest, sexiest, wildest and most innovative party and alternate film festival at Sundance." Lemmy plays Jerry, the race car driver.

»Metal Brigade« Various Artists
St. Clair Records (CHM44422)

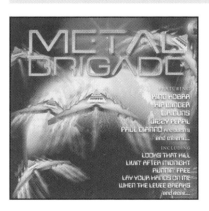

Released 2001
'Living On The Edge' - Mike Tramp from White Lion / 'Fool In The Rain' - King Cobra / 'Lay Your Hands On Me' - Jani Lane & Eric Turner from Warrant / 'Daniel' - Kip Winger / 'Ramble On' - Great White / 'Journey To The Centre Of The Mind' - Phil Lewis with Jake E. Lee / 'Running Free' - Paul Di'Anno with Steve Grimmett, Bernie Torme & Lea Hart / 'Livin' After Midnight' - Maro Torien with John Morris / 'Smash Alley' - Faster Pussycat / 'Looks That Kill' (Spahn Tanch Remix) -

Jizzy Pearl from Ratt / 'Good Rockin' Tonight' - Lemmy Kilmister with Johnny Ramone / 'I Wanna Be Your Man' - L.A. Guns

Johnny Ramone, who had been privately battling prostate cancer, died in Los Angeles on 15 September 2004. It was the same day as the first Ramones Museum opened in Berlin, Germany. Proud of all the tracks he has recorded through his career, Lemmy had a special place in his heart for The Ramones, especially this cover of 'Good Rocking Tonight' with Johnny; a jump-blues song first recorded in 1947 by Roy Brown, who also wrote it, it was later made famous when recorded and released on Sun Records by Elvis Presley in 1954.

September and October heralded another American tour for Motörhead with Mudhoney in support. In early November, four shows in South Africa were set and announced, but were later cancelled due to promoter problems.

The dates, two in Johannesburg and two in Cape Town, would perhaps have opened doors for others to follow, rather like Russia, but it wasn't to be. The year 2002 began quietly, but in early April Motörhead and Morbid Angel set out on a lengthy American tour which took them to the middle of the following month.

Black Flag »Rise Above«
Sanctuary Records (SMRCD264)

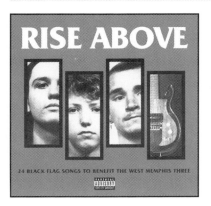

Released 13 June 2002
Tracks: 'Rise Above' / 'Nervous Breakdown' / 'Fix Me' / 'American Waste' / 'I've Had It' / 'I've Heard It Before' / 'Room 13' / 'Wasted' / 'Jealous Again' / 'TV Party' / 'No Values' / 'Gimmie, Gimmie, Gimmie' / 'Depression' / 'Six Pack' / 'Police Story' / 'Revenge' / 'Thirsty & Miserable' / 'What I See' / 'No More' / 'Black Coffee' / 'Slip It In' / 'Annihilate This Week' / 'My War' / 'Nervous Breakdown'
Recorded at Cherokee Studios, Los Angeles, California, May to July 2002; produced by Henry Rollins; executive producer, Heidi May.

»Rise Above« was formulated by Henry Rollins, with the proceeds going to the West Memphis Three Defence Fund. The West Memphis Three were three men who were convicted as teenagers in 1994 of the murder the previous year of three boys in West Memphis, Arkansas, USA. A number of TV documentaries based on the case have been televised, as well as fund raisers by celebrities and musicians who believed the three to be innocent. The artists involved include Henry Rollins, Lemmy, Iggy Pop, Nick Oliveri, Ice T, Tom Araya and others who gave their time for the cause. All songs on the album were originally recorded by Black Flag. 'Thirsty & Miserable' features Lemmy on vocals.

Motörhead played summer festivals through Europe and Scandinavia, followed by five dates in Brazil in late September. Mid-October saw the five-date Hammered UK tour take in a prestigious date at Wembley Arena, with Hawkwind supporting. As ever, European shows followed until late November, with a one-off festival appearance in Japan in the middle of that month.

2003 saw two American headlining tours for Motörhead during April and May, one with The Dwarves in support, and the other with Anthrax. A limited number of summer festivals were played as Motörhead spent July and August on the Iron Maiden / Dio / Motörhead American tour, which included a show at Madison Square Gardens.

Ace Sounds »Still Hungry«
Ace Sounds Records (SASCD001)

Released 30 June 2003
Tracks: 'Jet From California' - featuring Jason Perry / 'Back Up' - featuring Benji / 'One Way Love' - featuring Lemmy Kilmister / 'There's No Pleasin' Some People' - featuring Saffron / 'No Fear Of Falling' - featuring Shingai Shoniwa / 'Skiers Of Texas' - featuring JJ Burnel / 'Glass Ceiling' - featuring Ben Edwards / 'Your Face Hurts' - featuring Yap / '45 Grave' - featuring Cliff Jones / 'Prisoner' - featuring Skye / 'This Is The Last Time' - featuring Smokey Bandits / 'Mind's Taken Over' - featuring Kim Nail / 'Phoenix' - featuring Shingai Shoniwa / 'We Be' - featuring Smokey Bandits

The solo album from former Skunk Anansie guitarist Ace – Martin Kent – featured 'One Way Love', written by Ace / Lemmy Kilmister.

According to the sleeve notes, Ace recalls that he "called Lemmy and he said, 'it's a tricky one, but I'll do it!' I flew out to LA and hung out with him for a few days and had a real laugh. We went and recorded it one afternoon and then went straight down to the Rainbow Bar, and then went to his place until late. The next day I felt so ill I fell asleep in the afternoon and missed an appointment for my new tattoo."

»Down And Out With The Dolls«
Hart Sharp DVD (29567 0042-2)

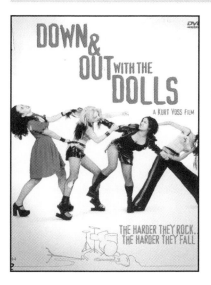

Released 28 October 2003. Running time 87 minutes

Described as "an underground comic book come to life" all-girl band the Paper Dolls move into a house and after a two-day binge a dead body is found. The film features numerous cameos and Lemmy plays Joe, a guru-in-the-closet. His best role to date, he comes across as a lovable and friendly character; certainly his most all-round film appearance since »Eat The Rich«.

Skew Siskin »Album Of The Year«
Ulftone Music (UTCD 078)

Released 24 November 2003

Tracks: 'We Hate' / 'Girl On A Mission' / 'Shake Me' / 'All Fired Up' / 'Hate Lies' / 'Lips' / 'White Trash' / 'Jesus Of Cool' / 'Much 4 U' / 'The Goddess' / 'Strike Me Blind' / 'War And Peace Song' / 'Another Good Man' / 'Torn Apart'

Nina C. Alice: vocals, Jim Voxx: guitars, Spray: bass, Damien Insane: drums

Recorded at Monongo Studios, Berlin, Germany; produced and arranged by Jim Voxx and Nina C. Alice

On this Skew Siskin album Lemmy provided the backing vocals on 'Shake Me', was involved in the lyric writing for 'Shake Me', 'All Fired Up' and 'White Trash', produced Nina C. Alice's vocals on 'All Fired Up' and co-produced her vocals on 'Shake Me' and 'White Trash'.

The Hammered UK tour with The Wildhearts and Young Heart Attack started in early October, quickly followed by the European leg with Skew Siskin. Lemmy spent a couple of days at Skew Siskin's Monongo Studios in Berlin in mid-December, recording tracks for his proposed solo album. The early months of 2004 were passed with Motörhead rehearsing, writing, and then recording what would later be released as the »Inferno« album.

Probot »Probot«
Southern Lord Records (SUNN30CD)

Released 16 February 2004
Tracks: 'Centuries Of Sin' with Cronos / 'Red War' with Max Cavalera / 'Shake Your Blood' with Lemmy / 'Access Babylon' with Mike Dean / 'Silent Spring' with Kurt Brecht / 'Ice Cold Man' with Lee Dorian / 'The Emerald Law' with Wino / 'Big Sky' with Tom G. Warrior / 'Dictatosaurus' with Snake / 'My Tortured Soul' with Eric Wagner / 'Sweet Dreams' with King Diamond
Recorded at Studio 606, Virginia, in 2003
Probot was a heavy metal project running adjacent to The Foo Fighters by its leading light and front man, Dave Grohl. Dave recorded the backing tracks, and then invited various heavy metal musicians and vocalists to come along and finish off the songs. So on 'Shake Your Blood' Dave had recorded the guitar and drums himself, but of course, Lemmy played bass in his own inimitable style, and wrote the lyrics. The music video was filmed in November 2003, and released shortly afterwards. It features 66 women from the Suicide Girls adult entertainment website. The video features Dave Grohl on drums, Lemmy Kilmister on lead vocals and bass, and Robert 'Wino' Weinrich (who also sang on 'The Emerald Law' on the album) on lead guitar. Lemmy said in the press release that the video performance was "just like a tour in the Sixties, when things were a lot more fun."

Young Heart Attack »Tommy Shots«
XL Records (XLS 183CD)

Released 29 March 2004
Tracks: 'Tommy Shots' / 'Get It Hot' / 'Sunset Sinner'
Jennifer Stephens: vocals, Frenchie: guitar, Steven T Hall: bass, Joey Shuffield: drums
Young Heart Attack are a gang of hard-living disciples from Austin, Texas, who remind

you of such greats as The Who, The MC5, The Rolling Stones, Led Zeppelin and AC/DC rolled into one. After a special guest slot on Motörhead's 2003 Hammered UK tour, they struck up great relationships with the band members, so much so that they asked Lemmy to sing guest vocals on one of their EP tracks, a cover version of AC/DC's 'Get It Hot'.

In the album's liner notes, vocalist Jennifer Stephens said: "Lemmy came into town and did the song, and he was a real pro. He did his shit and was really relaxed. He did his bass and vocals in two takes, and then gave us some good advice. 'Every riff has been written, you can try as hard as you want to come up with something new, but rock 'n' roll is not that hard.'"

As you can imagine from the credentials above, it's a rocking good balls-out number, and why else would Lemmy have become involved if this was not the case. However, as noted earlier, Motörhead tune down their instruments a half-step to accommodate Lemmy's vocal range. On 'Get It Hot', rather like on Fast Eddie Clarke's 'Laugh At The Devil', the instruments were tuned at normal concert pitch, and thus Lemmy had to sing in a higher register to remain in tune.

»Spin The Bottle – An All-Star Tribute To Kiss«
Koch Records (KOC-CD-9545)

Released 27 April 2004
Featuring: Lemmy Kilmister, Jennifer Batten, Dee Snider, Tim Bogart, Samantha Moloney, CC Deville, Aynsley Dunbar, and many others
Tracks: 'Detroit Rock City' / 'Love Gun' / 'Cold Gin' / 'King Of The Night Time World' / 'I Want You' / 'God Of Thunder' / 'Calling Dr. Love' / 'Shout It Out Loud' / 'Parasite' / 'Strutter' / 'I Stole Your Love'
Produced by Bob Kulick & Bruce Bouillet
'Shout It Out Loud' features Lemmy: vocals and bass, Jennifer Batten: guitar, Samantha Maloney: drums.

You couldn't wish for a better Kiss track featuring Lemmy, and he did indeed 'Shout It Out Loud'; a fine performance. Also included is a bonus DVD where the majority of the stars involved talk about the first time they heard about Kiss, Lemmy is featured, of course.

The Hindi Guns 'We Mess Up The System' from the »Patriot Act« EP French Fan Club Records (FFC-KVEP-01)

Released 2004
Tracks: 'We Mess Up The System' / 'Rise' / 'She's All Right' / 'Run Through The Jungle'
Band members: Deedee Chariel, Roger Campos, Mikael Jehanno and Kurt Voss
The Hindi Guns are a West Coast punk band founded by film director / screenwriter / musician / songwriter Kurt Voss.
'We Mess Up The System' features voice samples of Lemmy but also of Henry Rollins "extracted for promotional purposes from the forthcoming French Fan Club Records documentary titled 'Gun Club: The Jeffrey Lee Pierce Story." It's an excellent track with great backing, and even though Lemmy simply said what he said as part of an interview, it fits here perfectly. A great novelty track.

Dates in Brazil and Argentina for Motörhead followed in mid-May, with summer festival dates across Europe scheduled afterwards. The »Inferno« album was released in June.

Ramones »Raw«
BMG Image Entertainment DVD (82876 61324 9)

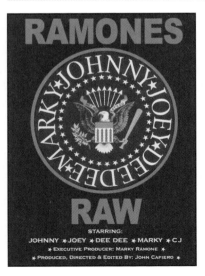

Released 28 September 2004
Produced, directed and edited by John Cafiero; executive producer Marky Ramone
A DVD with over five hours of rare material covering the career of the Ramones (including vintage concert footage professionally shot on film in 1980), it features a short excerpt with Lemmy and Joey Ramone circa 1979, and the Ramones playing Motörhead's 'R.A.M.O.N.E.S.' song over the main feature closing credits.
A great DVD, highly recommended.

Lixx Array »Mud In Your Eye«
Mind Blown Records (MDB-1010-3)

Released 30 September 2004
Tracks: 'Mud In Your Eye' / 'Addiction To Pain' / 'Lost Along The Way' / 'Mr. Angry' / 'For The World To See' / 'Young Rose' / 'Joining Of Hands' / 'Dirty Dancing' / 'Rely On' / 'Lover's Moon' / 'Strike Back' / 'Sweet Samantha' / 'When It Rains It Pours'

Rusty Dades: lead vocals, Blake Hastings: electric and acoustic guitars, keyboards and backing vocals, Rob Swanson: bass guitar, backing vocals, Barry McGill: drums and percussion

Produced by Eric E Garten and Lixx Array

Formed in the summer of 1988 by Blake Hastings, Los Angeles-based Lixx Array have high-quality production, layered guitar grooves, powerhouse choruses and catchy harmonies. The album features Lemmy on vocals on the title track.

Sean Dawson of Mind Blown Records related this story to me: "Lemmy does a great mid-section rap on the 'Mud In Your Eye' song. Blake Hastings, the guitarist in Lixx Array, had the chance to go to Lemmy's apartment in Hollywood back in 1992. Blake and Lixx Array were managed by Rob Jones, and Rob was also working with Motörhead at the time.

Lemmy dug the tune and the lyrical content, and said come over to his apartment, 'bring your four-track and we'll do it right here in my home'. Wish I was there, but heard it was a moment in time that was so damn surreal. Lemmy is a legend!"

In early November, Motörhead were joined by Sepultura for the Inferno UK tour. American female rockers Meldrum joined the tour for the European leg through The Netherlands, Germany and Scandinavia.

In February 2005, Motörhead won their first Grammy for their cover of Metallica's 'Whiplash'. From early March through to early May, the band played two American tours, firstly with Corrosion Of Conformity as support, and then Priestess.

A mass of summer festival appearances across Europe followed, with their 30th Anniversary show at Hammersmith Apollo sandwiched in on 16 June.

Nina Hagen »Punk & Glory« DVD
CreARTive film Entertainment (BEST Nr: CREDVD001)

Released 2005; director's cut, running time approx. 112 minutes
A fascinating film by Peter Sempel about Nina Hagen, with interview material with Lemmy.

»Charlie's Death Wish«
A Vital Fluid Release DVD (VFR-DV-6022)

Released 10 May 2005
A kill-or-be-killed explosive action and humour movie in the tradition of »Kill Bill« featuring 'scream queen' Phoebe Dollar and Ron Jeremy, together with Lemmy, Dizzy Reed (Guns N' Roses), Tracii Guns (LA Guns) and a cameo by John Clarke (»The Jagged Edge«).

»Lloyd Kaufman's Make Your Own Damn Movie«
Troma DVD (9237)

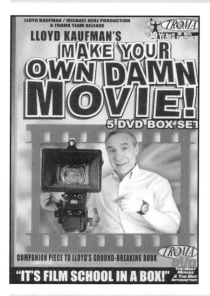

Released 31 May 2005 (five DVD box set)
Lloyd Kaufman, president of Troma Studios and creator of The Toxic Avenger, has written, produced and/or directed scores of successful movies and shares thirty years of moviemaking know-how – from raising money, scriptwriting and casting to production, how to do special effects and distribution. With his involvement in a number of the Troma films, Lemmy is featured at various points within this extravaganza.

»The Comic Strip Presents« The Complete Collection
(9 DVD Box Set) 4 DVD (C4DVD10141)

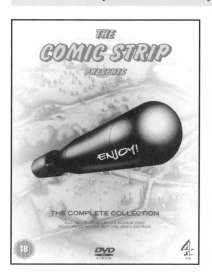

Released 14 July 2005
The Comic Strip's anarchic humour certainly shook up 1980's television and this box set, starring Keith Allen, Robbie Coltrane, Adrian Edmonson, Dawn French, Rik Mayall, Nigel Planer, Peter Richardson, Jennifer Saunders, and Alexi Sayle, rounds up all 39 episodes: »Five Go Mad In Dorset«, »War«, »The Beat Generation«, »Bad News Tour«, »Summer School«, »Five Go Mad On Mescalin«, »Dirty Movie«, »Susie«, »A Fistful Of Travellers' Cheques«, »Gino«, »Full Story And Pics«, »Eddie Monsoon«, »Slags«, »The Bullshitters«, »The Supergrass«, »Consuela«, »Private Enterprise«, »The Strike«, »More Bad News«, »Mr Jolly Lives Next Door«, »The

Yob«, »Didn't You Kill My Brother«, »Funseekers«, »South Atlantic Raiders«, »South Atlantic Raiders Part II«, »GLC«, »Oxford«, »Spaghetti Hoops«, »Les Dogs«, »Red Nose Of Courage«, »The Crying Game«, »Wild Turkey«, »Detectives On The Edge Of A Nervous Breakdown«, »Space Virgins From Planet Sex«, »Queen Of The Wild Frontier«, »Gregory«, »Diary Of A Nutcase«, »Demonella«, »Jealousy«, »Four Men In A Car«, »Four Men In A Plane«

»South Atlantic Raiders Part II« (originally broadcast 8 February 1990) features Lemmy playing the part of a rebel soldier named Rico.

Throw Rag »13ft And Rising«
BYO Records (78856-2)

Released 1 August 2005
Tracks: 'Swingset Superman' / 'She Don't Want To (She Don't Care)' / 'Lil' Danny' / 'Trouble' / 'Bobby Wayne' / 'Tonight The Bottle Let Me Down' / 'Rotten Me' / 'Highway 86' / 'Radio Romantica' / 'Sad Girl' / 'So. 5th St. (Country of O.G.)' / 'Sex War' / 'The Promise' / 'Children Of The Secret State' / 'Rule Maker'
Exclusive Europe only bonus content: 'Mission's Message' (enhanced live video recorded at The House of Blues, Anaheim, California)

Captain Sean Doe (The Wheeler): vocals, Jacko 'The Cobra' Washboard: vocals, jaw harp, saw, school bell, bugle, Dead (Dino) McQueen: guitar, vocals, Franco Fontana (New Rome Emperor): bass, vocals, Chango The Urban Commando: drums

Recorded at Maple Studios, Santa Ana, California; produced, engineered and mixed by Cameron Webb

Throw Rag are a four-piece punk band from Salton Sea, California, formed in 1993 by Sean Wheeler. Lemmy provided backing vocals on a cover of American country singer Merle Haggard's song 'Tonight The Bottle Let Me Down'.

MC5 »Sonic Revolution' – Live At London's 100 Club –
A Celebration Of The MC5«
Image Entertainment (82876 61322 9) DVD

Released 10 August 2005
Tracks: 'Main Title' / 'Skunk (Sonically Speaking)' – with Wayne Kramer / 'Gotta Keep Movin'' – with Nicke Royale / 'Shakin' Street' – with Michael Davis /

'Tonight' – with Dave Vanian / 'Looking At You' – with Dave Vanian / 'High School' – with Michael Davis / 'Poison' – with Wayne Kramer / 'The American Ruse' – with Nicke Royale / 'Rocket Reducer No. 62 (Rama Lama Fa-Fa-Fa)' – with Wayne Kramer / 'Sister Ann' – with Lemmy Kilmister / 'Ramblin' Rose' – with Wayne Kramer / 'Kick Out The Jams' – with Ian Astbury
Recorded live at the 100 Club, 13 March 2003
'Sister Ann' features Lemmy Kilmister on vocals & harmonica.

Early October 2005 saw Motörhead on a European tour with Mondo Generator as support. Late October and into November, they played the Inferno UK tour with Girlschool as support.

The after-show party for the Bristol Colston Hall gig on 30 October took place at a pole/lap-dancing club in the city centre. Super-fan Mick Stevenson had put forward the idea of visiting the club after enjoying a previous visit on an earlier tour. Mick had been to the club (which was called Temptations, I think), and told the boss that Motörhead were in town, and could a small crowd of us pay a visit. The boss agreed, and also waived the £20 per person door fee to enter the premises.

Mick returned with the news, so a crowd of us joined Lemmy, Mikkey and tour manager Eddie Rocha, walking across the fairly deserted, chilly, frosty, October urban city landscape. It was something of a unique experience strolling along the pedestrian precincts and pavements with Lem and Mikkey ahead of us, and I took time to pinch myself to make sure that this was actually happening. People we happened to see took little or no notice of us, despite Lemmy's distinctive clothing, boots, and cowboy hat. A couple of beefy bouncers stood on the door of the club, but when Mick stepped forward and they recognised him, it was all smiles and welcome to the venue.

Lemmy tended to visit such places in most of the cities Motörhead played, as a way of relaxing and winding down after the gig. So he was used to it, but this was new territory for some of us. A few local strip shows had come my way in my thirties, and they were fun: three girls who stripped twice, interspersed by a blue comedian. But things had moved a long way from those seedy nights to the classiness, and welcomed warmth, inside this club.

To the right were tables and chairs, to the left, a stage with a pole, and an astoundingly lithe and acrobatic female hanging from it, seemingly defying gravity, it appeared. Ahead, the bar, and to the left of that, a curtained-off area where the actual lap dances took place in privacy.

Lemmy quickly latched on to a dark haired young lady whom it seemed he had become acquainted with on a previous visit. We ambled up to the bar with Mikkey, bought drinks, and soon had some of the lap dancers prowling around us on the hustle. In such an environment, there should have been just one thing on every red-blooded male's mind, but during the show back at the Colston Hall, as guests, we had been herded into an upstairs area which had brought with it an unusual view of the stage. When we attended Motörhead shows in the past, Mikkey has been just a blur of arms and hair when viewed from the usual seating areas, but where we had been placed, we looked right down on him and his drum kit. (On the minus side – if there ever is one at a Motörhead gig – we could barely see Phil, and only managed a few quick glimpses of Lemmy.) The energy he put into the show was astounding, and really opened my eyes as to just how physical a rock drummer has to be. He could have fed the National Grid if he'd been wired up to a dynamo. I took the time to tell him so, and suggested at some point it might be an idea to have a camera above him so that everyone could witness what a powerhouse he was. Of course, Mikkey, being Mikkey, was flattered, but to him it was just another show, and what he did to earn a living. But having no other option but to watch Mikkey, it opened my eyes as to just how much energy he must put into each show, and how darned fit he must be.

Some of the aftershow attendees were being hustled for a lap dance by these stunning women. It only cost £10 for five minutes behind that curtained-off area, and some, who shall remain anonymous, enjoyed the fun to the maximum. Along with being astounded at Mikkey's performance, the evening had me astonished yet again – as not once was I hustled for a lap dance. The Motörheadbanger I was in conversation with told me not to worry about it: "after all," he pointed out, "you are their number one going in, but of little or no interest when they have done their business and you walk out again." Maybe they saw my wedding ring and avoided married men, or maybe I was the ugliest fellow they had ever clapped eyes on; nevertheless, it would have done my ego good if I had been hustled – just the once.

Mick Stevenson thought it was hilarious, and in fun threatened to call Jane and tell her where I had been. I laughed back, I have known Mick for decades and it as just his pop at having a laugh. But as I told him, I would tell Jane when I got back home, anyway, as I knew that she would not have objected if I had paid for a dance. My bottom line, which amused Mick was, that you can't turn back the clock, and by the time Jane found out, it would be an unreversable page in history. But are lap dances that wonderful, I asked myself. Some chick, dancing naked just for you, yet you are not permitted to touch them. It seemed to me like an old Punch magazine *joke I remember, with two schoolboys, one has a bag of toffees, and he's saying to his friend, 'No, you can't have a toffee, but you can listen to the bag when I blow it up and pop it!' And that's what the lap dance business is all about: a great deal of promise, but thereafter being sent home charged up, hoping your partner might still be awake – doubtful! – to benefit from it. So, other than self-relief, it would have been an exercise in extreme disappointment anyway.*

Later, we said our goodbyes and headed on home: another eventful evening at a Motörhead gig...

In early December, Motörhead played six Australian dates with Mötley Crüe.

The Ramones »Weird Tales Of The Ramones« Rhino Records Box Set (8122-74662-2)

Released 16 August 2005
85 songs featured on three CDs compiled by Johnny Ramone, and one DVD containing »Lifestyles Of The Ramones«, a documentary featuring their music videos up to 1990 and interviews with the band. Also included is the »Weird Tales Of The Ramones« comic book which is packed with artwork and stories by an array of artists, and is a joy to behold
CD1: 'Blitzkrieg Bop' / 'Beat On The Brat' / 'Judy Is A Punk' / 'I Wanna Be Your Boyfriend' / 'Loudmouth' / '53rd & 3rd' / 'Havana Affair' / 'Now I Wanna Sniff Some Glue' / 'Glad To See You Go' / 'Gimme Gimme Shock Treatment' / 'I Remember You' / 'Carbona Not Glue' / 'Oh Oh I Love Her So' / 'Swallow My Pride' / 'Commando' / 'Pinhead' / 'Sheena Is A Punk Rocker' (ABC single version) / 'I Don't Care' (single version) / 'Rockaway Beach' / 'Cretin Hop' / 'Here Today, Gone Tomorrow' / 'Teenage Lobotomy' / 'Slug' (demo) / 'Surfin' Bird' / 'We're A Happy Family' / 'I Just Want To Have Something To Do' / 'I Wanted Everything' / 'Needles & Pins' (remixed single version) / 'I Wanna Be Sedated' / 'Go Mental' / 'Don't Come Close' / 'I Don't Want You' / 'She's The One' / 'I'm Against It'
CD2: 'Rock 'N' Roll High School' (Ed Stasium mix) / 'I Want You Around' (Ed Stasium mix) / 'Do You Remember Rock 'N' Roll Radio?' / 'I'm Affected' / 'Danny Says' / 'The K.K.K. Took My Baby Away' / 'You Sound Like You're Sick' / 'She's A

Sensation' / 'All Quiet On The Eastern Front' / 'Outsider' / 'Highest Trails Above' / 'Psycho Therapy' / 'Time Bomb' / 'Mama's Boy' / 'I'm Not Afraid Of Life' / 'Too Tough To Die'/ 'Wart Hog' / 'Howling At The Moon (Sha-La-La)' / 'Daytime Dilemma (Dangers Of Love)' / 'Endless Vacation' / 'My Brain Is Hanging Upside Down' ('Bonzo Goes To Bitburg' - UK 12" version) / 'Somebody Put Something In My Drink' / 'Animal Boy' / 'I Don't Want To Live This Life (Anymore)' (UK B-side) / 'Love Kills' / 'Something To Believe In' (single version)

CD3: 'I Wanna Live' / 'Bop 'Til You Drop' / 'I Lost My Mind' / 'Garden Of Serenity' / 'I Believe In Miracles' / 'Pet Sematary' (single version) / 'Punishment Fits the Crime' / 'Merry Christmas (I Don't Want To Fight Tonight)' (single version) / 'Main Man' / 'Strength To Endure' / 'Poison Heart' / 'I Won't Let It Happen' / 'Censor-shit' / 'Journey To The Center Of The Mind' / '7 And 7 Is' / 'When I Was Young' / 'I Don't Wanna Grow Up' / 'Scattergun' / ''Makin' Monsters For My Friends' / 'The Crusher' / 'Spiderman' / 'Life's A Gas' / 'She Talks To Rainbows' / 'Any Way You Want It' / 'R.A.M.O.N.E.S.'

DVD »Lifestyles Of The Ramones And More!«: 'Do You Remember Rock 'N' Roll Radio?' / 'Rock 'N' Roll High School' / 'We Want The Airwaves' / 'Psycho Therapy / 'Time Has Come Today' / 'Howling At The Moon (Sha-La-La)' / 'Something To Believe In' / 'I Wanna Live' / 'I Wanna Be Sedated' / 'Pet Sematary' / 'Merry Christmas (I Don't Want To Fight Tonight)' / 'I Believe In Miracles' / 'Strength To Endure' / 'Poison Heart' / 'Substitute' / 'I Don't Wanna Grow Up' / 'Spiderman' / 'Blitzkrieg Bop' (live).

The set features the video of The Ramones' cover of The Who's 'Substitute' with a special guest appearance by Lemmy (which was banned by MTV), and The Ramones' version of Motörhead's 'R.A.M.O.N.E.S.'

»Lemmy – England«
Castle Music / Sanctuary Records Group Promo Sampler CD
(CMZPR 1259)

Released 4 October 2005
A special CD celebrating Lemmy's longstanding and eventful musical life, compiled by Steve Hammonds and Jon Richards and given away on 4 October 2005 to guests at the Café de Paris, London, when Classic Rock magazine's Roll Of Honour bestowed upon Lemmy both the Living Legend and Lifetime Achievement Awards.

Tracks (from across Lemmy's career): 'I Don't Need Your Kind' (The Rocking Vickers) / 'The Dark Lord' (Sam Gopal) / 'Silver Machine' (Hawkwind) / 'Motörhead' (Hawkwind) / 'Iron Horse/Born To Lose' (Motörhead) / 'Overkill' (Motörhead) / 'Ace Of Spades' (Motörhead) / 'Please Don't Touch' (HeadGirl) / 'No Class' (Motörhead) / 'Eat the Rich' (Motörhead)

»Numbers From The Beast – An All-Star Salute To Iron Maiden«
Restless Records (REST 73798)

Released 17 October 2005
Featuring: Lemmy Kilmister, Phil Campbell, Mikkey Dee, Michael Schenker, Dee Snider, Bob Kulick, Jason Bonham, Joe Lynn Turner and many more.
Tracks: 'Run To The Hills' / 'Wasted Years' / 'Wrathchild' / 'Flight Of Icarus' / 'Fear Of The Dark' / 'The Trooper' / 'Aces High' / '2 Minutes To Midnight' / 'Can I Play With Madness' / 'The Evil That Men Do' / 'The Wickerman'
Recorded at The Office Studios, Van Nuys, California; produced by Bob Kulick & Brett Chassen

An exciting tribute album to the legendary Iron Maiden with some well-chosen cover versions, too (and a cover illustration by Derek Riggs).
'The Trooper' features Lemmy: vocals and Phil Campbell: guitar, alongside Rocky George: guitar, Chuck Wright: bass and Chris Slade: drums.

»Ringers: Lord Of The Fans«
Sony Pictures DVD (CDR 41273)

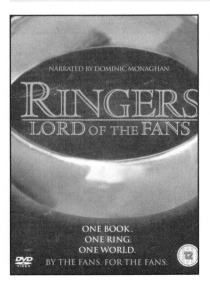

Released 21 November 2005
Special Edition: One Book. One Ring. One World. By The Fans, For The Fans.
»Ringers: Lord Of The Fans« describes how J.R.R. Tolkien's epic fantasy »The Lord Of The Rings« has influenced pop culture for fifty years. Produced in association with TheOneRing.net and narrated by »The Lord Of The Rings« trilogy star Dominic Monaghan, this award-winning film traces the impact of Tolkien's new mythology with eye-popping visuals, animation, and candid interviews with director Peter Jackson, actors Elijah Wood, Viggo Mortenson and Sir Ian McKellan and many others. Lemmy is featured in the main film and also in the extras' featurettes, and as director Carlene

Cordova noted in the DVD's booklet, "we were so thrilled to have Lemmy from Motörhead come in on this!"

»Thunderfingers – A Tribute To The Legendary John Entwistle Of The Who«
MVD Visual DVD (DR-4537)

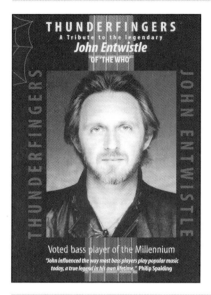

Released 28 November 2005
As the title cleverly says, this DVD is a tribute to John Entwistle, probably the most highly regarded bass player of all time, and who was voted 'Bass Player of the Millennium'. Entwistle had died on 27 June 2002 following a drug overdose.

The DVD includes an interview with Entwistle by Gordon Giltrap in which he talks openly about his unique and revolutionary style of playing, his influences, the other members of The Who, »Tommy«, and his amazing guitar collection. There are several interview extracts with Lemmy who had known him since the early 1960s when The Rocking Vickers and The Who – then still known as The High Numbers – often crossed paths on the gig circuit of the day.

Hawkwind »Take Me To Your Leader«
Dark Peak Records (HWDP1CD)
Limited Edition CD and DVD

Released 28 November 2005
CD: 'Sprit Of The Age' / 'Out Here We Are' / 'Greenback Massacre' / 'To Love A Machine' / 'Take Me To Your Leader' / 'Digital Nation' / 'Sunray' / 'Sighs' / 'Angela Android' / 'A Letter To Robert' / 'Paradox 2005'
The audio CD features: Dave Brock, Alan Davey, Richard Chadwiock with Jason Stuart, Simon House, Arthur Brown, Matthew Wright, Lene Lovich, Jez Huggett and

James Clemas. Engineered, mixed and produced by Dave Brock and Alan Davey, it's dedicated to John Peel and Tommy Vance.

DVD (limited edition of 2,000): interviews with Dave Brock, Alan Davey and Richard Chadwick alongside 'Spirit Of The Age' (promo version) / 'Silver Machine' (with Lemmy on bass guitar and vocals, recorded live at The Ruisrock Festival, Finland, 10th July 2004) / 'The Right To Decide' (live 1992) / 'Spirit Of The Age' (live 2004) / 'Psychedelic Warlords' (live 2004)

Years ago, anyone spotted in a concert hall or in the audience at a festival with a camera or tape recorder would be deemed a bootlegger, plucked from the crowd by roadies, and have their equipment unceremoniously destroyed before being ejected forcibly from the event. But with modern day technological advances, and with most people owning a mobile phone, filming at concerts and gigs has become far too big to police with any great effect. Bands now hold their hands up in surrender, and watch as their songs are uploaded onto sites like YouTube. With live sound mixes bordering on the excellent, and groups having the good sense to release live albums on a fairly regular basis, these amateur uploads often capture rare events within the life of a band, and the clip of 'Silver Machine' here is one such instance. Any concert promoter with foresight and a bit of knowledge of rock music history is clever enough to book Hawkwind and Motörhead not only on the same bill, but also on the same day; it's pretty much a foregone conclusion that Hawkwind will invite Lemmy into their set to create that ultimate few minutes of nostalgia that is their mutual 'Silver Machine' hit single, and give the crowd the thrill of a lifetime. Again.

Ozzy Osbourne »Ozzy Under Cover«
Epic Records Dual Disc (82876 74316 2)

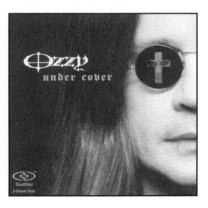

Released 28 November 2005

A new concept for the humble compact disc, the Dual Disc format featured an audio side and a DVD side. It didn't take off that well, and pretty much everything released on this format has since been issued as two separate discs.

CD Side: 'Rocky Mountain Way' / 'In My Life' / 'Mississippi Queen' / 'Go Now' / 'Woman' / '21st Century Schizoid Man' / 'All The Young Dudes' / 'For What It's Worth' / 'Good Times' / 'Sunshine Of Your Love' / 'Fire' / 'Working Class Hero' / 'Sympathy For The Devil' / 'Changes' (with Kelly Osbourne) – bonus track

Musicians: Ozzy Osbourne: vocals, Ike Bordin: drums, Jerry Cantrell: guitars, Chris Wyse: bass; guest musicians: Ian Hunter: vocals on 'All The Young Dudes', Leslie West: guitar solo on 'Mississippi Queen', Robert Randolph: pedal steel guitar on 'Sympathy For The Devil' and guitar solo on '21st Century Schizoid Man'
DVD Side: all songs from the album in enhanced stereo , 'In My Life' promo video clip and 'Dinner With Ozzy And Friends' video featuring Ozzy Osbourne, Harvey Leeds, Adrian Wilson, Rod MacSween, Jack Osbourne and Lemmy.
In the same way as David Bowie recorded his favourite songs by other artists on his 1973 »Pin Ups« album, Ozzy Osbourne took a similar path with »Ozzy Under Cover« but added the extra magic of inviting some of the original legendary performers to sing and/or play on certain tracks. The album was an expanded version of the fourth CD included in the »Prince Of Darkness« box set released earlier in the year. As a bonus, if you've ever wondered what music business personalities talk about when invited to 'Dinner With Ozzy' then this DVD is your opportunity to find out, as one of the guests was Lemmy; a thirty-minute feature of Ozzy telling classic stories with his closest friends.

»A Rock 'N' Roll Tribute To Motörhead – St. Valentine's Day Massacre«
Bad Reputation Records (070268311-2)

Released 5 December 2005
Tracks: 'Going To Brazil' ($ Green Dollar Colour $) / 'Boogey Man' (Skew Siskin) / 'Killed By Death' (Crucified Barbara) / 'Rock It' (American Dog) / 'Over The Top' (Crank County Daredevils) / 'Nothing Up My Sleeve' (Hellsuckers) / 'Bomber' (Mother Superior) / 'No Class' (Crystal Pistol) / 'Born To Raise Hell' (Voodoo Vegas) / 'Please Don't Touch' (Crucified Barbara & American Dog – bonus track) / 'B4' (Skew Siskin featuring Lemmy Kilmister – bonus track)

Extra Bonus Video: 'Please Don't Touch' (performed live by Crucified Barbara & American Dog)
Executive Producer - Eric Coubard
Liner notes by Alan Burridge
A fine tribute CD in itself with the added bonus of 'B4' featuring Lemmy on bass and joint vocals with Skew Siskin vocalist Nina C. Alice. This track was remixed by Skew Siskin to make it unique for this release.

In March 2006, with Meldrum as support, Motörhead played another American tour. On 25 May The Head Cat, Lemmy's rock 'n' roll band with Danny B. Harvey on guitar and Slim Jim Phantom on drums, played a one-off show in Anaheim, California.

MC5 'Sister Ann'
White Panther Records (CLP 2333)

Released 2006

A 45rpm red vinyl single, this was a limited edition pressing of 300 copies of the 'Sister Ann' track recorded at the 100 Club on 13th March 2003. The B-side is 'One Of The Guys', recorded by the MC5 in Detroit, Michigan, in 1967.

The MC5 developed a reputation for high-energy live performances, one of which was recorded and released in 1969 as their debut album »Kick Out The Jams«, which has now achieved legendary status. Here, on one single, you have the best of both worlds with two tracks spanning four decades.

»Real Rock Divas – Reality Check TV Volume 1«
MDI Distribution (617917818767) DVD

Released January 29 2006

From the RCTV archives come interviews with the likes of The Donnas, Sandy West, Lacuna Coil, Lita Ford, Doro, L7, Lunachicks and Bif Naked, amongst others. Lemmy is featured during the intro, plus the Bif Naked [born Beth Torbet in New Delhi in 1971] interview was filmed in Motörhead's dressing rooms during the Overnight Sensation American tour, and Lemmy is caught in the background of some of the interview footage.

»Flying High Again – The World's Greatest Tribute To Ozzy Osbourne«
Magick Records (CLP1585-2)

Released 27 February 2006
Featuring: Lemmy Kilmister, Richie Kotzen, Lita Ford, Dee Snider, Tim 'Ripper' Owens, Yngwie Malmsteen, Doug Aldrich, Jason Bonham and other artists
Tracks: 'Mr. Crowley' (Tim 'Ripper' Owens & Yngwie Malmsteen) / 'Shot In The Dark' (Children Of Bodom) / 'S.A.T.O.' (Icarus Witch & George Lynch) / 'Bark At The Moon' (Forever Say Die with Jeff Duncan) / 'Close My Eyes Forever' (Lita Ford) / 'Desire' (Lemmy & Richie Kotzen) / 'Crazy Train' (Dee Snider, Doug Aldrich & Jason Bonham) /
'Over The Mountain' (Mark Slaughter & Brad Gillis) / 'I Don't Know' (Jack Blades & Reb Beach) / 'Hellraiser' (Joe Lynn Turner & Steve Lukather) / 'Revelation (Mother Earth)' (November's Doom) / 'Goodbye To Romance' (Alex Skolnick Trio)
Produced by Bruce Bouillet & Bob Kulick; executive producer for the Cleopatra Label Group Brian Perera.

Along with writing lyrics to 'Desire' for Ozzy Osbourne, it must have been a special thrill for Lemmy to take an opportunity such as this to sing them himself. This is quite some track anyway, and this version, featuring Lemmy: vocals, Jeff Pilson: backing vocals, Ritchie Kotzen: lead guitar, Bob Kulick: guitar, Tony Franklin: bass, and Vinnie Colaiuta: drums, is excellent. 'Desire' was also released on another Ozzy tribute compilation titled »Bat Head Soup«.

The Head Cat »Rockin' the Cat Club«
Rockabilly Records / Cleopatra Records DVD (CLP 1531-9)

Released 25 April 2006
Recorded live at The Cat Club on Sunset Strip, on Tuesday 13 January 2006, and featuring Lemmy on acoustic guitar and vocals, Danny B Harvey on guitar and back-up vocals, Slim Jim Phantom on drums and back-up vocals, and Johnny Bowler on upright slap bass.
Tracks: 'Good Rockin' Tonight' / 'Lawdy Miss Clawdy' / 'Talkin' Bout You' / 'Something Else' / 'Reelin' And Rockin'' / 'Fool's Paradise' / 'Bye Bye Johnny' / 'Sick And Tired' / 'Bad Boy' / 'Matchbox' / 'Back In The USA' / 'Baby What You Want Me To Do?' / 'Blue Suede Shoes'

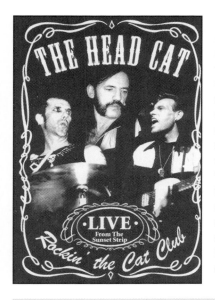

Executive Producer: Brian Perera.

Bonus features include interviews with Lemmy, Slim Jim and Danny B Harvey, and a photo slide show.

Captured on film at last! Due to Lemmy's commitments with Motörhead, The Head Cat played a maximum of maybe five shows a year, in America. So it made sense to film and release a performance on DVD so that the rest of the world could enjoy this 'whacked out rockabilly' music wherever in the world they lived. The thirteen classic rock 'n' roll songs were originally recorded and made famous by Elvis Presley, Eddie Cochran, Chuck Berry, Carl Perkins, The Beatles, Sam Cooke and Buddy Holly amongst others.

The Stray Cats 'Alley Cat Rumble'
Music Avenue Records (250143)

Released 24 April 2006

Acousticats – Studio Tracks: 'Stray Cat Strut' / 'Lust 'N' Love' / 'Mystery Train' / 'Summertime Blues' / 'Oh Boy'

Rumble At The Roxy – Live Tracks: 'Double Talkin' Baby' / 'Rumble In Brighton' / 'Baby What You Want Me To Do?' / 'Rev It Up And Go' / 'Beautiful Delilah' / 'Stray Cat Strut' / 'Rock Around With Ollie Vee' / 'Fishnet Stockings' / 'Jeanie, Jeanie, Jeanie' / 'Rock This Town'

Good Rockin' Cats – Bonus Tracks: 'Swing Cat Stomp' (Danny B. Harvey, Lee Rocker and Slim Jim Phantom) / 'Good Rockin' Tonight' (Danny B. Harvey, Lemmy Kilmister and Johnny Ramone) / 'St. James Infirmary' (Danny B. Harvey and Jeff 'Skunk' Baxter) / 'Viva Las Vegas' (Danny B. Harvey, Slim Jim Phantom and Johnny Ramone)

The concert was recorded on 2 September 1981 at The Roxy in Los Angeles, with the unplugged material recorded in 1991. The bonus track, 'Good Rockin'

Tonight', featuring Lemmy Kilmister and Johnny Ramone, was released on »Swing Cats« and »Metal Brigade« (both titles featured herein), but has well-deservedly been added to the superb tracks on this CD.

The CD booklet is flagged "Featuring Lemmy & Johnny Ramone" as an extra sales point.

»Metal – A Headbangers Journey«
Warner Bros DVD (80575)

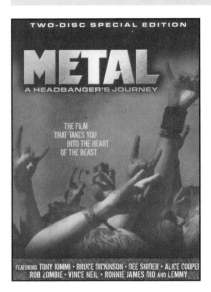

Released 23 May 2006

Featuring Tony Iommi / Bruce Dickinson / Dee Snider / Alice Cooper / Rob Zombie / Vince Neil / Ronnie James Dio and Lemmy

This ground-breaking film From Banger Productions, who would go on to release the »Metal Evolution« series in 2011 examines the history of heavy metal stereotypes, and looks for the truth behind the music. Shot on location in the UK, Germany, Norway, Canada and the U.S., for the fan this documentary is an exhilarating tribute as well as an outsider's window into a complex spectacle and fascinating subculture. Performances and inteviews feature, amongst others, Black Sabbath, Iron Maiden, Slayer, Motörhead, Rob Zombie, Alice Cooper, Ronnie James Dio, Rush, Slipknot and Cannibal Corpse.

The first disc of the two disc set is the main documentary which includes 'Ace Of Spades' in its entirety, plus interview segments with Lemmy, Jackie Chambers and Kim McAuliffe from Girlschool and Doro Pesch, while the 'Special Feature' disc has, amongst other things, a seven-plus minute interview chapter titled 'Lemmy At The Rainbow'.

The Ramones »We're Outa Here«
Radioctive Records DVD (ERDVD257)

Released 25 May 2006

The Ramones – Johnny, Joey, Marky and C.J. – filmed on 6 August 1996 at The Palace, Los Angeles, California

Tracks: 'Beat On The Brat' / 'Blitzkrieg Bop' / 'Suzy Is A Headbanger' / 'Gimme Gimme Shock Treatment' / 'Teenage Lobotomy' / 'Loudmouth' /

'Pet Sematary' / 'Love Kills' / 'Any Way You Want It' / 'Psycho Therapy' / 'I'm Affected' / 'Pinhead' / 'Rock 'N' Roll High School' / 'She's The One' / 'The K.K.K. Took My Baby Away' / 'Cretin Hop' / 'I Wanna Be Sedated' / 'R.A.M.O.N.E.S.' / 'Someone Put Something In My Drink' / 'Sheena Is A Punk Rocker' / 'Rockaway Beach' / '53rd & 3rd'

The legendary Ramones final live show captured on DVD, and a must for every rock fan's collection. There's a short interview clip with Lemmy, plus the concert footage features him onstage playing 'R.A.M.O.N.E.S.'.

The Head Cat »Fool's Paradise«
Rock-A-Billy Records (CLP 1642-2)

Released 27 June 2006
Re-release of fifteen tracks from the »Lemmy, Slim Jim & Danny B« CD released in 2000 (with tracks in a different running order): 'Fool's Paradise' / 'Tell Me How' / You Got Me Dizzy' / 'Not Fade Away' / 'Cut Across Shorty' / 'Lawdy Miss Clawdy' / 'Take Your Time' / 'Well... All Right' / 'Trying To Get To You' / 'Learning The Game' / 'Peggy Sue Got Married' / 'Crying, Waiting, Hoping' / 'Love's Made A Fool Of You' / 'Big River' / 'Matchbox'

Featuring Lemmy: vocals, acoustic guitar and harmonica, Danny B Harvey: lead guitar, bass, keyboards and backing vocals, and Slim Jim Phantom: drums, percussion and backing vocals.

2006 saw a host of summer festival dates for Motörhead yet again, including their support slot at the Foo Fighters' show on 17 June at Hyde Park, where Lemmy joined the Foos onstage during their set for 'Shake Your Blood', a song for which Lemmy wrote the lyrics and performed on Dave Grohl's »Probot« project. Motörhead's »Kiss Of Death« album was released in late August, followed by a UK tour supporting it in November, with female rockers Crucified Barbara and Clutch opening for them. The European leg of the tour had Meldrum and/or WE as support.

Dacia & The WMD »Dacia & The WMD«
MTM Music (0681-173)

Released 25 September 2006
Tracks: 'Who's To Say' / 'Rockabilly Bitch' / 'Stop And Stare' / 'Change The World' / 'Live To Tell' / '6' / 'Sorry' / 'My Reality' / 'How Long' / 'Intensify' / 'The Communist' / 'Losing You' (featuring Lemmy Kilmister) / 'First Time' / 'The Universe'
Dacia & The WMD (Dacia & The Weapons Of Mass Destruction) was the latest project for the multi-talented Dacia – known through her work with Tape – and her band (guitarist Alex Scholpp, drummer Alex Menichini, and bassist Ralf Botzenhart). Their self-titled debut album was produced by Skunk Anansie's guitarist Ace.

The song 'Losing You' was recorded with special guest Lemmy, Dacia's idea being to work with him in the direction of the Nick Cave and Kylie Minogue duet 'Where Wild Roses Grow'. And indeed, the track evokes some memories (without similarities in the music) of those two contrasting voices, with the soft, sympathetic vocal by Dacia countered by Lemmy's distinctive, smoky-edged voice. A superb song and an excellent debut album as a whole.

»Poultrygeist: Night Of The Chicken Dead«
Troma DVD and CD Soundtrack

Released 28 September 2006
Another offering from the weird 'n' wonderful world of Troma, in which the American Chicken Bunker, a military-themed fried-chicken chain, builds a restaurant on an ancient Indian burial ground with predictably messy results.
The film features a cameo appearance by Lemmy (as well as zombie chickens), and Motörhead music on the soundtrack.

»The Curse Of El Charro«
Showtime Entertainment (80161) DVD

Released 3 October 2006
Directed by Rich Ragsdale, »The Curse Of El Charro« is a gruesome story of love, murder and revenge, in which the the un-dead corpse of 19th Century land baron El Charro attempts to re-claim his re-incarnated true love. Lemmy makes a special guest appearance as Priest a.k.a. God.

»Scarface: The World Is Yours«
X-Box 360 Computer game (and other formats)

Released 13 October 2006
Based on the film and the exploits of Tony Montana the game allows you to reclaim your turf and rebuild your empire. Lemmy provides the voice for an arms dealer.

»Butchering The Beatles – A Head Bashing Tribute«
Restless Records (REST 73801)

Released 23 October 2006
Featuring: Lemmy Kilmister, Mikkey Dee, Phil Campbell, George Lynch, Bob Kulick, Doug Aldrich, Tommy Shaw and other artists
Tracks: 'Hey Bulldog' (Alice Cooper, Steve Vai, Duff McKagen, Mikkey Dee) / 'Back In The USSR' (Lemmy Kilmister, John 5, Eric Singer) / 'Lucy In The Sky With Diamonds' (Geoff Tate, Michael Wilton, Craig Goldy, Rudy Sarzo, Simon Wright, Scott Warren) / 'Tomorrow Never Knows' (Billy Idol, Steve Stevens, Blasko, Brian Tichy) / 'Magical Mystery Tour' (Jeff Scott Soto, Yngwie Malmsteen, Bob Kulick, Paul Stanley, Jeff Pilson, Frankie Banali) / 'Revolution' (Billy F. Gibbons, Vivian Campbell, Mike Porcaro, Greg Bissonette, Joe Fazzio) / 'Day Tripper' (Jack Blades, Tommy Shaw, Doug Aldrich, Marco Mendoza, Virgil Donati) / 'I Feel Fine' (John Bush, Stephen Carpenter, Mike Inez, John Tempesta) / 'Taxman' (Doug Pinnick, Steve Lukather, Tony Levin, Steve Ferrone) / 'I Saw Her Standing There' (John Corabi, Phil Campbell, CC Deville, Chris Chaney, Kenny Aronoff) / 'Hey Jude' (Tim 'Ripper' Owens, George Lynch, Bob Kulick, Tim Bogart, Chris Slade) / 'Drive My Car' (Kip Winger, Bruce Kulick, Tony Franklin, Aynsley Dunbar)
Produced by Bob Kulick and Brett Chassen

All three members of Motörhead playing on different tracks on the same album is reason enough to pick this one up, and Lemmy more than does 'Back In The USSR' justice.

Keli Raven featuring Lemmy Kilmister 'Bad Boyz 4 Life' e.p. records 2006

Released 24 October 2006
Keli Raven is a deep to the core singer, guitarist, bass player, percussionist and producer with influences ranging from The Beatles to Rush to The Smashing Pumpkins, Michael Jackson and Marilyn Manson. He's worked with such artists as Kiss, Tom Jones and Vinnie Vincent, and has developed a unique sound to his recordings. He has also shared the stage with friend Lemmy Kilmister.

His first first full-length album features the single 'Bad Boyz 4 Life', co-written by and featuring Lemmy who also appeared in the video for the song, which can be found on YouTube.

Regarding this liaison with Lemmy on 'Bad Boyz 4 Life', Keli told the author in November 2006: "I have known Lemmy for twenty years, and we have been close friends the whole time. Although I have done some live spots with him, I always wanted to collaborate with him on a record. Finally we both had time to co-write 'Bad Boyz 4 Life' and I'm blessed to have him on the new album as well as a continued brother and mentor in my life. Lemmy is a great man and I will always remain a loyal friend to him as he has to me!"

Foo Fighters »Hyde Park – Skin And Bones« DVD (RCA 88697032399)

Released 20 November 2006
Disc 1: Hyde Park electric set: 'In Your Honor' / 'All My Life' / 'Best Of You' / 'Times Like These' / 'Learn To Fly' / 'Breakout' / 'Shake Your Blood' / 'Stacked Actors' / 'My Hero' / 'Generator' / 'DOA' / 'Monkey Wrench' / 'Tie Your Mother Down' / 'Everlong'
Disc 2: 'Skin And Bones - Live in Hollywood' acoustic set: 'Intro' / 'Razor' / 'Over And Out' / 'On The Mend' / 'Walking After You' / 'Still' / 'Marigold' / 'My Hero' / 'Next Year' / 'Another Round' / 'See You' / 'Cold Day In The Sun' / 'Big Me' / 'What If I Do?' / 'Skin And Bones' / 'Ain't It The Life' / 'February Stars' / 'Times Like These' / 'Friend Of Mine' / 'Best Of You' / 'Everlong'

As previously mentioned, the Foo Fighters (Dave Grohl, Taylor Hawkins, Nate Mandel and Chris Shiflett) not only invited Motörhead to play at their June 2006 open-air show in Hyde Park, but they also invited Lemmy onstage during their set to sing on 'Shake Your Blood', which had been a part of Grohl's »Probot« project. It's one hell of a rocking song anyway, and proved to be a huge crowd pleaser when played on the night.

A great DVD in its own right, but particularly special for Lemmy's involvement.

Doro »Warrior Soul Winter Edition 20th Anniversary« DVD
AFM Records (AFM141-7)

Released 27 November 2006
Disc 1: Warrior Soul On The Road: 'Intro' / 'Earthshaker Rock' / 'Doro Rocks Hamburg' / 'Haunted Heart' / 'From Hamburg To Helmond' / 'The Twilight Zone' / 'You're My Family' / 'Hot In Helmond – Metal Mayhem In Madrid' / 'True As Steel' / 'From Madrid To Barcelona – Hello Langen' / 'Strangers Yesterday' / 'Für Immer' / 'Langen Farewell' / 'Love Me In Black' / 'Russia Special Part 1' / 'My Majesty' / 'Warrior Soul' / 'Russia Special Part 2' / 'All We Are' / 'Outro'
20 Years Anniversary – The Movie: 'Intro' / 'Rule The Ruins' / 'Always Live To Win' / 'Metal Racer' / 'East Meets West' (featuring Udo Dirkschneider) / 'Tausend Mal Gelebt' / 'White Wedding' (featuring Jean Beauvoir) / 'Egypt – The Chains Are On' / 'A Whiter Shade Of Pale' / 'Hellbound' / 'You've Got Another Thing Coming' (featuring Saxon) / 'Fall For Me Again' / 'Unholy Love' / 'Fight For Rock' (featuring Warlock) / 'Love Me Forever' (featuring Lemmy Kilmister

and Mikkey Dee) / 'Für Immer' / 'Born To Be Wild' (featuring Claus Lessmann) / 'All
We Are' (featuring Lemmy Kilmister, Mikkey Dee, Jean Beavoir, Udo Dirkschneider,
Saxon, Blaze Bayley, the Warlock guys, Claus Lessmann, Circe II Circle) / after show
Disc 2: 20 Years Anniversary – The Concert: 'Intro' / 'Rule The Ruins' / 'Always
Live To Win' / 'Metal Racer' / 'Hellbound' / 'True As Steel' / 'Burning The Witches' /
'Hellraiser' / 'East Meets West' (featuring Udo Dirkschneider) / 'Metal Tango' /
'Out Of Control' / 'Unholy Love' / 'A Whiter Shade Of Pale' / 'Whenever I Think Of
You' / 'Für Immer' / 'Fall For Me Again' / 'Tausend Mal Gelebt' / 'White Wedding'
(featuring Jean Beauvior) / drum solo / 'Bad Blood' (featuring Blaze Bayley) /
'Egypt – The Chains Are On' / 'Brutal And Effective' / 'Love Me In Black' / 'Earth-
shaker Rock' / 'Love Me Forever' (featuring Lemmy Kilmister & Mikkey Dee) /
'Fight' /'Burn It Up' (featuring Rhein Fire) / 'You've Got Another Thing Coming'
(featuring Saxon) / 'Alles Ist Gut' / 'All Night' (featuring Warlock) / 'Fight For Rock'
(featuring Warlock) / 'Evil' (featuring Warlock) / 'Born To Be Wild' (featuring Claus
Lessmann) / 'All We Are' (featuring Lemmy Kilmister, Mikkey Dee, Jean Beauvior,
Udo Dirkschneider, Saxon, Blaze Bayley, the Warlock guys, Circle II Circle
An excellent DVD (the first disc is a film shot by director Ronald Matthes, the
second the straight concert) which celebrates Doro's twentieth anniversary, with
appearances by Lemmy and Mikkey Dee, and many, many others.

A handful of shows by The Head Cat kick-started 2007. Motörhead then played
six dates on their Kiss Of Death South American tour, after which The Head Cat
took to the road again in mid-May.

Heideroosjes »Chapter Eight – The Golden State«
U-Sonic Records (USR 7007)

Released 12 March 2007
Tracks: 'What If' / 'My Funeral' / 'Lekker
Bolingbrook' / 'Homesick For A Place That
Does Not Exist' / 'Buckle Up' / 'I Don't Wan-
na Wake Up' / 'Ik Zie Je Later' / 'All Your
Government Does' / 'Forgotten Continent' /
'Ik Ben Niet Bang' / 'Embrace & Destroy' /
'Any Drug Will Do' / 'Primeur! Terreur!' /
'Cash Is King' / 'Shout Out For Freedom'
With a name taken from the wild Catsfoot
plant, Heideroosjes were a Dutch punk band
formed in 1989 featuring Marco Roelofs (vocals and guitar), Frank Kleuskens (gui-
tar), Fred Houben (bass) and Igor Hobus (percussion)
Recorded at Maple Sound Studios, Santa Ana, California in October / November

2006, and produced, engineered and mixed by Cameron Webb. Lemmy provides the spoken word intro to 'My Funeral'.

The Head Cat 'Tell Me How' / 'Take Your Time' No Balls Records (NBR 008)

Released 5 April 2007
Lemmy Kilmister: vocals and acoustic guitar, Danny B. Harvey: guitar and bass, Slim Jim Phantom: drums and percussion
Both tracks licensed from Cleopatra Records for this vinyl 7" release.

Meldrum »Blowin' Up The Machine« Frontier Records (FR PR CD 334)

Released 14 May 2007
Tracks: 'Purge' / 'Down Your Throat' / 'Scar' / 'Crème De La Crème' / 'Hang 'Em' / 'Miss Me When I'm Gone' / 'Another Kind' / 'Exploited' / 'Get Yours' / 'Get Me Outta Here' / 'Bite The Pillow'
Michelle Meldrum: guitars, Moa Holmsten: vocals, Frida Stahl: bass, with Gene Haglan: drums
Formed in Sweden in 1999, Meldrum recorded their debut album »Loaded Mental Cannon« in 2001. A year after »Blowin' Up The Machine« was released, founder and guitarist Michelle Meldrum died suddenly in a hospital in Burbank, California, from a cystic brain growth. On »Blowin' Up The Machine« Lemmy co-wrote 'Get Me Outta Here' and 'Miss Me When I'm Gone', on which he also sang backing vocals.
Moa Holmsten featured in Motörhead's 'Whorehouse Blues' video, and sings on a track written by Foo Fighter's leader, Dave Grohl, originally scheduled to be included on the solo album »Lemmy & Friends« on which Lemmy had been working off-and-on for quite some time but hadn't completed at the time of his death.

Summer festival dates began with a small French tour. On 16 June Motörhead took to the stage at Jarvis Cocker's Meltdown Festival. Cocker had been given the opportunity of selecting artists from the worlds of stage, music, theatre and dance, presenting them during two weeks of events in and around London. For some reason, the vocalist from the Britpop band Pulp chose Motörhead to play at one of the events at the Royal Festival Hall. Thank you, Jarvis; much appreciated!

For the sake of ease a rail trip was the most practical solution, as the Royal Festival Hall was but a stonesthrow from Waterloo station. I had been there a year or so before, with local MHB and friend Eddie Evans to see the MC5.

On arrival at the stage door, I met MHBs Darren Hooley (sadly no longer with us) and Mark Shaw. They had recently returned from seeing Motörhead in Brazil: now, that's fan commitment for you. We chatted for a while, with other fans and friends stopping by to say hi. Inside, Lemmy had been harboured in a room filled with TV cameras for his usual multitude of interviews. MHBs Robert Kiewik, Mick Stevenson, Chris Sage and Adrian Simpson, also known as The Superfans, were there milling around, so we enjoyed some time catching up with one another.

It became somewhat chaotic – as backstage at Motörhead gigs often is – with the media, keen to get their slot interviewing the band, taking no prisoners. Lemmy appeared briefly for a photo session, holding a Gibson SG which he had signed as a competition prize for one of the rock magazines; then, as he returned to the room for more TV interviews, he gave me a quick greeting, a handshake and smile, before disappearing yet again.

Phil and Mikkey had completed their interviews so the Superfans and I joined them in their dressing room for a catch-up. Always great to see them, but as London gigs are (and always have been) notorious for being packed to the rafters backstage with fans, friends, family, record company and management staff, we exited to find a café or restaurant for something to eat. There are quite a few eateries around the Waterloo station area, and we found one with which we were happy with the menu and prices, and tucked in.

It was still late afternoon / early evening and, being June, it was sunny and warm, so we went back to the venue and wandered inside, only to find the chaos had not abated, so walked out again. Mick Stevenson was behind me, and, behind him, were an anchor and camerman seemingly filming all of the events on Jarvis's calendar. The anchorman looked at Mick and I, microphone in hand, and the cameraman positioned himself behind him. Smiling, he asked us, "can you tell me why you're here today?"

"To see Motörhead, of course," Mick told him.

"Special to you, are they?" he ventured.

I thought, right, we're in here! A bit of publicity could do us some good, on film, too. "Well, we are the presidents of the Motörheadbangers, Motörhead's fan club," I replied.

But rather than pick up on his 'find' our interrogator just sort of wilted, as if we were the most boring bastards on planet Earth. Fuck you then, buddy! We didn't want to speak to you, anyway!

The gig went very well, of course, with Jarvis introducing the band, and Lemmy saying "this is a bit posh for us, isn't it!" It was an excellent set, but I must apologise here, as what happened after the gig has become a complete blank for me.

Too many gigs, too many great memories, I suppose, but being there, as ever, was a privilege.

Some weeks prior to this event, I'd had a phone call from some bloke who wanted to 'pay for my knowledge'. Apparently he was, at the time, negotiating with Motörhead, to film the Royal Festival Hall gig for DVD release. He wanted to pay me (quite handsomely at that) to go on the road with his film crew with the aim of tracking down some of the Motörhead luminaries from the past (like, for example, Larry Wallis, Lucas Fox and Motorcycle Irene) to interview them. Some would be difficult to find but, with connections, I was up for giving it a try: and, to be honest, for the pay packet he was offering, I was straining at the leash.

As ever, though, in the world of rock 'n' roll, I have learned not to believe in anything, especially a deal as tenuous as this, until it is actually happening. And of course, before things went much further, negotiations for the filming didn't happen, so everything fell by the wayside. But wouldn't it have been great, being driven around by a film crew, all expenses paid including hotels and food, and that heavy pay packet at the end of it? Never mind; it was a nice pipedream while it lasted...

Paul Inder 'You Don't Own Me'

Released June 2007
Recorded in April 2007, a track upon which Paul plays guitar and his father, Lemmy, plays bass, mouth harp and keyboards; at the time of writing this track is only available via Paul's Myspace site.

Ramones 'Solo Performances'
No Balls Records (NBR010)

Released 2007
7" red vinyl EP limited to 400 copies
Side A: 'Good Rockin' Tonight' (Lemmy Kilmister – Motörhead, Johnny Ramone, Danny B. Harvey & Slim Jim Phantom – Stray Cats) / 'Viva Las Vegas' (Johnny Ramone, Danny B. Harvey & Slim Jim Phantom – Stray Cats)
Side AA: 'Cherry Bomb' (Cherie Currie – The Runaways, Marky Ramone, Wayne Kramer – MC5) / 'Jump In The Fire' (Dee Dee Ramone)
Yet another re-release of the 'Good Rockin' Tonight' track (and why ever not?) with Lemmy's bass barking away. The other tracks are of equal legendary interest.

Skew Siskin »Peace Breaker«
Monongo Records (MO 07-05-007)

Released (in France) 7 July 2007
Tracks: 'Metal In Your Face' / 'We're An In-
stitution' / 'Ridin' With The Devil' / 'Trouble
Shooter' / 'Hit You Harder' / 'Who The Hell
Are You' / 'War, Fire, Guns & Blood' / 'I
Wanna Be Me' / 'Eva Braun Is Back In
Town' / 'I Don't Care' / 'Loser' / 'Can't
Hear You (Hey, Hey You)' / 'Shoot The Rats'
Nina C. Alice: lead and backing vocals, Jim
Voxx: guitar, Henning Menke: bass, Randy
Black: drums and percussion
Lemmy and Nina C. Alice co-wrote the lyrics
for 'Ridin' With The Devil', 'Trouble Shooter',
'Hit You Harder' and 'Who The Hell Are You'.
On 17 January 2014, the video for 'Ridin' With The Devil', with a cameo appear-
ance by Lemmy, was uploaded on YouTube.

The Warriors »Genuine Sense Of Outrage«
Victory Records (VR 342)

Released 13 August 2007
Tracks: 'Ruthless Sweep' / 'Life Grows
Cold' / 'The Stone Grinds' / 'The Price Of
Punishment' / 'Genuine Sense Of Outrage' /
'Destroying Cenodoxus' / 'New Sun Rising' /
'Your Time Is Near' / 'Silence Is Bliss' /
'Nothing Lasts' / 'Belly' / 'Odium Vice' /
'Mankind Screams'
Javier Zarate: guitar, Marshall Lichtenwaldt:
vocals, Matt Anderson: drums, Charlie
Alvarez: guitar, Roger Camero: bass
Recorded at Maple Studios and Hurley
Studios.
Produced by Cameron Webb, co-produced by Roger Camero
An American hardcore punk band from Oxnard in California, The Warriors'
unique sound is heavily influenced by bands like Rage Against The Machine and
Snapcase.
Guest vocals by Lemmy on 'The Price Of Punishment'.

Airbourne »Runnin' Wild«
Roadrunner Records (RR7963-8)

Released 25 June 2007
Limited edition CD with DVD and slipcase
CD Tracks: 'Stand Up For Rock 'N' Roll' / 'Runnin' Wild' / 'Too Much, Too Young, Too Fast' / 'Diamond In The Rough' / 'Fat City' / 'Blackjack' / 'What's Eatin' You' / 'Girls In Black' / 'Cheap Wine & Cheaper Women' / 'Heartbreaker' / 'Hellfire'
DVD Tracks: Wacken 2008 Concert: 'Hellfire' / 'Fat City' / 'What's Eatin' You' / 'Girls In Black' / 'Cheap Wine & Cheaper Women' / 'Heartbreaker' / 'Blackjack' / 'Runnin' Wild'
Music promos: 'Runnin' Wild' / 'Too Much, Too Young, Too Fast' / 'Diamond In The Rough'
Joel O'Keeffe: vocals and lead guitar, Ryan O'Keeffe: drums, David Roads: guitar and backing vocals, Justin Street: bass and backing vocals
Album produced by Bob Marlette
Airbourne are an Australian rock band formed in 2001. After touring together and friendships being forged, Lemmy enjoyed a cameo role as the truck driver in their 'Runnin' Wild' video. A 'clean' version of the clip was released on the »Metal Hammer Golden Gods of 2008« DVD which was given away for free with the September 2008 edition of Metal Hammer magazine.

Motörhead 'Overkill' (Exclusive Version) / Lemmy & Ted Nugent 'Tie Your Mother Down' Cleopatra Records (CLP 1934)

Released September 2007
7" green vinyl single limited to 300 copies
Side 1: 'Overkill' (exclusive version) – recorded by Lemmy, Mikkey Dee and Phil Campbell for the »Guitar Hero« computer game. It was the first time that this line-up had recorded a Kilmister / Clarke / Taylor song in the studio
Side 2: 'Tie Your Mother Down' – recorded by Lemmy and Ted Nugent for the »Dragon Attack« Queen tribute album in 1997, with Lemmy providing vocals and Ted Nugent on guitar, backed by Tommy Aldridge (drums), Rudy Sarzo (bass guitar) and Bob Kulick (guitar). Both tracks were produced by Bob Kulick.

After two shows in Japan in August, Motörhead, Rose Tattoo and Airbourne played an Australian tour in October.

Saxon 'I've Got To Rock (To Stay Alive)' / 'Going Nowhere Fast'
SPV Records (SPV 98063 CDS)

Released 19 October 2007
CD single and download with both tracks from the Saxon album »The Inner Sanctum«. 'I've Got To Rock (To Stay Alive)' featured special guests Lemmy, Angry Anderson and Andi Deris.

Saxon »To Hell And Back Again« DVD
SPV Records (SPV 99997 2DVD)

Released 12 November 2007
A double DVD fold-out Digipack with booklet. DVD 1: 'To Hell And Back Again (The Movie)', 'To Hell And Back Again (The Soundtrack)' – running time 176 minutes DVD 2: Video clips which include 'I've Got To Rock (To Stay Alive)' featuring Lemmy, Angry Anderson, and Andi Deris as well as Saxon featuring Doro Pesch performing 'You've Got Another Thing Coming', live at Rocksound Festival and live at Rock For Asia – running time 120 minutes.
Frequent touring partners since 1979's Bomber UK tour, Saxon and Motörhead are stalwarts of the heavy rock scene, so it was no surprise, but by the same token a nice surprise, to see Lemmy adding his vocals to this great song and video.

In November 2007 the Alice Cooper / Motörhead / Joan Jett and the Blackhearts tour played major arena shows across the UK. A batch of German dates followed in late November with Skew Siskin, and a Scandinavian tour saw out the year. Into 2008, and in January there were three dates from The Head Cat, and the following month Motörhead started recording a new studio album. Three more Head Cat dates followed in April, along with the announcement that the new Motörhead album would be titled »Motörizer «.

»Sheep In Wolves' Clothing«
Motörheadbangers Fan Club CD (MHB002)

Released 1 April 2008
Featuring cover versions of Motörhead songs as opposed to the originals, the idea for »Sheep In Wolves' Clothing« came to me after Mad Dogs played me a cover of 'Capricorn' which sounded like a cross between Pink Floyd and Hawkwind.

An entry on the Fan Club Motorblog brought offers of more songs for the project: Sonja Kristina is lead vocalist for Curved Air; The Deviants are Mick Farren, who wrote the 'Lost Johnny' lyrics anyway, along with guitarist Andy Colquohoun, and Philthy Animal Taylor on drums; The Underbelly are an offshoot of Blue Öyster Cult; Bridget Wishart and Alan Davey are Hawkwind players; and Girlschool (with Fast Eddie Clarke) gave us a mix of 'Metropolis' (which they then re-mixed again for their »Legacy« album).

Full tracklist: 'Capricorn' – Mad Dogs / '1916' – The Sweet Zeroes / 'I Don't Believe A Word' – Sonja Kristina / 'Lost Johnny' – The Deviants / 'Back At The Funny Farm' – The Underbelly / 'Ace Of Spades' – Spirit's Burning & Bridget Wishart / 'Orgasmatron' – Hobbyhorse / 'Damage Case' – Lissy Abraham / 'Stay Clean' – Alan Davey's Gunslinger / 'Metropolis' – Girlschool.

Project organised and co-ordinated by Alan Burridge.

Album booklet artwork, mixing and production by Tim Way.

The 500 copies of the CD were pressed from glass masters by an official manufacturer, not burned on a home PC.

Lemmy is featured on background vocals during the mid-section of Girlschool's unique version of 'Metropolis'.

Plenty of summer festival dates across Europe followed, before Motörhead joined The Metal Masters US tour with Judas Priest in August. No time for breath, in early September they played The Volcom tour of North America, headlining over The Misfits, Airbourne and Valiant Thor.

Nashville Pussy »Live! In Hollywood« DVD
MVD Visual (DR-4561)

Released 29 September 2008
Recorded Live at The Key Club, Hollywood; total running time 70 minutes.
Tracks: 'Pussy Time' / 'Going Down Swinging' / 'High As Hell' / 'Piece Of Ass' / 'Come On Come On' / 'Good Night For A Heart Attack' / 'She's Meaner Than My Momma' / 'Go Motherfucker Go' / 'I'm Gonna Hitchhike Down To Cincinnati And Kick The Shit Outa Your Drunk Daddy' / 'One Way Down' / 'Hell Ain't What It Used To Be' / 'Hate And Whiskey' / 'I'm The Man' / 'Nutbush City Limits' / 'The Bitch Just Kicked Me Out' / 'She's Got The Drugs' / 'Shoot First, Run Like Hell' / 'Lazy White Boy' / 'Snake Eyes'
Bonus: 'Pussy's Home Movies: Adventures In France (Canal Plus TV show live, or Blane 'Gets Some' with Marianne Faithful) / Australia with Pete Wells / Mancow Morning Radio Show Live Performance / Interview by Psychobabble TV / Aqua Teen Hunger Force Movie Alternate Intro / Jamming with Blaine / Get Some Studio Sessions with Daniel Rey and Ruyter / Nashville Pussy interviewed by Lemmy Kilmister / Fan Footage Canada
Blaine Cartwright: guitar and vocals, Ruyter Suys: guitar and vocals, Karen Cuda: bass and vocals, Jeremy Thompson: drums
Nashville Pussy are from Atlanta, Georgia, and their style has been variously described as psychobilly, Southern rock, hard rock and cow punk, with lyrics usually focussed on sex, drugs, fighting, drinking and rock 'n' roll. Beloved by Lemmy and Motörhead, the bands have often toured the States together. Guitarist Ruyter Suys has become well known for her Gibson SG guitar which has the front (neck) pick-up completely removed, and usually ends up playing their shows in her underwear. She also tears the strings from the guitar with her bare hands! The kind of lady you would be scared to take home to meet your parents, but she's in your dreams at night. A great idea here is in moving Lemmy to the opposite side of the camera and microphone, where he asks the band all of the usual interview questions rock bands have to suffer. Nashville Pussy are a great band though, and this DVD showcases why every rock fan needs to see them live sooner rather than later.

Various Artists »We Wish You A Metal Christmas And A Headbanging New Year« Armoury Records (ARMCD501)

Released October 2008
Tracks: 'We Wish You A Merry Xmas' – Jeff Scott Soto, Bruce Kulick, Bob Kulick, Chris Wyse, Ray Luzier / 'Run Rudolph Run' – Lemmy Kilmister, Billy F. Gibbons, Dave Grohl / 'Santa Claws Is Coming To Town' – Alice Cooper, John 5, Billy Sheehan, Vinny Appice / 'God Rest Ye Merry Gentlemen' – Ronnie James Dio, Tony Iommi, Rudy Sarzo, Simon Wright / 'Silver Bells' – Geoff Tate, Carlos Cavazo, James Lomenzo, Ray Luzier / 'Little Drummer Boy' – Dug Pinnick, George Lynch, Billy Sheehan, Simon Phillips / 'Santa Claus Is Back In Town' – Tim 'Ripper' Owens, Steve Morse, Juan Garcia, Marco Mendoza, Vinny Appice / 'Silent Night' – Chuck Billy, Scott Ian, Jon Donais, Chris Wyse, John Tempesta / 'Deck The Halls' – Oni Logan, Craig Goldy, Tony Franklin, John Tempesta / 'Grandma Got Ran Over By A Reindeer' – Stephen Pearcey, Traci Guns, Bob Kulick, Billy Sheehan, Greg Bissonette / 'Rockin' Around The Xmas Tree' – Joe Lynn Turner, Bruce Kulick, Bob Kulick, Rudy Sarzo, Simon Wright / 'Happy Xmas (War Is Over)' – Tommy Shaw, Steve Lukather, Marco Mendoza, Kenny Aronoff / 'O' Christmas Tree' – Doro Pesch, Michael Schenker, Tony Franklin, Frankie Banali / 'Auld Lang Syne' – Girlschool: Kim McAuliffe, Jackie Chambers, Enid Williams, Denise Dufort
Recorded at Office Studios, Van Nuys, California; produced by Bob Kulick and Brett Chasson; executive producer Wendy Dio
Lemmy puts in a spirited performance with Billy Gibbons and Dave Grohl on 'Run Rudolph Run'.

The Motörizer UK tour, with Saxon and Danko Jones in support, began in late October, followed by the European leg which also took in some Scandinavian shows.

Girlschool »Legacy« Wacken Records (SPV 92732CD)

Released 10 November 2008
Tracks: 'Everything's The Same' / 'Other Side' / 'I Spy' (Girlschool Mix) / 'Spend, Spend, Spend' (Eddie Ojeda – lead guitar and solo) / 'Whole New World' (Neil Murray – bass, Phil Campbell – lead guitar solo) / 'Just Another Day' (Phil Campbell –

guitar solo) / 'Legend' (Neil Murray – bass) / 'Still Waters' / 'Metropolis' (Motörhead cover – Fast Eddie Clarke – first guitar solo) / 'Don't Mess Around' (J.J. French – guitar solo) / 'Zeitgeist' (Phil Campbell on guitar) / 'Don't Talk To Me' (Lemmy Kilmister on bass, vocals and triangle)

Bonus Tracks: 'I Spy' (Dio / Iommi Mix – Ronnie James Dio on vocals, Tony Iommi – lead guitar) / 'Emergency' / 'London'

Kim McAuliffe: guitar and vocals, Denise Dufort: drums, backing vocals, Enid Williams: bass and vocals, Jackie Chambers: guitar and backing vocals

Recorded at Sonic One Studios, Llangennech, South Wales; produced by Girlshool and Tim Hamill

A great album featuring a stunning selection of music biz guests and friends, including Lemmy on bass, vocals and triangle on 'Don't Talk To Me'. Lemmy and Kim also shared the writing credit for the lyrics.

2009 began with a handful of dates by The Head Cat, and in March Motörhead played the Desert Rock Festival in Dubai.

Queen V »Death Or Glory«
Royal Noise Records (8-84502-30845-7)

Released 26 February 2009

Tracks: 'Continental' / 'Revolution Baby' (featuring Jon Paris) / 'My Machine' (featuring Tom Morello) / 'Cry For A Minute' / 'One & Only' (featuring Vernon Reid) / 'Survival' (mixed by Ron Saint Germain) / 'Good Enough' (mixed by Ron Saint Germain) / 'Twisty Tie' (featuring Jon Paris) / 'One More Time' (mixed by Ron Saint Germain) / 'Runaway' / 'Wasted' (featuring Lemmy Kilmister)

Queen V (V. Stigeler): lead vocals, Chris Altenhoff: bass, Tommy Diehi and Jon Weber: drums, Tristan Avakian and Tony Lewis: guitars, Steve Mosto: keyboards, pianos, organs, Jon Paris: harmonica, Phil Scholl: percussion. Lemmy is featured on the track 'Wasted'.

»Down And Dirty with Jim Norton«
HBO Entertainment (3000020342)

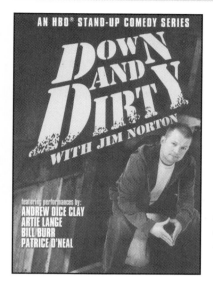

Released 7 April 2009
An HBO Stand-Up Comedy Series DVD with Jim Norton. Running time 120 minutes.
The DVD features Jim Norton, formerly of HBO's »Lucky Louie« introducing some of the comedy circuit's most outspoken and dirtiest comedians, priming the audience with his own unique brand of humour and paving the way for the likes Artie Lange, Bill Burr, Patrice O'Neal and Andrew Dice Clay, along with some of the edgiest up-and-coming comics around.
Lemmy appears frequently as master of ceremonies, with a wall of Marshall amps and cabinets behind him, to introduce the comedians. This was recorded whilst Motörhead were recording their »Motörizer« album, which Lemmy mentions.

Motörhead played a collection of dates in South America, including Argentina, Columbia and Brazil.

»Guitar Hero – Metallica«
Xbox 360 and other formats computer game

Released 29 May 2009
Lemmy provided his voice, and Motörhead (Lemmy Kilmister, Phil Campbell and Mikkey Dee) a new recording of 'Ace Of Spades'.

Anvil »The Story Of Anvil«
Universal (8260326) DVD

Released 15 June 2009
Aged 14, school friends Steve 'Lips' Kudlow and Robb Reiner made a pact to rock together forever. Their band Anvil was at one point seemingly poised to break through to the big time, particularly when they released »Metal On Metal« in 1982. A hugely significant release, »Metal On Metal« influenced bands like Metallica, Slayer and Anthrax, all of whom went on to sell millions of records. Unfortunately Anvil's career stalled and they went slowly into obscurity.

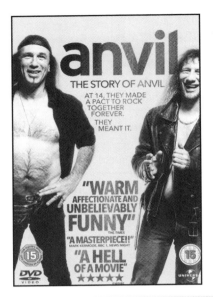

Directed by Sacha Gervasi »The Story Of Anvil« follows the band as they attempt one last shot at the big time with their thirteenth album »This Is Thirteen«. Described as "an inspirational, heart-warming and uplifting tale of two best friends who refuse to give up on their dream" the film is a pretty accurate reflection of life in a band.

The DVD includes two short interview clips with Lemmy; Anvil of course had supported Motörhead in the UK in 1983.

The summer festivals across Europe had become a favourite by now, not only for Motörhead but also the attending crowds. In late August, though, the band set out on another American trek with Rev Horton Heat and Nashville Pussy opening for them.

»Hardware« (Special Edition)
Optimum Releasing (OPTD1583) DVD and Blu-ray

Released 13 October 2009
A re-issue of the 1990 film written and directed by Richard Stanley and starring Dylan McDermot, Stacey Travis, John Lynch, William Hootkins and Iggy Pop as Angry Bob. Lemmy is featured in the film as a riverboat taxi driver. He also provided his services for a new trailer for the promotion of this DVD release. It would have been great to have had that trailer as an extra on the DVD itself, but it can be found on YouTube.

»Brutal Legend«
Video game for X-Box 360 (and other formats)

Released 16 October 2009
With Jack Black as roadie Eddie Riggs (who gets pulled into a fantasy world inspired by the most outrageous album covers and populated by music-hating demons) the game is an action caper which allows you to save the world through the power of rock. Not only do you get your own customisable car to drive, and armies of followers to command, but you can also team up with rock superstars like Ozzy Osbourne and Lemmy, each of which can help out with their own monster-slaying moves. Alongside the voices and likenesses of the likes of Jack Black, Tim Curry, Rob Hal-

ford, Ozzy Osbourne and Lita Ford, »Brutal Legend« also features the bass playing, voice and likeness of Lemmy as The Kill Master.

On 11 November 2009, the No Sleep 'Til Moscow tour hit Plymouth in the south-west of the UK. This was one gig I needed to attend. Almost exactly thirty years before, on 10 November 1979, the Bomber tour had kicked off at Bracknell Sports Centre, the first night I met the band – the Lemmy / Fast Eddie / Philthy line-up – and this was something I needed to celebrate with Lemmy.

For whatever reason, I decided to travel by rail, and found it to be the best option as some of the most outstanding countryside in Dorset, Somerset and Devon can be enjoyed from the tranquil seat of a railway carriage. I had also booked a room at a hostel close to the railway station, as an overnight stay was essential. My wife Jane and Amy, our granddaughter by our son Steven, waved me off at our local Hamworthy Junction station. First stop and change at Dorchester South meant a five-minute walk through this market town (and home of the Eldridge Pope brewery) to Dorchester West station.

A somewhat rusty and ancient diesel loco begrudgingly chortled to a stop at the platform. It had two carriages, and the loco was coming close to being sent to the scrapyard by the look of it, but the driver must have had the confidence in her. It was clapped-out, but took us, with what sounded like a huge amount of effort, to Castle Cary in Somerset. Another change, to a somewhat better train, took me onward to Plymouth. As I said, the scenery is breathtaking, and at various intervals runs parallel to the coast, with the sea (well, the English Channel) a stones-throw away. By the time we arrived at Plymouth it was pouring with rain, big lumps, and Burridge does not like getting wet. Having spent many years in the warehousing trade unloading and loading lorries in the rain, by hand or by driving a fork lift truck, I'd had enough. Plus, although my room at the hostel was said to have been 'close to the station' I hadn't a clue where exactly it might be. So a taxi was essential. I sat inside and gave the driver the address. He tossed his head, and raised his eyebrows. I found out why when the two-minute journey brought me to the hostel, just around the corner. Oh, well; whatever. Going to see Motörhead is fun; who cares?

It was still hammering down and the hostel door had no protection from the weather, so by the time I had rapped on the door several times, and walked across the frontage to wave to someone whom I could see through the window to let me in, I was soaked anyway.

Hostels are strange places, but the two men and young lady were nice enough to find my room key, make a cup of coffee, and be easy-going with the chat in asking why I was in Plymouth. Rather than going through the whole story, I edited it down to 'going to see Motörhead at the Pavilions.' That was enough. One of the guys had vaguely heard of them; the other one and the girl had not. The youth of today, eh? Where the fuck have they been living? In a convent? Ah well, their loss.

After checking out the (very basic) room, I took what I needed for the gig out of my travel bag, and went back downstairs. It was by now after 6 pm, not long to go, but again I had no clue where the Pavilions were, and wet as I was, there was no way I would be getting wetter by walking. The girl, despite her ignorance of the best rock 'n' roll band in the world, found a cab company and called them for me. I thanked them for the coffee and their help, and went to the front door to watch for the cab. The rain was still coming down, as we say in the UK, 'like stair rods', so from the door along the short path to the cab at the roadside meant another soaking.

Dark, raining, dreary... It seemed from the ride that the Pavilions were quite a long way from the railway station. Inside the venue, I phoned tour manager, Eddie Rocha. He invited me backstage and gave me a hallowed pass, for which I am always grateful, but as ever, I'd again covered my ass by having a ticket – just in case. Eddie is a great guy if he knows you love the band and won't be a pain in the butt. I have always been on my best behaviour backstage – face it: a privileged place to be – and in the dressing rooms, the band members' 'lounge' for the evening. We would not expect to invite a guest or guests into our lounge and them to be a pain in the butt. Some fans, however, have overstepped the mark in the past, blotting their copybook in the process, and once out of this close circle it's difficult getting back in, as they found out to their cost.

Eddie showed me to Lemmy's dressing room. He and Phil were inside, talking, and were as pleased to see me as I was them, and we exchanged handshakes and welcomes. I had written a couple of books about my locality, and had taken copies of the title »Bournemouth Rocks!« for them. It's basically a journey through all of the bands I had been to see live in the Bournemouth and Poole area, from Mantovani and The Shadows with my parents at age 14 through to and including my first Motörhead gigs. Lem and Phil seemed thrilled to own a copy, and of course, I had been there to see The Move and Jimi Hendrix package tour, on which Lemmy had been a roadie for Hendrix. Amongst the illustrations is a copy of the itinerary for the tour, published all those years ago in either New Musical Express or Melody Maker. Lemmy was astouded when he saw this. "Fuck me!" he said. "That's all the dates and venues I was on! I haven't seen that for years!" He was chuffed and proud enough to show it to everyone and anyone who happened to walk through the door. Phil thanked me for his copy, but before he went off to 'put a capped tooth back in with super glue', he and Lemmy agreed that bass tech Tim Butcher could have Mikkey's copy, as "Mikkey doesn't like reading much". As long as it was read and enjoyed, that's all that mattered, but I had never seen Lemmy so excited over anything in all my time of knowing him.

He and I were left alone for some 45 minutes or so. We talked about the Hendrix days, and bands like The Creation whom we both liked, especially their singles, 'Making Time' and 'Painter Man', and their equally good B-sides. We spoke of The Ritz, a Bournemouth blues club on the seafront; I'd not seen Lemmy's appearance there with Sam Gopal, but we had been very much 'in each other's presence' when he was roadie and I was a fan at the concerts at the venue by The Nice.

I asked a few questions about tracks he'd appeared on, which are now included in this book. I pointed out that he had been a pioneer in breaking down barriers around appearances on other artists' records. In the 1960s, usually for contractual reasons, if an artist appeared on another artist's record, it had to be kept secret. Even when records like Donovan's 'Hurdy Gurdy Man' made the charts, and everyone wanted to know who was playing guitar, it was years until it was revealed to be Jimmy Page, who was just a paid session player at the time. Likewise Donovan's 'Goo-Goo Barabajagal' – Donovan and the Jeff Beck Group were both signed to producer Mickie Most and, although Beck's band played the backing, again it was kept a close secret. But Lemmy blew that apart with his participation with many of the early tracks listed herein. 'Ballroom Blitz' with The Damned was more straightforward in that both bands were, at the time, signed to Chiswick Records. Lemmy did exactly what he wanted to do, and not what some record company expected or told him to do. There's no way he wanted to be tied up in some record company political red-tape bullshit. "It's written into my contract now," he told me. "If I want to do a track with someone, I can just do it." Lemmy broke the mould. Today, it is fairly common practice, but I think Lemmy's tenacity had a great deal influence in opening up this once strictly taboo area of the music scene.

The Damned and Girlschool were special guests on the tour, and together we went out behind the stacks to watch the Girls' soundcheck for a few minutes. Lemmy disappeared, so I went back to his dressing room to write down their set list for the evening, which I had noticed on a printed out A4 sheet in his room. Little did I realise that Lem was in the bathroom, until I heard the toilet flush. "You're playing 'Dirty Love' tonight?" I asked when he re-appeared.

"Yeah, we're going to give it a try; see how it goes."

I then explained the reason why I had made it to this particular show, and its 30 year connection with us at the start of the Bomber tour. He shook his head in disbelief. "That's amazing," he said, shaking my hand. "Thanks for sticking with us, Al."

"Thanks for having me along. What else could I do? It's been great. Watching The Shadows back in the Sixties I wondered what it had taken to get them on stage that night. Where had they played the day before? Where would they be playing tomorrow? Where would they be staying? How did they get from A to B? And thanks to you and the band, I found it out."

It was time to leave him in peace until after the show. Out in the arena, I bumped into MHBs Kostas Makras and his lady, Anna Panta, and they suggested we went for a drink. Kostas and Anna are two of the Motörhead superfans who go to every gig on the tour, and any more besides if they can. We have been friends for some time through their fan club membership, and through meeting up at gigs. Kostas, who has always been interested in my writing, and Anna (with that lovely beaming smile) are both always a joy to be with. We enjoyed swapping stories for a while over a few beers, and then returned to the venue to watch Girlschool and The Damned, and of course, the Motörhead show.

After a few songs, Lemmy told the crowd that the Bomber tour had started thirty years before, and that there was at least one other person who was with him then, and was also with him tonight. "This one is for Al Burridge, this is 'Dirty Love'!"

Kostas and Anna looked at me with mouths agape. I guess I just looked surprised yet honoured. Lem went through a stage where he would dedicate pretty much every song to someone: me, Mick Stevenson, members of the road crew, loads of people and fans, but then tired of it, and hadn't done so for quite a few years. So it was a very special moment, which I thanked him for after the show.

As ever, we had to hang about for an hour or so whilst the band came down from the hyper-adrenaline rush of the gig. They say that AC/DC's Angus Young takes about four hours to do so after his punishing onstage routine, and most performers need this degree of quiet time after a show. After we'd given the band the thumbs-up for the gig, Mikkey said he felt a bit restless and wanted an aftershow party. We went to a couple of bars, which was fun, and it was great that so many people enjoyed talking to him, including us, of course.

Let me digress and take a few moments to just note a couple of Motörhead facts, as I think they are interesting. You may wonder why Lem always smoked Marlboro cigarettes. Well, singers have to look after their voice, and as most smokers will know, changing brands of cigarette usually affects the throat. By sticking to Marlboro, Lemmy could to avoid this, because, in his words, "you can get Marlboro in every country in the world, and they always taste the same, so it avoids sore throat problems."

Most hard and heavy rock bands have long hair. Agreed, these days, trend and fashion in recent years has altered this to bald heads and a beard, but in history it's been long hair, especialy for Lemmy's generation. So he developed the habit of having a quick shave around his chin half an hour or so before going onstage, and this avoids his hair sticking to the little bristles which would have grown in a couple of hours or so. This does not happen with longer facial hair. With freshly shaven skin, a quick flick of the head moves it back, yet if you try this with a little stubble there you're helpless behind a curtain of hair. You can of course stop playing for a moment to wipe it away, but this screws the song up.

Another amusing but useful fact Fast Eddie Clarke shared with me on another occasion was: "if you get a groupie backstage, make sure you get her to drink, a short of spirits before kissing her, as you never know what favours she had to give the roadie before she got to you." Think about it...

Trying to get a cab back to the hostel brought with it a whole new learning curve for me. Not a mobile phone fan, I have one just for emergencies, an ancient Nokia. At around 2am, back outside the venue, a cab pulled up, so I walked over. The driver let the window down and asked my name. I told him.

"Ah, no, that's not the name I have to pick up."

"But I need a cab..."

"Sorry, man, we get mugged, so you have to call the office and book through them, so they have your name and phone number to trace if we have any problems."

"But you're here, and I need a lift..."

What an odd world we live in these days. Being a stranger in town I asked if he'd give me his firm's card so that I could give them a call. He did so, and then drove off. It started raining again, so I walked over towards a hotel which had a covered porchway so that I could at least make the call in the dry. "Five minutes," the woman on the end of the line told me. In about two minutes, the same cab driver I'd spoken to before arrived. I smiled at him. Agreed, these guys don't want to be beaten up and robbed, but he could clearly see the irony in my eyes.

Next morning I got up early, the habit of a lifetime in the working world. No rain, so I did as I had been asked at the hostel, leaving the room tidy and the key on the pillow, making sure the door was locked behind me, and walked to the railway station. My train, which would go through to Castle Cary, then change for Weymouth, went at 07.50. Already, the platform was a bustle of office types who would be commuting to Basingstoke or London to work, and the next train, after the Castle Cary change, would take them to their destination, terminating at London Waterloo.

I arrived at Castle Cary station: in the middle of Somerset, it was quiet, and peaceful, yet chilly. An announcement came over the tannoy that the train through to Weymouth would be twenty minutes late. Well, that didn't make an ounce of difference to me, but the mumble of pissed-off commuters, who now had deeply engrained frowns etched into their foreheads, filled the air; like Queen Victoria, they were not amused.

The train did indeed arrive twenty minutes late as promised, so we scrambled on, not worrying that it was yet another well-worn ancient diesel, one of the first generation built to replace steam locomotives in the Sixties. It chortled and rasped like an old man with the death's rattle in his throat when the driver hit the throttle to move off. When he achieved some degree of speed, he coasted the engine, as if knowing the clapped-out old relic needed as much tender loving care as he could give it to make sure we reached Weymouth.

Jane and Amy would be waiting at Hamworthy Junction at 11.30. They would wait, I knew, but the Weymouth to Waterloo runs every half hour, so they would not know that I would be on the midday train instead. I tried calling Jane on our home number on the mobile, but out in the rural countryside between Castle Cary and Weymouth there was no signal. But as soon as that old dragon of a diesel loco stopped at Weymouth railway station, and we hastily boarded our up-to-the-minute ultra-modern electric train, we also had a phone signal.

Of course, Jane was happy that I had let her know about the timetable change; partners worry when we don't arrive on time, don't they? But almost on the dot of 12, they were on the platform smiling and waving as the train stopped, and I jumped off. It had been well worth the twenty-four hour round trip to remind Lemmy of our personal anniversary, and I think he appreciated it. I certainly did.

Flip Skateboards »Extremely Sorry«
Volcom Ent #04570

Released 16 November 2009
The soundtrack to the third film of skateboard tricks by California-based Flip Skateboards company
Track one: 'Intro' (featuring Geoff Rowley and Lemmy) – first verse of 'Orgasmatron' as spoken word
Track two: 'Stand By Me' (featuring Lemmy and Dave Lombardo) – the Ben E. King soul classic with bass and vocals by Lemmy
Other tracks: 'Drum Solo' (featuring Dave Lombardo) / 'This Is Forever' / 'Scream My Name' (featuring Jim Lindberg) / 'When Is Now' / 'Lead The Storm' / 'Ignition' / 'Love Shroom' (featuring Mack Winston) / 'Arizona Lead In' / 'Desert Convoy' / 'The End Of The Beginning' (featuring Black Mountains) / 'Burn Out Like Fireflies' (featuring Sounder) / 'The Process Of Extinction' (featuring Early Man) / 'Swagger Rich' (featuring Warren G & Snoop Dogg).

With The Damned and Girlschool in support, Motörhead played the UK leg of their No Sleep 'Til Moscow tour, which naturally then moved through Germany and Finland with two final dates in St Petersburg and Moscow. The first week of February 2010 then saw The Head Cat record their second album, which would later be released under the title »Walk The Walk, Talk The Talk«. Lemmy then hooked up with his former guitarist Würzel.

Leader Of Down

A band formed by ex-Motörhead guitarist Würzel, whose name came about when Würzel misheard the lyrics of Status Quo's UK Number 1 'Down Down'. Lemmy wrote lyrics for and recorded vocals in LA on 14 February 2010 over two backing tracks previously recorded in London. The songs 'Mr. Würzel' and another whose title is unknown were to be for the B-side of a single and an album track.
Würzel passed away on 10 July 2011, and it is unknown whether any of the Leader Of Down music and video archive will ever be released.

»LA Ink« Series 2 starring Kat von D
Revelation (PAR61395)

Released 22 February 2010
Three-DVD box set of Series Two of the TV show consisting of thirteen episodes plus extras. The TV series stars tattooist Kat von D and staff at her Los Angeles tattoo shop, with essential 'soap-opera' shenanigans amongst the staff to keep

the viewing interest levels up – it would be pretty boring just watching punters being tattooed! Lemmy and Kat had been friends for a long time, and occasionally attended functions in and around Los Angeles together. Lemmy appears in the episode »It's All About The Family« (originally broadcast 8 January 2009) in which Kat touches in the now battle-worn 1979 'Born To Lose – Live To Win - Ace Of Spades' tattoo on Lemmy's left forearm.

With little peace for the wicked, in March Motörhead started work on another studio album, which would later be released as »The World Is Yours«.

Slash »Slash«
(Classic Rock magazine limited edition 'Fan Pack' /
Roadrunner Records)

Featuring as issue of Classic Rock magazine dedicated to Slash, plus an advanced limited edition copy of the album, and a patch
Released 8 April 2010
Tracks and guest artists: 'Ghost' (Ian Astbury) / 'Crucify The Dead' (Ozzy Osbourne) / 'Beautiful Dangerous' (Fergie) / 'Back From Cali' (Myles Kennedy) / 'Promise' (Chris Cornell) / 'By The Sword' (Andrew Stockdale) / 'Gottem' (Adam Levine) / 'Doctor Alibi' (Lemmy Kilmister) / 'Watch This' (Dave Grohl and Duff McKagan) / 'I Hold On' (Kid Rock) / 'Nothing To Say' (M. Shadows) / 'Starlight' (Miles Kennedy) / 'Saint Is A Sinner Too' (Rocco DeLuca) / 'We're All Gonna Die' (Iggy Pop)
Slash (real name Saul Hudson), is a British-American musician and songwriter, who was the former lead guitarist with Guns N' Roses. His first solo venture was Slash's Snakepit (with whom he recorded two albums) and later he co-founded Velvet Revolver, which re-established him as a mainstream performer. »Slash« was his first 'real' solo album. Lemmy wrote the lyrics and provided vocals for 'Doctor Alibi', which he has performed live with Slash and his band at various gigs and functions.

Danko Jones 'I Think Bad Thoughts' video
CO5 Music Promo CD (BTR ITBT US).

Uploaded to YouTube 12 May 2010
Music Tracks: 'I Think Bad Thoughts' (Radio Edit) / 'I Think Bad Thoughts' (Album Version) / 'Full Of Regret' (video clip)

From Toronto, Ontario, Canada and formed in 1996, the band are: Danko Jones: vocals and guitar, John 'JC' Calabrese: bass guitar, and Atom Willard: drums. They performed live around the north-eastern United States and Canada for two years as the opening act for a multitude of bands, their reputation spreading by word of mouth, and in 1998 they released a self-titled six-track EP. In 2008, with their fourth album »Never Too Loud« they toured the UK, Germany, France, Belgium, The Netherlands and Luxembourg with Motörhead.

Following on from the friendship forged on the 2008 Motörizer tour where Danko Jones were special guests, Lemmy Kilmister starred in the band's 'Full Of Regret' video alongside Mike Watt of The Minutemen and actors Elijah Wood and Selma Blair. "It's like a mini-movie," a band spokesperson said. "Mr. Kilmister plays a mob impresario who hires Wood and Ms Blair to take out Danko Jones."

Danko Jones himself said "we are humungous Motörhead fans. Having Lemmy in our video is a total honour that we do not take lightly. As you can see in the video, Lemmy is a total professional and natural actor."

The video was released on the »I Think Bad Thoughts« promo CD.

Saxon »Heavy Metal Thunder – The Movie« Coolhead Productions (TOWN31DVD)

Released 7 June 2010
Running time approximately six hours
This feature-length documentary film tells the full warts-and-all story of thirty years of heartache, earache, success and excess. Produced by critically acclaimed documentary filmmakers, Coolhead, it not only has contributions from members of Saxon past and present, but also from the likes of Lars Ulrich, Lemmy and Fast Eddie Clarke, promoter Harvey Goldsmith, Doro Pesch and members of Airbourne and Amon Amarth. The double-DVD also features freshly-uncovered archive material, including the band performing in 1979 on Motörhead's Bomber tour, recording sessions and interviews from the »Crusader« and »Innocence Is No Excuse« albums and a classic concert from 1981, along with stunning headline performances at Wacken in 2000, and the now legendary inaugural St George's Day show in London.

Interview footage with Lemmy is included, as well as Saxon's reminiscences of tales of debauchery on their tours with Motörhead through the years.

Various Artists »Harder & Heavier – '60s British Invasion Goes Metal« The Orchard (CIR-9164)

Released 8 June 2010

Tracks and artists: 'Paint It Black' (Dee Snider, George Lynch, Tony Franklin, Frankie Banali) / 'The Mighty Quinn' (Mickey Dolenz, John 5, Billy Sheehan, Gregg Bissonette) / 'It's Not Unusual' (Dez Fafara, Bob Kulick, Rudy Sarzo, Simon Wright) / 'Twist And Shout' (Lemmy Kilmister, Scott Ian, Gregg Bissonette, Andrea Becker) / 'She's Not There' (Doug Pinnick, Carlos Cavazo, Rudy Sarzo, Simon Wright) / 'We Gotta Get Out Of This Place' (Tim 'Ripper' Owens, Andreas Kisser, Chris Chaney, Vinny Appice) / 'All Day And All Of The Night' (Joe Lynn Turner, Brad Gillis, Rudy Sarzo, Simon Wright) / 'Wild Thing' (Brett Scallions, Doug Aldrich, Tony Franklin, Frankie Banali) / 'Do Wah Diddy Diddy' (David Johansen, Tracii Guns, Rudy Sarzo, Simon Wright) / 'I'm A Man' (Terry Reid, Richie Kotzen, Tony Franklin, Frankie Banali, Doug Katsaros) / 'My Generation' (Mike Tramp, Jeff Labar, Tony Franklin, Frankie Banali)

Recorded and mixed at Office Studios, Van Nuys, California; produced by Bob Kulick and Brett Chassen

Bob Kulick is an American guitarist and Grammy Award-winning record producer, best known for his work with Diana Ross and Kiss (for whom his brother Bruce was a former lead guitarist) amongst many others. Bob also produced Motörhead's cover of the Metallica song 'Whiplash' which won the band the 2004 Grammy Award for Best Metal Performance.

'Twist And Shout' features Lemmy: bass and vocals, Scott Ian: guitars, Greg Bissonette: drums and Andrea Becker: backing vocals.

Lemmy (and no doubt the rest of the musicians involved in this album) enjoyed doing something like this because, for the day or two it took to record his track, he was having fun doing something a bit different to the usual routine. And, let's face it, we have all heard the originals of these songs often enough – perhaps not enough to get bored with them, but to welcome a different version. This is just the album for that moment. A great selection of songs which is well worth owning.

Summer 2010 saw Motörhead play a large number of festival dates across Europe.

»Jimi Hendrix The Guitar Hero«
Classic Rock magazine limited edition 'Fan Pack'
(CRP02DVD-12-10)

A special issue of Classic Rock magazine dedicated to Jimi Hendrix with a DVD
Released 14 September 2010: running time approximately 109 minutes.

Narrated by Slash, a long-time Hendrix acolyte, this film is less a biography than the first film ever to focus on the music itself and the impetus of the master who created it. As such it's an excellent documentary, which includes various interview segments featuring Lemmy, commenting on his memories of Jimi in the mid-Sixties as roadie and friend.

Although still working on »The World Is Yours«, Lemmy spent time in September playing more dates with The Head Cat. Two shows in Japan followed in October for Motörhead, and then the UK tour, with Michael Monroe, started in early November. The album was released midway through January 2011, along with »Lemmy The Movie«.

»Lemmy – 49% Motherf**ker, 51% Son Of A Bitch« EOne DVD (EOS51472)

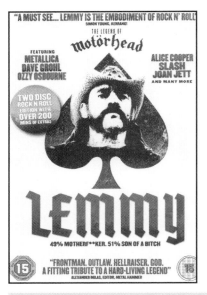

Released 24 January 2011
Directed by Greg Olliver and Wes Orshoski and featuring Metallica, Dave Grohl, Ozzy Osbourne, Alice Cooper, Slash, Joan Jett and many more, the film explores the life and career of "heavy metal pioneer and cultural icon Lemmy Kilmister".
The DVD/Blu-Ray has been certified Gold for 50,000+ sales in the United States and 25,000+ sales the United Kingdom, Germany, France and Finland. It also won the DVD/Film Of The Year category at the Classic Rock Awards in London in November 2011.

Foo Fighters 'White Limo' from »Wasting Light« (Roswell/RCA B004LUHQ1G)

Released 12 April 2011
Tracks: 'Bridge Burning' / 'Rope' / 'Dear Rosemary' / 'White Limo' / 'Arlandria' / 'These Days' / 'Back & Forth' / 'A Matter Of Time' / 'Miss The Misery' / 'I Should Have Known' / 'Walk'
Dave Grohl: vocals, guitar, Nate Mandel: bass, Taylor Hawkins: drums, Chris Shiflett: guitar and backing vocals, Pat Smear: rhythm guitar
Produced by Butch Vig

In 2010 Dave Grohl built a recording studio in his San Fernando Valley garage, and hired Nirvana's »Nevermind« producer, Butch Vig to oversee the Foo Fighters' seventh album (recorded entirely on analogue tape).

The video for 'White Limo' was released and uploaded to YouTube as a St Valentine's Day gift to fans on 14 February 2011. Lemmy has a role in the short promo as the bad-ass limo driver who always gets the girl.

A massive American tour with Clutch and Valiant Thor in support saw Motörhead on the road through to early March.

Lemmy, Girlschool, Rudy Sarzo and The Livewire Youth Music Band 'Emergency 2010 – Young People Rock for Haiti'

Released as a download track on 25 February 2011

Arrangements were made by youth work coordinator Andy Rance, during the Motörhead / Girlschool / The Damned 2009 UK tour, for the track to be recorded as a charity song with proceeds going to help the Haiti Earthquake victims. The Livewire Youth Music Centre is in Saltash, Cornwall, England. AC/DC vocalist Brian Johnson is patron for the Livewire Youth Music project. Other support comes from the likes of AC/DC, Jimmy Page, Thin Lizzy, The Answer, Airbourne, Girlschool, Steve Vai, Phil Collins, Judas Priest, Funeral For A Friend, Avril Levigne, Motörhead, Blink 182, Pete Townshend, Mick Jagger, Led Zeppelin, Peter Gabriel and Iron Maiden.

The track was dedicated to the memory of Kelly Johnson and Ronnie James Dio.

Michael Monroe »Sensory Overdrive«
Spinefarm Records (SPI388CD)

Released 14 March 2011

Tracks: 'Trick Of The Wrist' / 'Got Blood?' / 'Superpowered Superfly' / 'Modern Day Miracle' / 'Bombs Away' / 'All You Need' / 'Later Won't Wait' / 'Gone Baby Gone' (featuring Lucinda Williams) / 'Centre Of Your Heart' / 'Debauchery As A Fine Art' (featuring Lemmy Kilmister)

Michael Monroe: lead vocals, harmonica & sax, Sam Yaffa: bass and background vocals, Ginger: guitar and background vocals, Steve Conte: guitar and background vocals, Karl Rockfist: drums and background vocals

"Michael Monroe is a Finnish rock musician and multi-instrumentalist, who became famous as the lead singer for Hanoi Rocks," I commented at the time for a MHB's review. "The Michael Monroe band were special guests on Motörhead's 35th Anniversary UK tour in autumn 2010. They were very impressive musically, with an outstanding sound in the concert halls. Despite every venue being of different interior design, somehow Michael Monroe managed to find a way of scaling the walls like Spiderman during instrumental breaks in the music. You have to wonder what he held on to on some occasions, as it seemed as if he quite literally scaled bare walls (although apparently he has fallen on occasions). He and his band are excellent, and although these theatrics are thrilling to the rock audience, they are not essential, as the music is more than enough as entertainment."

On 11 September 2010, whilst recording sessions for the album at Swing House Studios in Hollywood were underway, Lemmy collaborated and sang with Monroe on 'Debauchery As A Fine Art'. The song is credited to Monroe / Kilmister, and Lemmy's lyrical input is rather obvious. In November 2011 »Sensory Overdrive« won Classic Rock magazine's 'Album Of The Year' award.

'Hollywood Hillbillies' Sharynlee featuring Lemmy Kilmister

Sharynlee is a bluegrass, country, country-rock and gospel singer-songwriter. Born in Danville, Virginia, she began a solo recording career in the Eighties, and then moved out west to become a Country Music Show headliner in Las Vegas. She plays rhythm mandolin, and what she calls other hillbilly percussion instruments, including the washboard, jug and tambourine, and was considered for four Grammy nominations in 2012.

To the surprise of many, Sharynlee and Lemmy recorded a single together. It was released as a download track on 15 March 2011, and is also available on the Sharynlee website (and YouTube). It's a charming and typically country and western style song (as familiar to the genre as the twelve-bar blues is to rock music) with pedal-steel guitar in the backing. Another string to Lemmy's bow, and a great duet by the two stars. On her website, Sharynlee said : "we can't say thank you enough times to all of you who have shown me and Lemmy Kilmister (Motörhead / The Head Cat) nothing but a huge amount of support for our single 'Hollywood Hillbillies'. We were just happy to be able to go into the studio as two dear friends who love music, and have the opportunity to do a song together. Now look where things are. On the radio. People buying the single. You guys reaching out to us. Thank you, thank you, thank you – from the heart."

Motörhead played four shows in Australia, then more over in South America.

The Head Cat »Fool's Paradise«
CD+DVD Deluxe Box Set (limited edition of 500)
Cleopatra Records

Released 2 May 2011
Re-issue of the revised fifteen-track album and the »Rockin' The Cat Club« DVD in a limited edition box set with colour poster and pin-badge – The Head Cat's recorded legacy for Cleopatra Records in one deluxe box set, plus collectors' goodies.

Motörhead supported Foo Fighters on a short arena tour in America. Summer festival dates followed, then came four dates on the Spanish leg of Judas Priest's 'farewell' tour.

The Head Cat »Walk The Walk... Talk The Talk«
Niji Entertainment (NEG007)

Released 7 July 2011
Lemmy Kilmister: bass and vocals, Slim Jim Phantom: drums, Danny B. Harvey: guitars and piano
Tracks: 'American Beat' / 'Say Mama' / 'I Ain't Never' / 'Bad Boy' / 'Shakin' All Over' / 'Let It Rock' / 'Something Else' / 'The Eagle Flies On Friday' / 'Trying To Get To You' / 'You Can't Do That' / 'It'll Be Me' / 'Crossroads'
Recorded at Sage and Sound Studios, Hollywood, California
Produced and engineered by Cameron Webb; assistant engineer: Wesley Michener.

A second album, and a new record label for The Head Cat, with 'American Beat' and 'The Eagle Flies On Friday' as band-penned songs amongst ten classics.

Diamond Baby 'The Last Rock Star' promo video clip

Diamond Baby were put together by Guns N' Roses / Velvet Revolver drummer Matt Sorum, under the name Baron von Storm, and featured his girlfriend Ace Harper (aka Ace Of Diamonds) on vocals. The video has cameo appearances by Motör-head's frontman, Jane Lynch from »Glee« and actors Juliet Lewis and Verne Troyer, and was uploaded to YouTube on 17 July 2011. Sorum described the music as 'electro-rock', and it is pleasant in a poppy kind of way.

The Head Cat played their first dates outside the USA, with one show each in London and Berlin (on 16 and 18 October respectively).

»Mind Of The Demon' – The Larry Linkogle Story«
Breaking Glass Pictures (BGP289)

Released 29 November 2011
Running time 63 minutes
"In the 1990s, infamous dirt bike rider Larry Linkogle began a revolution. Fed up with the culture of motocross racing, he and his friends set out to create a new sport. The high-stakes, often death-defying world of freestyle motocross was born, and took fans of extreme sports by storm. Though Linkogle rose to legendary status with his record-breaking stunts and rock-and-roll life-style, his inner demons and self-destructive behaviour eventually led to his demise," runs the promo text, and whether you like motorbikes or not – and I'm guessing most Motörhead fans do – this is quite an eye-opening documentary. Larry has the same attitude as Lemmy had in that despite so-called advice, he had to do what's in his heart and soul re-gardless of what other people might think. But crashes happen, and Larry became addicted to all kinds of legal and illegal pain killers, an addiction which almost killed him. The story goes that as soon as discussions started regarding this film, Larry said "we must get Lemmy to do the narration." On its original theatrical release it won the Bel Air Film Festival award for Best Jury International Documentary.

Motörhead played some dates in Europe to kick off their UK tour with The Anti Nowhere League and The UK Subs. Duff McKagen's Loaded supported the band throughout the European leg, whilst Dead Man's Curse accompanied them for the Scandinavian shows. 2012 then started with just over a month on the road in America, second on the bill to Megadeth on the Gigantour.

Nashville Pussy »From Hell To Texas – Tour Edition«
SPV Records (SPV 306090 2CD)

Released 23 January 2012
CD 1: 'From Hell To Texas' / 'Drunk Driving Man' / 'Ain't Yo Business' / 'I'm So High' / 'Late Great USA' / 'Speed Machine' / 'Dead Men Can't Get Drunk' / 'Why, Why, Why' / 'Lazy Jesus' / 'Stone Cold Down' / 'Pray For The Devil' / 'Give Me A Hit Before You Go'

CD 2 – Live And Loud In Europe: 'Say Something Nasty' / 'From Hell To Texas' / 'Ain't Your Business' / 'Piece Of Ass' / 'Come On, Come On, Come On' / 'Hate And Whiskey' / 'Late Great USA' / 'I'm So High' / 'Struttin Cock' / 'Snake Eyes' / 'I'm The Man' / 'Why Why Why' / 'The Bitch Just Kicked Me Out' / 'Drunk Drivin' Man' / 'Go Motherfucker Go' / 'Goin' Down'
Produced by Daniel Rey
Blaine Cartwright: guitars, vocals, Ruyer Suys: guitars, backing vocals, Karen Cuda: bass, backing vocals, Jeremy Thompson: drums.
Lemmy appears as Jesus as the guest voice on the 'Lazy Jesus' track.

Dates on the summer festival circuit follow, and, in early July, Motörhead played the Rockstar Energy Drink Mayhem Festival tour at major venues throughout America.

Doro Pesch »Raise Your Fist«
Nuclear Blast Records (27361 27260)

Released 22 October 2012
Tracks: 'Raise Your Fist In The Air' / 'Cold Hearted Lover' / 'Rock Till Death' / 'It Still Hurts' (featuring Lemmy) / 'Take No Prisoner' / 'Grab The Bull (Last Man Standing)' (featuring Gus G) / 'Engel' / 'Freiheit (Human Rights)' / 'Little Headbanger (Nackenbrecher)' / 'Revenge' / 'Free My Heart' / 'Victory' / 'Hero'
'It Still Hurts' is a stunning duet by Doro and Lemmy. It was written and produced by Andreas Bruhn and Doro Pesch, with Lemmy's vocals recorded by Chris Rakestraw at Sunset Lodge Studio, Los Angeles. The digi-pack booklet features photos of Lemmy Kilmister and Phil Campbell with Doro band members, and another of Lemmy and Doro together on the 'It Still Hurts' lyrics page. Recalls Doro of the song: "we had 'It Still Hurts', and I thought that it would sound great as a duet with Lemmy. So I sent it to him in March [2012], and he liked it, and recorded his vocals in L.A. I love it. I am thrilled with it, and so pleased that Lemmy wanted to sing another song with me. It would be nice if it was released as a single, but I am just grateful to share another track with him on the album."

»Metal Evolution«
Banger Films / Tricon Films and Television DVD (EREDV958)

Released 19 November 2012
With a running time of 495 minutes »Metal Evolution« is the biggest, most comprehensive documentary series ever made on the history of heavy metal and hard rock. Featuring countless interviews with members of the likes of Black Sabbath, Deep Purple, Iron Maiden, Metallica, The Kinks, Van Halen, Kiss, Alice Cooper, Soundgarden and Slayer (some 300 or so interviewees crop up) this eleven-episode series saw Sam Dunn criss-crossing the globe to explore the history of the genre. From the streets of the UK to the bars on Sunset Strip, the beer-soaked festivals of Germany to soccer stadiums in Chile, Dunn examined the pioneers of British and American hard rock, as well as the modern-day luminaries worldwide that keep it alive today. Episodes: 1. 'Pre-History of Metal' / 2. 'Early Metal US' / 3. 'Early Metal UK' / 4. 'New Wave of British Heavy Metal' / 5. 'Glam Metal' / 6. 'Thrash Metal' / 7. 'Grunge' / 8. 'Nu Metal' / 9. 'Shock Rock' / 10. 'Power Metal' / 11. 'Progressive Metal' Everyone reading this book would do well to get hold of a copy of this DVD box set of the whole series. It features various interview segments with Lemmy, naturally, and Dunn also filmed Motörhead's concert in Chile for their »The World Is Ours, Volume 1« DVD release.

2012 ended with the now legendary UK and European tours, with Anthrax in support. Motörhead also release two DVD collections titled »The World Is Ours, Volume One« which featured the band at indoor venues, and »The World Is Ours, Volume Two« at festival appearances, both heartily welcomed by the fans. The following year began with Motörhead back in the studio recording what would become the critically acclaimed and best selling »Aftershock« album. But after a few summer festivals, the band cancelled any outstanding gigs as well as the autumn UK and European tour due to Lemmy's health issues.

Huntress »Starbound Beast«
Napalm Records (NPR 191)

Released 28 June 2013
Tracks: 'Enter The Exosphere' / 'Blood Sisters' / 'I Want To Fuck You To Death' / 'Destroy Your Life' / 'Starbound Beast' / 'Zenith' / 'Oracle' / 'Receiver' / 'Spectra Spectral' / 'Alpha Tauri' / 'Running Wild' [bonus track, Judas Priest cover]
Jill Janus: vocals, Blake Meahl: guitars, Ant 'Pockets' Crocamo: guitars, Ian Alden: bass, Carl Wierzbicky: drums.
Jill Janus spoke about the track entitled 'I Want To Fuck You To Death', the lyrics for which were written for her by Lemmy. "I met Lemmy through my former band, Chelsea

Girls. We'd play hard rock and metal covers featuring guest celebrities. Lemmy was always friends with the girls, and he played 'Ace Of Spades' with us and it blew my mind. We stayed in touch and would meet up at the Rainbow for drinks. So I asked him over Jack and Cokes if he'd write lyrics for a Huntress song, and he said 'sure.' A few weeks later, I met him at the studio during Motörhead recording sessions. Lemmy handed me two pieces of notebook paper with the lyrics for 'I Want To Fuck You To Death'. I am beyond honoured. To me, this is a love song. It is the most romantic song I have ever heard." Lemmy said of the collaboration: "the first time I heard Jill's voice with the Chelsea Girls, it was phenomenal. I wrote the lyrics from her point of view, the Huntress. 'I Want To Fuck You To Death' was inspired by her, and written for her. I've always had a soft spot for her, and a hard spot, too."

Classic Rock Magazine issue #190 November 2013

Published 9 October 2013
Lemmy featured on the cover, together with a nine-page interview/photospread and free CD titled »Rock 'N' Roll« featuring fifteen of Lemmy's favourite songs.
Tracks: 'Ballroom Blitz' – Motördamn / 'Great Balls Of Fire' – Jerry Lee Lewis / 'Peggy Sue Got Married' – The Head Cat / 'Good Golly Miss Molly' – Little Richard / 'That'll Be The Day' – Buddy Holly & The Crickets / 'Peter Gunn' – Duane Eddy / 'Learning The Game' – The Head Cat / 'Heartbreak Hotel' – Elvis Presley / 'Big River' – The Head Cat / 'C'mon Everybody' – Eddie Cochrane / 'Because Of You – Skunk Anansie' / 'Sweet Little Sixteen' – Chuck Berry / 'Matchbox' – The Head Cat / 'Sweet Nothin's' – Brenda Lee / 'Debauchery As A Fine Art' – Michael Monroe

Emigrate »Silent So Long« (Vertigo Records 0602537978625)

Released 17 November 2014
Tracks: 'Eat You Alive' (featuring Frank Belle) / 'Get Down' (featuring Peaches) / 'Rock City' (featuring Lemmy Kilmister) / 'Hypothetical' (featuring Marilyn Manson) / 'Rainbow' / 'Born On My Own' / 'Giving Up' / 'My Pleasure' / 'Happy Times' (featuring Margaux Bossieux) / 'Faust' / 'Silent So Long' (featuring Jonathan Davis).
Richard Z. Kruspe: vocals, lead guitar, Olsen Involtini: rhythm guitar, Arnaud Giroux: bass guitar and backing vocals, Margaux Bossieux: rhythm guitar and backing vocals, Joe Letz: live drums, Mikko Siren: studio drums

Emigrate is a European alternative metal band based in New York, led by Richard Z Kruspe, lead guitar player of the band Rammstein.

'Rock City' features a great vocal performance from Lemmy.

»Gutterdämmerung«
A Shoot The Artist Films presentation of a film
by Bjorn Tagemuse

To be released sometime in 2016

Starring Henry Rollins, Iggy Pop, Lemmy Kilmister, Nina Hagen, Slash, Jesse Hughes, Grace Jones, Tom Araya, Volbeat, Mark Lanegan, Olivia Vindall and Tuesday Cross (described in the trailer as "the most epic cast in rock 'n' roll history"), the film is set in a world where God has saved the world from The Devil's 'Grail of Sin' – the evil guitar. An evil Puritan priest (Rollins) manipulates a naïve girl into retrieving the guitar to destroy it. At the time of writing, "the loudest silent movie on Earth" is supposed to be touring with a live narrator and a live band providing the soundtrack.

Going to Motörhead's gig at the Bournemouth International Centre on 15 November 2012 had been ruled out. Doctors and a consultant had announced as yet undiagnosed multiple sclerosis, and knowing a local Motörhead fan and personal friend suffering with it, I could do no more than agree. The medical world had now also decided that a complaint suffered in 1989, when I lost the use of my hands for five months, had been the start of it, and that the interim years had been a form of remission. But now I had difficulty walking 100 yards, never mind getting from the BIC car park to the venue and spending four or five hours on my feet.

Motörhead publicist Ute Kromrey heard that I wouldn't be attending the show via our emails, and also noted the fact that I hadn't asked for a pass. When I told her why, she said "I will call you in ten minutes." She did. "It is all organised, Alan." "What?" "You will be collected by Robert and Kelly Kiewik and driven to the venue. There, I have organised a wheelchair for you, and Robert and Kelly will be your carers for the evening."

The last thing I needed was to be wheeled around in a wheelchair. I am a very independent person, and detest having things done for me. But it was either that, or stay at home. Ute made me promise that I would go along; no excuses. So I had to put my pride in a jam jar and leave it at home; after all, this was making another Motörhead gig possible. Around 2 pm, Robert and Kelly pulled into the drive, and after handshakes, hugs, conversation and a cup of tea, we were off.

The eight-mile journey passed pretty quickly. After turning into a dead-end road on the left of the venue Robert pulled up, stepped out, and found someone to ask where we needed to go. The BIC car park is to the right of the venue, and between the curb stones, a gap, which we slid through. Now out the back of the venue, the Motörhead juggernauts and crew busses came into view, along with the vista of the legendary

Bournemouth beach and pier. Bass guitar tech Tim Butcher's cheery face appeared as Robert pulled up and parked. The two old friends shook hands and conversed, then disappeared inside the venue. Kelly gave me a hand to get out of the car, and as I took in the ozone, a couple of MHBs walked up for a handshake, a chat, and a photo.

Robert came back to the car with the wheelchair and, somewhat reluctantly, I sat in it to be wheeled inside the back/stage door entrance. Being Motörhead super-fans, Robert and Kelly knew most if not all of the crew, and we quickly realised the band were on their way from the previous night's gig at Portsmouth. With the crew still going in and out the doors were open, and despite this being mid-November, it wasn't that cold, but it was chilly in a draught, so they pushed me through past some doors outside Anthrax's dressing room.

Twenty or so minutes later, Mikkey Dee, Lemmy, and Lem's PA Steve Luna appeared to greet the three of us. Lemmy invited us into his dressing room. His usual rider was laid out there on a table: two cartons of Marlboros, two bottles of Jack Daniels, a bottle of Marmite, an assortment of cheese and biscuits and Kinder eggs, and, on the floor, a large cooler filled with ice, beer and Coca Colas. After pleasantries had been exchanged, Robert and Kelly excused themselves and went off on their investigation around the venue. Lemmy had an iPad to which he plugged in an external speaker. "Have a listen to my solo album, Al," he suggested, lighting a Marlboro and smiling.

Now, I'm not saying this just because of the occasion, or the thrill of the legend with whom I was sitting, but I had known him for 33 years by that time, and I knew that he would expect an honest opinion, not a load of bullshit to pander to his ego. But without exception, all of the tracks blew me away. I asked who produced it, because the production was quite stunning. "Jim Voxx, Skew Siskin," he replied, between playing air guitar and singing along to some of the lyrics. Needless to say, we were listening to it at quite some volume – not as many decibels as Motörhead on-stage, obviously, but, for the size of the dressing room, not far off in comparison to the band in a concert hall: after my 34 years of listening to Motörhead, and his 37 years of being in Motörhead, neither of us could claim our hearing was perfect.

The Joan Jett track has a stunning guitar solo in it. Knowing Joan is a competent rhythm player, I asked "who the hell played that solo?" "My son, Paul [Inder]," he smiled; "good, isn't he!" Damn right he is!

In such a situation, it wasn't the right time or the right place to ask for track listings and suchlike. It was time to enjoy it with the Boss. But we were interrupted after the third or fourth song by Robert, Kelly and Steve, coming back to let Lemmy know that it was time for the soundcheck. My two carers pushed and escorted me out into the concert hall, where we enjoyed the band getting their sound crafted to perfection for the evening show. There were quite a few fans, super fans, and MHBs with passes to chat to, but hearing my name being called by one of the crew with "Lemmy wants you back to finish hearing his album!" my escorts did the honours, and took me back to the dressing room.

Believe me, like any Motörhead album, every track is excellent, no holds barred, just as you would have expected from Lemmy Kilmister. Whilst we were sitting there watching Lem take slugs of his booze and enjoy a cigarette or two, some past conversations came to mind, along with the lyrics he wrote for the 'Dr. Alibi' track, which he recorded with Slash for his solo album.

Lemmy often maintained that to give up a habit which one has had for many years is not a good thing, as the natural reaction of our body to its sudden starvation will be 'where is it? I want it!' and if it doesn't get it, then it will kick you in the ass with something nasty. My supposed bout of multiple sclerosis happened after 38 years of smoking which had to cease for a heart operation. I had inherited a faulty heart valve from my mother, who'd died when three of her four valves blew out. So, in late 2006, I had given up smoking for the open-heart surgery. Yet despite the things the medical profession tells us about smoking, tests had shown that my heart, arteries, veins, and everything else, had been untouched by my habit. But to be fair to the medical profession, the brilliant surgeon who did the operation, and the cost to the NHS, it was of course the right thing to do. Somehow, I'd got it fixed in my head that I was – and always would be now – a non-smoker. It didn't even bother me when Lemmy sat there smoking: I had, I thought, gone past the point of wanting one during those six years of abstinence.

But about three years through that period, I began suffering chronic migraines, which saw me in bed for a minimum of twelve hours straight with the room blacked out and this crucifying pain across the top of my skull. Sometimes, I would suffer three per week, and all through that waking pain (just couldn't sleep through pain like that!) and misery, I would be thinking, "this is terrible, surely it must be affecting me or my system somehow. That amount of pain cannot just be suffered: there just has to be some kind of price to pay".

Gradually, my walking began getting worse. A short walk to the village shops to post the mail and buy a newspaper became more of a struggle month by month. Several visits to the doctor, and an appointment with the appropriate consultant at Poole Hospital, brought the news that the odd illness which I had suffered back in 1989 had also been a form of multiple sclerosis, and it had returned, this time affecting my legs rather than my hands. This diagnosis was no surprise, as my local long-time friend and gig companion, Eddie Evans, was also suffering multiple sclerosis. I had watched his gradual decline, and my symptoms were just the same. Oddly, he too had given up smoking at the insistence of a girlfriend, had suffered immense migraines, and ended up with this terrible debilitating disease, and is now bedridden.

All through my non-smoking years, I had been very much still pro-smoking rather than anti-, and had told my family that if it was at all possible on my deathbed, if they could get me a cigarette and a shot of my favourite bourbon, Southern Comfort, it would make my last gasp of breath a sheer delight. Just before Christmas 2012, watching TV with my wife Jane and son Steven, I said "wow! I could murder a cigarette!" This was not the first time such an exclamation had been voiced. I still missed them, but didn't want to ruin that six years of abstinence with just one puff.

Steve excused himself and went out. He's 33 years old so we don't ask where; he's big enough now! He returned thirty or so minutes later, and tossed a pack of twenty Chesterfield blue and a lighter on my lap. It was quite a shock. He knew that I would choose Chesterfield as I had spoken about them being one of the cheapest cigarettes on the market (at some £3 per packet less than most brands) and wondering why everyone in this recessionary era didn't smoke them.

With a week in Southampton Hospital for tests at the end of January 2013 lined up, I thanked him, and said that I would wait until after coming home, rather than having to get to the outside of the building for a smoke in my condition. There was no way that I could walk that distance from the ward to the hospital entrance, so best be patient for a few months more, but I respected and was grateful for his kind gesture.

So, the Chesterfields and the lighter went in an appropriate space in my CD rack, and when I was back home from the tests I waited for the results before returning to my habit. Eventually, they admitted that they didn't actually recognise my illness as multiple sclerosis, but as the symptoms were so damned similar they put it in that pigeon hole so that I, my family, and the medical world, knew roughly what we are dealing with, and would in the fullness of time, try and treat.

It wasn't a shock to hear the multiple sclerosis diagnosis. After seeing Eddie go down with it, all I knew was that if there was any way else that I could die other than rotting away to a corpse in bed, then that's the route I would prefer to take. Smoking once more might give me a stroke or a heart attack, but it would be preferable to fading away with a long and miserable death with multiple sclerosis. It was difficult walking outside the back door with that first cigarette between my lips, and the lighter in my hand. One draw on the filter tip and six years would be wiped out, but bearing in mind the above logic, it seemed a better way to go. The migraines, by the way, had never gone away. The doctor had (begrudgingly, because of their cost) given me tablets, and every couple of days when I felt the migraine coming on I would take one. Three days into smoking five or six cigarettes a day, the migraines stopped, and have never returned. With my replacement heart valve, I take Warfarin, and have regular hospital blood tests to check that my blood is of the right consistency – too thin, you get very cold; too thick, it clogs the valve and you have a stroke or heart attack. But I had decided to opt for the Lemmy's 'Dr. Alibi' logic completely. With Warfarin, they recommend one pint of beer per day, or one pub shot of a short. So as long as there's no blood test the following day, I chose to enjoy a couple of beers rather than the prescribed one. After visiting some friends whom we had enjoyed Christmas dinner with, and my disappointing them by not enjoying a Southern Comfort and Coke, another return social visit saw me drink third of a litre bottle with no ill-effects, and no hangover. This in itself was amazing. Before my heart operation I would have two beers and a hefty glass of Southern and Coke every evening, and it was as if my body not only remembered that, but actually felt pleased to have things returned to normal. It would have been awful to have had to go through the late-teens misery of getting drunk, going to bed, and the room going around and around until I threw up; so it was and is a blessing that our system remembers its past, and apparently enjoys returning to what it must have regarded as 'normal'.

Having eliminated the migraines, my walking has also stabilised. I haven't managed to walk to the village shop and back yet, but it is on my agenda. I have informed my doctor and the consultant of my return to my old vices. They had no problem with it, because they know how cruel multiple sclerosis can be, and would no doubt even allow a patient to take heroin if they so desired; any death other than the lingering misery of one's muscular system decaying with multiple sclerosis is better than that. And there is no chemotherapy as there is with cancer; no magic bullet for this one. It's just visits from the nurse, and physiotherapy once a month, until the sufferer just fades away.

But Lemmy Kilmister, you see, had the whole world worked out. He knew what happens if we give up long-term vices, and I thank him wholeheartedly for saving me from, quite literally, a fate worse than death by taking up my vices again. Life is so much more bearable now. Other than being a rock star, a legend, and an icon, Lemmy, of course, was also a human being, with frailties, just like everyone else. These were well documented in the media, and his fans were behind him all the way.

As this book illustrates beyond any doubt, Lemmy made the most of any and all opportunities on offer, delving into many diverse musical genres and succeeding in achieving songwriting, musical, and vocal skills way beyond the confines of the band he founded all those years ago. Ian Fraser Kilmister – Lemmy to us all – was a very special man indeed (and we don't get many of those) who gained respect over the decades from his many musical peers, from the countless journalists who once lambasted him but who later treated with deference and civility, and from his countless hundreds of thousands of fans across the globe. The world was his, indeed.

Lemmy Kilmister »Lemmy & Friends«
(working title for Lemmy's proposed solo album)

Tracks recorded are two with The Damned, two with Skew Siskin, two with The Reverend Horton Heat, one with Joan Jett, one with members of Metallica, and one with Dave Grohl; Lemmy was also hoping to record one track each with Jeff Beck and Skin from Skunk Anansie. Outside of recording and touring with Motörhead and The Head Cat, this had been Lemmy's 'hobby' for several years. It would be welcomed by fans if it is released, and enjoyed as yet another facet of his wide and varied musical career. On 2 July 2013, the track 'Don't Matter To Me' from this album was uploaded to YouTube.

Appendix One

Lemmy in North Wales, by Martin Peel

By way of a timeline, this essay was sent to me by Martin with a letter dated 28 September 2012.

My name is Martin Peel. I'm a few months younger than Lemmy Kilmister, or Lemmy Willis as we knew him at the time and, like him, was active in music in the North Wales area in the early 1960s. I'm still active on a full-time basis in music to this day.

I am not a Motörhead fan. I have purchased a CD or two out of curiosity, and went to see them play in Llandudno a couple of years ago, but would never call myself a fan. The reason for this 'chronicle' is to correct inaccuracies both in »White Line Fever« (which for example omits the lead singer of The Motown Sect) and circling around the internet. Note that any dates quoted in full are from my research into back copies of The North Wales Weekly News held on microfilm in the County Records Office. The rest are from my own recollections and recollections of others from those times that I still see.

In the summer of 1962 I joined my first group, Danny Jay and the Jaguars, con-sisting of pupils from John Bright Grammar School in Llandudno. I replaced Tudor Williams on rhythm guitar, as he had joined a group from Colwyn Bay called The Olympics. At this time, there must have been around two dozen groups in the Llan-dudno / Colwyn Bay area, most of them playing Cliff Richard and The Shadows tunes.

The group I was in used to frequent the Venezia Coffee Bar in Llandudno, as did most of the local acts. Around this time, a guitarist who had just moved to Conwy be-gan coming into Llandudno. I recall one night in The Boat Cellar in Craig-y-Don (Llan-dudno) this guitarist showing me the lead guitar for The Shadows' 'Frightened City' in the interval between the sets of The Jets, the band that night. This guitarist then started turning up in the Venezia, and he was known as 'Lemmy'.

The local music shop was called Wagstaffs, and one Saturday afternoon a group from Mochdre near Colwyn Bay came into the shop. It turned out they were called The Dee Jays, and Lemmy played rhythm guitar with them. I never got to hear them, and the only gig of theirs advertised in the local paper was at Payne's Café Royal, Llandudno, on 12 October 1963. By this time, I was in another school group called Power Five, and I recall going to an audition one Saturday afternoon held in Benl-lech, Anglesey, by Oriole Records. The auditions were held in an old cinema, and many groups played, including my own and Lemmy's. No group from that particular afternoon was successful. The only North Wales group signed was Dino and the

Wildfires, from Pwllheli: they had a single or two released on Oriole, on which their name was changed to The Wackers, to try to capitalise on the Mersey Beat thing. Such is life!

Lemmy continued to hang around Llandudno, and on occasion we both used to go and see visiting bands, such as The Artwoods at The Washington, and Peter Jay and the Jaywalkers at the Rhos Abbey Hotel, Rhos-on-Sea, Colwyn Bay, on 2 May 1964. I think Lemmy was, by this time, living with his stepfather in Greenfield Road, Colwyn Bay. I assume we would have got a bus to Rhos-on-Sea to get to the gig, and then walked the long distance home to Llandudno (me) and Colwyn Bay (Lemmy). I recall us both talking to Jay's band members at the bar.

Around August 1964 my group, Power Five, had broken up due to the others going off to study in universities, and me being now in an office job. Wanting to carry on playing, I approached Lemmy about starting a group with Barry Jones (ex-Power Five) on drums, Dave 'Tempy' Templeton (a friend from The Venezia) on bass, Lemmy on lead guitar and vocals, and me on rhythm guitar. We used to practice at a church house in Deganwy (near Llandudno) once or twice a week, and then Lemmy would go off to work the night shift at the Hotpoint factory in Llandudno Junction. His stepfather had got Lemmy the job, but he only worked there for a week or so. The material we used to rehearse included many of the popular R&B tunes of the day, such as Jimmy Reed's 'Baby What You Want Me To Do' and Muddy Waters' 'Got My Mojo Working', various rock 'n' roll covers, and 'You Can't Do That' by The Beatles. It is interesting to read Lemmy's quote that he saw The Beatles at The Cavern in Liverpool in 1963 when he was 18. Perhaps he also saw them when I did, when they played for a week at The Odeon in Llandudno, also in 1963?

We never gigged with this band. We had no proper equipment or transport, except for Tempy's car, and after a few weeks Lemmy informed me that I was not of the standard required to play in the group which I formed and I was replaced by Tudor Williams, whose last group The Cossacks had broken up. I am not sure if the group ever had a name. I recall that the night I was 'sacked' we went to see Victor Brox Blues Train at The Washington in Llandudno. Victor Brox went on to work with Alexis Korner and Aynsley Dunbar, appeared on the first double album recording of »Jesus Christ Superstar« and many more projects. By the 1980s, Victor was again Manchester-based, and I did a few gigs with him. I remember Victor telling me he offered Lemmy a try-out with the Blues Train when Lemmy first went to Manchester, but Lemmy declined as he did not think he was good enough.

Barry Jones played around North Wales until the early 1980s, but then re-located to London on the insistence of his wife (a Londoner herself). Tempy emigrated to Australia: I heard he had been playing in an Australian band entertaining troops in Vietnam, and then got a job as a taxi driver in Sydney, where he received an injury in a car accident which eventually proved fatal. After his short time with Lemmy, Tudor packed up playing. I lost contact with him in the 1970s.

Throughout the period described, Lemmy played a silver-glitter guitar, which I assume was Italian in origin.

Soon after this, Lemmy went to Manchester together with a Llandudno local known as Ming (due to the fact he had, as a child, spent time in China, where his father had worked). At the time, Ming was living in a cave on The Great Orme, having disappointed his parents by dropping out of accountancy training. It would be at about this time that Lemmy joined The Rainmakers, but I do not recall him mentioning this group during his frequent visits back to North Wales. Also at this time, one Robbie Watson began making the journey from Beaumaris (Anglesey) to Llandudno and, it would appear, became friendly with Lemmy.

Another local venue was Rhos Pool, near Colwyn Bay. Rhos Pool was an old-style lido open-air bathing pool, which also occasionally had live gigs in the café adjoining the pool itself. On 28 July 1965 The Pretty Things played there, supported by a Manchester group called The Motown Sect, and a local group called The Panzies. I didn't know it at the time, but Lemmy was playing rhythm guitar in The Motown Sect and probably singing. I didn't attend the gig, nor the one on 30 August 1965, when The Panzies and The Motown Sect supported Kris Ryan and the Questions. I assume I may have been playing elsewhere. However, I did attend a gig at the Winter Gardens Ballroom, Llandudno on 8 October 1965, when The Motown Sect were supported by The Panzies. I recall that Stu, the lead guitarist, was playing a cherry Gibson 345 stereo, and Lemmy by this time had a sunburst Gibson 330.

Soon after this, vocal duties in The Motown Sect were taken over by Haydn Bannister, who had been singing with The Panzies, and the bass was now played by another Llandudno musician, Glyn Davies, whose nickname was Glunk (but is incorrectly referred to in »White Line Fever« as 'Glun'. To add to the North Wales connection, they also relied on another Llandudno local, Ritchie Yates, to drive them around in his van.

To me, it remains a mystery why Haydn Bannister is not mentioned in Lemmy's autobiography. When »White Line Fever« was published I called Ming to tell him that he was in Lemmy's book, and his first question was "does he mention Haydn?" When I said no his reaction was "that's unbelievable!" Ming, by the way, still lives in Colwyn Bay, and is now retired after a career in the Civil Service and related activities.

My next contact with The Motown Sect was in late 1965 or early 1966 when, one Saturday afternoon, I was sitting in The Venezia Coffee Bar wondering what to do that weekend as my band had no gigs. My indecision was soon answered when Ritchie, The Motown Sect roadie, came into the coffee bar, obviously very worried. His van had broken down on the way to Manchester to meet the group, and he had hitch-hiked back to Llandudno to try and find someone to help out. I agreed, we took my own van to where Ritchie's Ford Thames had blown its big-end bearings, and we proceeded to Manchester with The Sect equipment in my Bedford.

Upon reaching Manchester, we met the group at Barratts Music Shop. However, the group had all their followers with them so, packed with about sixteen people and The Sect's equipment, we made our way to Bury Palais. Following the gig, I spent the evening at a flat shared by Lemmy and Glyn, while Haydn entertained a young lady in my van parked outside.

On Sunday I took the gear to Mr Smith's Club, where they had a gig, and left it there, and returned with Ritchie to North Wales. Soon after this, a friend of the group named Jake (whose father owned The Venezia Coffee Bar, and himself managed The Ritz Restaurant) arranged for The Motown Sect to do a demo for Robert Stigwood (the famous impresario and entertainment entrepreneur, and manager of The Bee Gees and Cream, amongst others) at The Ritz.

On the arranged evening, Jake's equipment (a Ferrograph-sized reel-to-reel tape recorder) was set up, and I agreed to pick up Stu and Kev (the drummer) from Llandudno station. The train arrived, and Stu, plus his Gibson and AC30 amp, struggled down the platform, but Kev had not bothered to come! The recording session went ahead, with Lemmy playing drums on a kit which had been borrowed for Kev's use, and me playing rhythm guitar instead of Lemmy. I remember we played the Motown song 'Leaving Here' and Howling Wolf's 'Smokestack Lightning' which featured an extended solo by Stu who was an outstanding player. I later heard that Robert Stigwood had wanted to sign The Motown Sect based on what he heard on the demo, but Stu's parents intervened and made him a Ward of Court, as they wanted him to complete his engineering apprenticeship. Soon after this, The Motown Sect drifted apart; what is there left for a group if you've turned down Robert Stigwood!

Lemmy then (in 1965) as has been widely reported, joined The Rocking Vickers in Blackpool. I recall that on one of his visits to Colwyn Bay, he showed us a copy of the 'Dandy' single, and his new Fender Telecaster guitar.

Glunk packed up playing and found work on the pipelines during the 1970s oil boom, and subsequently moved to Thailand. When I saw him on a visit home in the early 1990s, he said "it's nice to see Lemmy still playing the same stuff!" Last I heard about Stu was that he was playing with a group in Manchester called The Brooklyn Freight. He was someone who truly had the potential to 'get somewhere' as a guitarist.

Haydn Bannister drifted back to North Wales musical activity, and eventually joined a group called Uncle Herbert's Big Soul Band, in which he replaced Jon Lloyd-Hughes who'd moved to London and got some work playing harmonica for Alexis Korner, before going into record production work in Germany. Also in Uncle Herbert was Pete Flaherty on drums, Steve Griffiths on bass, Mike Hall on organ, and me on lead guitar. Haydn was an excellent frontman, and we were very busy. However, Haydn had started hanging out with Robbie Watson, and was often late turning up for gigs – "we were watching the waterfall" – to the extent that Pete had to take lead vocals on a number of occasions. During this time, Lemmy used to roadie for us on his visits back to North Wales. I think the last time I spoke to him was when he played me the Sam Gopal album at his parent's flat Greenfield Road, Colwyn Bay.

Around 1968, I grew tired both of people using my Vox Super Twin as a PA system, and of people scrounging lifts from me, and I left the band and started playing solo in folk clubs doing blues material. I was replaced by Adney Tingel. When the band finally broke up I often saw Haydn, and he always said "hey, Martin, let's start a band." However, his lifestyle caught up with him, and he was found dead from an overdose in a flat in the Colwyn Bay area in the early 1980s. The tale I heard was that he died sitting in a chair, and it was a day or so before anyone realised he was dead.

Of the other members of Uncle Herbert's Big Soul Band, Pete, the drummer died of cancer in the early 2000s. Steve, the bass player, was last seen playing in a soul band in the early 2000s. Mike, on keyboards, went to Leeds College of Music, and from there into a career playing on cruise liners. Adney packed up playing after The Herberts broke up, and I went into blues and jazz (as mentioned earlier, I worked with Victor Brox in the 1980s), and currently teach guitar in schools.

In »Lemmy the Movie« Dave Grohl says that Lemmy keeps part of his past secret: here are those days as they happened. No doubt Lemmy would have called me if he'd disagreed.

Martin Peel

I later had the opportunity to ask Lemmy about The Beatles in Llandudno as described by Martin.

"Yes, I saw them," he recalled, "and I met George and John in Llandudno. It was like the Llandudno branch of The Beatles' fan club. So the night before they went onstage at the (Llandudno) Odeon, I sneaked into their hotel, and met them. I'm not sure what I expected, and of course, they didn't know me; I was just some fan. But they were really great under the circumstances. This was in 1963, like he said, the height of Beatlemania, and it was totally crazy. You can't imagine what that was like – even the Daily Mirror had a full page, every single day, detailing what The Beatles were doing. John Lennon said that you have to be bastards to get through all of the shit in the music business, and The Beatles were the biggest bastards of all, but they were completely cool as far as I am concerned."

Appendix Two

Lemmy and The Rocking Vickers, by Kevin Parrott.

This was uploaded on 30 October 2011 to my message board. I've attempted, via email, to contact Kevin on several occasions to ask permission to reproduce his thoughts in this book. As there's been no reply, I have assumed that as Kevin was happy publishing his essay on the message board, then he would be happy to have it reproduced here.

There have been a number of versions of how Lemmy joined the Rocking Vicars (or Vickers): this is what really happened. In 1965, I was in a band called the Fat Sound. Our manager was a really great guy called Dave Baxter, and he kept a pub called The Albion, in Stalybridge, Cheshire, near Manchester. We were a soul, Stax style band, and rehearsed at Dave's pub. At the time I had a day job, and Dave called me at work to say that the drummer of a local band called The Motown Sect had come into the pub and asked if there was any chance they could borrow our van to get to a gig in North Wales. He knew that we were based at The Albion, and hoped that there might be goodwill between bands. I believe the venue they were to play was the Picture House, at Pentre Broughton.

There was no way that any of The Motown Sect could drive our van, as none of them had passed their driving test, so kind-hearted Dave drove, and I went along for the trip. We first picked up the drummer and his kit from his parents' house on the Hattersley estate, near Hyde, a lad nicknamed Hector. I can't remember how we collected the rest of the group in the van. The cinema was about half-full of young kids, and The Motown Sect played on the floor in front of the first row of seats with the cinema screen with curtains closed behind them and all the house lights up. I can't remember if they did one or two sets; probably two. I think I remember Lemmy playing rhythm guitar on a Hofner acoustic with a pick-up. On the way home in the van, Lemmy and I discussed our love of Buddy Holly, and he told me that he'd seen Buddy live in Liverpool on the 1958 tour. I believe Lemmy said he'd travelled from his home in Colwyn Bay to see Buddy at the Liverpool Empire.

Dave and I did the favour of this North Wales trip with The Motown Sect on one more occasion before they split. On one of the trips home from Pentre Broughton, the van lost a wheel after coming around a roundabout outside Chester. A couple of the bolts on the wheel hub had sheered off, and we watched the wheel roll in front of us, and come to rest in the roadside ditch as the van took a dive to one side and ground to a halt. Dave found some nuts and bolts in the toolbox and miraculously put the wheel back on the hub and got us home. I believe The Motown Sect split up soon after.

Meanwhile, in February 1966, The Fat Sound got the job backing the singer Karol Keyes. Karol's real name was Carol Hirsch, who became actress Luan Peters, and the singer with 5000 Volts, and the Australian girl in the »Fawlty Towers« episode 'The Psychiatrist'. We changed the name to The Big Sound; nothing to do with Simon Dupree and the Big Sound, it was just that Karol didn't like the word 'fat'. The Big Sound was then managed by Karol's manager Joan Lewis, sister of Alan Lewis, who was manager of the Four Pennies. This was with Dave Baxter's blessing. It was during early 1966 that, through Joan, we met Jack Venet, manager of The Rocking Vickers. Joan called him The Pot Man, as his business was selling pottery seconds of plates, dinner services, and the like, on Bury Market. We got to know The Vickers quite well. I remember Harry Feeney driving us in our van to London. I can't remember why he drove us, but he may have needed a lift, so volunteered.

Around this time, The Rocking Vickers were having problems with one of their guitar players. Both The Big Sound and The Vickers were booked together on the same bill at the Palais de Dance, Gas Street, in Ashton under Lyne, probably around March 1966. The Vickers' guitar player was late, and they feared he might not turn up at all. They thought he might be suffering from a nervous breakdown, as he'd appeared not too well for a few weeks. They asked me to stand in, so I was frantically rehearsing with them in the dressing room, when he eventually turned up. However, that night Jack Venet either fired him, or he left of his own accord.

I mentioned to Jack and The Vickers that I knew this guy who had the image and attributes to take his place, and they asked me if I could get hold of him. The following day I called Dave Baxter. Dave still had Hector, The Motown Sect drummer's, phone number. Hector got hold of Lemmy, who wasn't doing anything, and he went along and passed the audition. The rest, as they say, is history.

We met up with the Vickers a couple of weeks later, and Lemmy thanked me for the break.

Kevin Parrott

Appendix Three

Lemmy wrote an introduction or foreword to the following books:

»The Illustrated Collector's Guide To Motörhead«
by Alan Burridge with Mick Stevenson
Collector's Guide Publishing – 8 December 1994

»Straight Whisky« by Erik Quisling and Austin Williams
Bonus Books – 1 July 2003

»Orgasmatron – The Heavy Metal Art Of Joe Petagno«
Feral House Books – 1 August 2004

»The Official Heavy Metal Book Of Lists« by Eric Danville
Backbeat Books – 7 December 2009

»Direct Your Own Damn Movie« by Lloyd Kaufman
Focal Press – 20 February 2009

»The Motörhead Collector's Guide« by Mick Stevenson
Cherry Red Books – 23 May 2011

»Motörhead – Live To Win« by Alan Burridge
Cleopatra Books – 10 September 2012

Also worth noting is »The Simpson's Tree House Of Horror #16« – Bongo Comics Group. The October 2010 edition featured a full-length cartoon story, written by Lemmy, which includes Simpsons-styled caricatures of Lemmy, Phil Campbell, and Mikkey Dee.